FIDELER SOCIAL STUDIES

Families
Family life: sharing, caring, and working together
A Chartbook of discussion pictures

Families Around the World
How families live in communities around the world.

Our Needs
The needs of people in families and in communities

Our Earth
Our Earth, its geography, its people and communities.

Great Americans and Great Ideas
Biographies of thirteen great Americans.
The great ideas that built our nation.

The United States
The people, geography, and history of the United States. The Northeast, The South, Midwest and Great Plains, The West, Pictorial Story of Our Country. Depth Studies.

American Neighbors
The people, geography, and history of Canada, Mexico, Caribbean Lands, and South America. Depth Studies.

World Cultures
The people, geography, and history of ten world regions. British Isles, Germany, France, Soviet Union, China, Japan, India, Southeast Asia, Africa, South America. Depth Studies.

Inquiring About Freedom
United States history. Depth Studies of the "freedom" concepts that built our nation.

Contributors to The West

JOHN FRASER HART
   Professor of Geography
   University of Minnesota
   Minneapolis, Minnesota

G. ETZEL PEARCY
   Chairman, Department
    of Geography
   California State College
   Los Angeles, California

WILLIAM H. WAKE
   Professor of Geography
   Fresno State College
   Fresno, California

BETTY-JO BUELL
MARGARET S. DeWITT
MARY A. DOWNEY

EVELYN M. DOWNING
RAYMOND E. FIDELER
SUSAN R. GROOVER
MARGARET F. HERTEL

MARY MITUS
CAROL S. PRESCOTT
BEV J. ROCHE
MARY JANE SACK

VIRGINIA A. SKALSKY
BARBARA M. SMITH
MARION H. SMITH
JUDY A. TAYLOR

ALICE VAIL
JOANNA VAN ZOEST
LISA WRIGHT

THE WEST

Jerry E. Jennings, Editor

Jerry E. Jennings is an author and editor of textbooks for young people. A graduate of Michigan State University, Mr. Jennings continued his education at Columbia University in New York. Through extensive travel and study, he has gained a comprehensive knowledge of our country and its people. Mr. Jennings has a deep interest in young people and a desire to share with them important concepts of American life and culture in terms they can readily understand.

COPYRIGHT 1979, THE FIDELER COMPANY

All rights reserved in the U.S.A. and foreign countries. This book or parts thereof must not be reproduced in any form without permission. Printed in the U.S.A. by offset lithography.

Earlier Edition Copyright The Fideler Company 1974.
LIBRARY OF CONGRESS CATALOG CARD NUMBER: 78-54256
ISBN: 0-88296-077-6

THE FIDELER COMPANY   GRAND RAPIDS, MICHIGAN • TORONTO, CANADA

CONTENTS

Part 1 Land and Climate

1. A Global View............... 4
2. Land....................... 12
3. Climate.................... 26

Part 2 People

4. People..................... 42
5. Cities..................... 52
6. Citizenship and Government.. 62
7. The Arts................... 74

Part 3 Earning a Living

8. Farming.................... 80
9. Natural Resources and Energy.... 92
10. Industry.................. 112

Alaska and Hawaii............. 124
Index......................... 129
Acknowledgments............... 132

States of the West

Arizona....................... 134
California.................... 135
Colorado...................... 137
Idaho......................... 139
Montana....................... 140
Nevada........................ 141
New Mexico.................... 142
Oregon........................ 143
Utah.......................... 145
Washington.................... 146
Wyoming....................... 148

Pictorial Story of Our Country

Our Country................... 2
1. People Build Communities in America 4
2. American Communities Form a Nation   20
3. The Nation Grows................. 30
4. The Union Is Saved............... 41
5. Our Country Becomes a World Leader 46
6. Years of Amazing Change.......... 56

Index......................... 65
Acknowledgments............... 66

Thinking Aids

Skills Manual
  Thinking.................... 1
  Solving Problems............ 2
  Learning Social Studies Skills....... 3
  Learning Map Skills......... 10
Needs of People............... 17
Great Ideas That Built Our Nation 19
Word List (Glossary).......... 35
Acknowledgments............... 48

Maps, Charts, and Special Features

Parts 1, 2, and 3
Our Earth, 5
The United States, 7
The United States, 8-9
Main Groups of States, 10
Land Regions, 24
Average Yearly Rainfall, 27
Average January and July Temperatures, 30
The Seasons of the Year, 34-35
Average Length of Growing Season, 38
United States Population Distribution, 46
Six Metropolitan Areas, 53
Cities of the West, 61
Seven Important Beliefs That Build
  Strong Communities, 64
Responsibilities of Citizens in a Strong
  Community, 68
Seven Social Problems, 70
Major Types of Farming in the United States, 82
Fruits and Nuts, Vegetables, Sugar Beets, Wheat, 86
Cattle and Calves, and Sheep and Lambs, 87
Water Resources, 94
Copper, Lead, Uranium, and Oil, 96
Where We Get Our Energy, 97
Lumber Production, National Forests in the West, 107
Leading Fishing States in the West, 108
Main Industrial Areas of the West, 115
Alaska, 125

Pictorial Story of Our Country
Routes of Indian Settlers, 5
Routes of Explorers and Traders, 7
Routes of Spanish Explorers, 10
Dutch and Swedish Settlements, 13
Thirteen British Colonies, 17
Before and After the French and Indian War, 21
How Our Country Grew, 34
The United States and Mexico in 1821, 35
Routes to the West, 36
A Divided Country, 43
Our Changing Nation, 57
The United States, 60-61

THE WEST

The Golden Gate Bridge across San Francisco Bay, in California. This bay is an arm of the Pacific Ocean.

Part 1

Land and Climate

In the western part of the United States is a huge area of land known as the West. It covers almost one third of our country.

If you were to travel through the West, you would see many interesting sights. You would find snowy mountains and beautiful green valleys. You would find deserts and thick forests, rolling plains and steep-sided canyons. You would also see the blue water of the Pacific Ocean.

The chapters in Part 1 tell more about the land and climate of the West. As you read, try to find answers to the following questions:
- How many states are there in the West? What are their names?
- What are the four main land regions of the West? What is the land in each of these regions like?
- How does the climate differ from one part of the West to another? What causes these differences in climate?
- How do land features and climate affect the way people live in different parts of the West?

Along the Pacific coast of California, near the town of Carmel. The part of our country that we call the West extends all the way from Canada on the north to Mexico on the south. To the west, it is bordered by the huge Pacific Ocean.

The city of San Diego, California, as seen from an airplane. When you fly several miles above the earth's surface in an airplane, you can sometimes see places as far as 100 miles (161 km.) away. But even at this height, you can see only a very small part of the earth. Why is this so?

1 A Global View

Our earth from an airplane

Have you ever taken a trip in an airplane? If you have, you will remember the excitement you felt as the plane left the airport runway and began climbing high into the air. Before long, you were flying miles above the earth's surface. Below you were cities, farms, and forests. From your window, you looked out over a wide area. If it was a clear day, you were able to see as far as 100 miles (161 km.)† away. But the earth is so large that even at this height you could see only a small part of its surface.

Our earth from space

Until a few years ago, no one had ever been able to see more than a small part of the earth at one time. Then, in the late 1950's, the United States and the Soviet Union* began to send different kinds of spacecraft far away from the earth. Some of these spacecraft have carried persons called astronauts. Others have carried cameras or scientific equipment. So far, most of the spacecraft that have been launched have traveled around the earth. But some have journeyed to the moon or to other planets,* such as Mars and Venus.

*See Glossary
† km. means kilometer

4 The West

Eastern Hemisphere

Western Hemisphere

From a spacecraft many thousands of miles out in space, it is possible to get a view of our earth as a whole.

The picture on page 6 shows a view of the earth from far out in space. This picture was taken from a United States spacecraft known as the ATS III. When the picture was taken, the spacecraft was more than 22,000 miles (35,000 km.)† away from the earth.

Continents and oceans

As you study the picture on page 6, you will notice that some of the earth's surface is hidden by clouds. In some

Our earth. The surface of our earth is covered partly with land and partly with water. The largest bodies of water are called oceans, and the largest masses of land are known as continents. Five of the earth's six continents are shown on the maps above. The continent of Antarctica is located around the South Pole, so it does not show on either of these maps.

The West 5

The earth from space. This photograph of the earth was taken from a United States spacecraft.

places, however, you can see land. The largest masses of land are called continents. In other places, you can see water. The largest bodies of water are oceans. They make up about three fourths of the earth's surface.

The Eastern Hemisphere

If you look at the top map on page 5, you can see the continents of Africa, Eurasia, and Australia. The western part of the great continent of Eurasia is called Europe, while the eastern part is known as Asia. Many people consider Europe and Asia to be two separate continents. The map shows that the continent of Africa lies to the south of Europe. A small part of Australia can be seen to the east of the Indian Ocean.

The Western Hemisphere

The other side of the earth is known as the Western Hemisphere. The bottom map on page 5 shows that the continents of North America and South America are located in the Western Hemisphere.

Now look at the picture of the earth on page 6. With the help of the globe in your classroom, find South America in the picture. At the top left of the picture, you can also see part of North America. Much of this continent is hidden under a layer of clouds.

The United States

The map below presents a closer view of North America. Most of our own country, the United States, is on this continent. Our nearest neighbors in North America are the countries of Canada and Mexico.

Our country is made up of fifty states. Two of these, Alaska and Hawaii, are separated from all the others. Alaska lies to the northwest of Canada, on the North American continent. Hawaii is a group of islands in the Pacific Ocean. The part of our country that is made up of the other forty-eight states is called the conterminous* United States. (See map below.)

The West

The map at the top of page 10 shows that the West is a group of eleven states in the western part of our country. The West is very large in area, covering

The United States

This map shows the location of the fifty states that make up our country. Two of these, Alaska and Hawaii, are separated from the others. Alaska is in the far northern part of North America. Hawaii is an island state in the Pacific Ocean. The other forty-eight states form the part of our country known as the conterminous* United States.

7

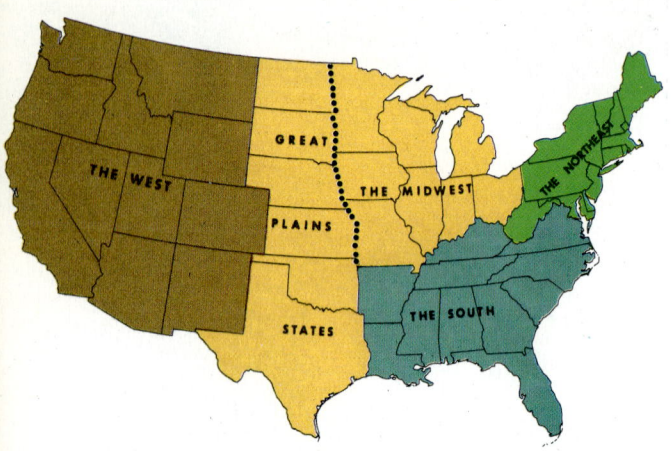

Main groups of states. The states in the conterminous United States may be divided into groups. The map above shows one way in which these states may be grouped.

almost one third of the United States. It extends all the way from Canada on the north to Mexico on the south. To the west, it is bordered by the huge Pacific Ocean.

A changing region

More than one hundred years ago, a newspaper editor in New York City wrote, "Go West, young man, go West." At that time, the part of the United States known as the West was still largely a wilderness. Almost the only people who lived in much of the West were small groups of Indians.

During the years that followed, many Americans did "go West." In some places, they found barren deserts and rugged mountains. But in other places, they found fertile lowlands with a pleasant climate. There were also rich deposits of minerals and valuable forests. Sparkling rivers flowed down from high mountain peaks. These provided water for dry farmlands. Many of the newcomers liked the West so well that they decided to stay there. Today, more than 38 million people make their homes in the West.

In the following chapters, you will discover more facts about the land, the climate, and the natural resources of the West. You will also find out why so many people have chosen to make their homes in this important part of our country.

2 Land

Imagine that you have just received a letter from a cousin who lives in another country. Your cousin has seen American movies that took place in the West. She wants to know more about this part of the United States. How would you answer your cousin's letter?

You might begin by telling your cousin that the West is a group of eleven states in the western part of our country. Then you might tell her that there are three important facts she should know about the West. Some of the maps in this book will help you understand these facts and explain them to your cousin.

A land of wide open spaces

The map on page 46 shows how many people live in different parts of the United States. Each dot on the map stands for ten thousand people. In a few places along the Pacific Ocean, there are thick clumps of dots. But in most parts of the West, there are very few dots. This map shows us that few people live in much of the West. In this chapter, you will discover some of the reasons why most of the West's people are crowded into a few small areas.

A dry land

By looking at the map on page 27, we can see how much rain falls in different parts of our country. Notice that only a small part of the West receives more than 20 inches (51 cm.)† of rainfall each year. Most farm crops need at least this amount of rainfall in

† cm. means centimeter

Dry land in Arizona. The West has large areas in which few people live. One reason why much of the West has so few people is the lack of rainfall here. What are some other reasons?

The West 13

order to grow well. We can tell from the map, then, that most of the West is very dry.

Now we know one reason why so much of the West is thinly populated. People need water to live. They need water for drinking, bathing, and many other uses. The lack of rainfall helps to explain why few people live in most parts of the West.

A land of mountains and high plateaus

The land in the West is higher and more rugged than the land in other parts of the United States. Look at the map on pages 8 and 9. This map shows how high the land in our country rises above the level of the sea. Notice that much of the land in the West is more than 5,000 feet (1,524 m.)[†] above sea level. In some places, high mountains tower above deep valleys. Between the groups of mountains are broad areas of high ground called plateaus. The pictures on pages 18 and 19 show us views of two different plateaus—the Columbia Plateau and the Colorado Plateau.

Four main regions

The West may be divided into four main parts, or regions. (See map on page 24.) The easternmost part of the West is made up of broad plains, like the one shown in the picture at right. Rising west of the plains are the Rocky Mountains. Still farther west is a huge land region that is made up largely of plateaus. It is called the Plateau Country. Between this region and the Pacific Ocean are long mountain chains separated by valleys.

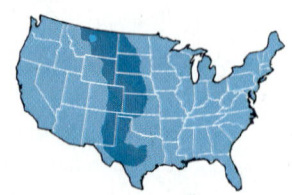

The Great Plains

The region known as the Great Plains forms a wide band extending from Canada in the north to Mexico in the south. The land in the Great Plains slopes gently upward from east to west. At the western edge of this region, some places are more than 1 mile (1.6 km.)[†] above sea level.

[†] m. means meter
[†] km. means kilometer

14 The West

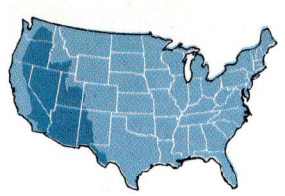

The Plateau Country

The Plateau Country is a large region that is bordered by mountains on the east, north, and west. High plateaus cover much of this region, but there are mountains and valleys in some places. This is the driest region of the West. There are few cities or large towns in the Plateau Country.

The Grand Teton Mountains of Wyoming are part of the Rocky Mountains region. Some of the rugged peaks in this region are so high that they are covered with snow all year long. Few people live in the Rocky Mountains region of the West. What do you think are the reasons for this?

The Columbia Plateau

At the northern end of the Plateau Country is the Columbia Plateau. It is named for a large river that flows through the area. Many thousands of years ago, hot, melted rock called lava poured from openings in the earth and formed the Columbia Plateau. As the lava cooled, it hardened. Little by little, wind and water wore away some of the rock to form a dark soil that is very good

Harvesting wheat on the Columbia Plateau. This picture was named for the great Columbia River. Compare the map on page 24 with the map on pages 8 and 9. What other major river also flows through this plateau?

Using Natural Resources

See Great Ideas

Fertile soil is one of the natural resources found in parts of the West. For example, the soil found on the Columbia Plateau is especially good for growing crops. Do research to discover how this soil was formed, and why it is so fertile.

The Grand Canyon is in the Colorado Plateau. Millions of years ago, the land in this area was almost flat. As time passed, the Colorado River cut deeper and deeper into the earth's surface, forming the Grand Canyon. Today, this canyon is more than a mile deep in some places.

for growing crops. If we visited the northern part of the Columbia Plateau today, we would see rolling hills covered with wheat fields. In other parts of the plateau, we would see cattle grazing on grassy plains.

The Colorado Plateau

In the southeastern part of the Plateau Country is the Colorado Plateau. It is made up of many plateaus that lie several thousand feet above sea level. Here much of the land is almost flat. In some places, however, fast-flowing rivers such as the Colorado have cut deep, straight-sided valleys called canyons. One of these, the Grand Canyon, is more than a mile (1.6 km.) deep in some places. On the Colorado Plateau, there are masses of brightly colored

The WEST 19

Joshua trees and yucca in southern Nevada. This area is part of the Basin and Range Country. Hundreds of short mountain ranges and wide valleys make up this region of the West.

rock that have been carved into strange shapes by wind and rivers. Pine forests cover the highest parts of the plateau. In other places there are wide stretches of grassland. Few roads or railroads cross this plateau. It is hard to build bridges across the deep canyons.

The Basin and Range Country

To the west and south of the Colorado Plateau there are hundreds of short mountain ranges. A range is a row of connected mountains. Between these ranges are wide basins.*

This whole area is called the Basin and Range Country. Here much of the land is so dry that few plants will grow on it. In some places the ground is dotted with sagebrush, or with cactus and other plants that can live without much water. From an airplane, the Basin and Range Country looks dusty-gray or tan. Only where water is available for irrigation* are there green farmlands. The deserts of southern California are part of the Basin and Range Country.

The northern part of the Basin and Range Country is called the Great Basin. Mountain streams that flow into the Great Basin have no way to escape to the sea. Their water collects in low spots and forms lakes. The hot sun dries up some of the water in these lakes.

20 The West

the West. The map on page 24 shows us that this region contains two long mountain chains extending from north to south. The two mountain chains are separated by long valleys.

The chain of mountains to the east has two parts. In the north is the Cascade Range. In the south is the Sierra Nevada. The peaks of these mountains are very high and steep sided.

The Cascade Range

The Cascade Range extends through Washington and Oregon into northern California. Several high, cone-shaped peaks tower above the other mountains in this area. These were formed many thousands of years ago by lava pouring out from openings in the earth called volcanoes.* Today the highest peaks of the Cascade Range are blanketed with glistening snow and ice the year around. In many places, the lower mountain slopes are covered with thick forests. There are few farms or towns in this rugged mountain area. The only low passageway through the Cascade Range is the valley of the Columbia River.

The Sierra Nevada

The Sierra Nevada gets its name from two Spanish words meaning "snowy range." This mountain range is more than 400 miles (644 km.) long. It was formed millions of years ago, when movements deep in the earth caused a huge block of stone to tilt upward into the sky. Only a few railroads and main highways cross the high, rugged Sierra Nevada. In the southern part of this range is Mount Whitney, the highest

When this happens, salt and other minerals are left behind. Therefore, some lakes in the Great Basin are very salty. The largest is Great Salt Lake. It is so salty that fish cannot live in it. Sometimes a lake dries up entirely, leaving a large patch of glistening white salt.

Pacific Mountains and Valleys

Between the Plateau Country and the Pacific Ocean is another land region of

The West 21

peak in the conterminous* United States. It rises 14,495 feet (4,418 m.) above the level of the sea.

The Central Valley

To the west of the high Sierra Nevada and the Cascade Range are two long valleys. One of these is the Central Valley of California, a broad lowland surrounded by mountains. This valley is about 50 miles (80 km.) wide and 450 miles (724 km.) long. In the Central Valley, the land is almost flat and the soil is fertile. This is one of the most important farming areas in the United States. Orchards, pastures, and fields of crops cover much of the land here.

Two important rivers flow through the Central Valley. One of these is the Sacramento River, which flows through the northern part of the valley. The other is the San Joaquin River, which flows through the southern part. (See the map on page 94.) These

Yosemite National Park is in a rugged mountain range called the Sierra Nevada. This range lies almost entirely in California. It is more than 400 miles (644 km.) long. In the southern part of the Sierra Nevada is Mount Whitney. It is one of the highest peaks in the United States.

two rivers join together near San Francisco Bay, and their waters flow into the bay.

The Puget-Willamette Lowland

The other valley is located in Washington and northern Oregon. It is called the Puget-Willamette Lowland. In the northern part of this valley is an inlet of the Pacific Ocean called Puget Sound. The Willamette River flows through the southern part of the valley. Here the soil is fertile, and much of the land is level enough for farming. If we were to fly over this valley in an airplane, we would see below us a patchwork of farms, meadows, and forests. We would also notice many towns and cities.

Mountains along the coast

A long chain of mountains extends from north to south along the Pacific coast of our country. These mountains

The Central Valley of California (right) lies to the west of the Sierra Nevada. This broad lowland is one of the most important farming areas in the United States. Why is this so? This chapter and Chapter 8 have information that will help you answer this question.

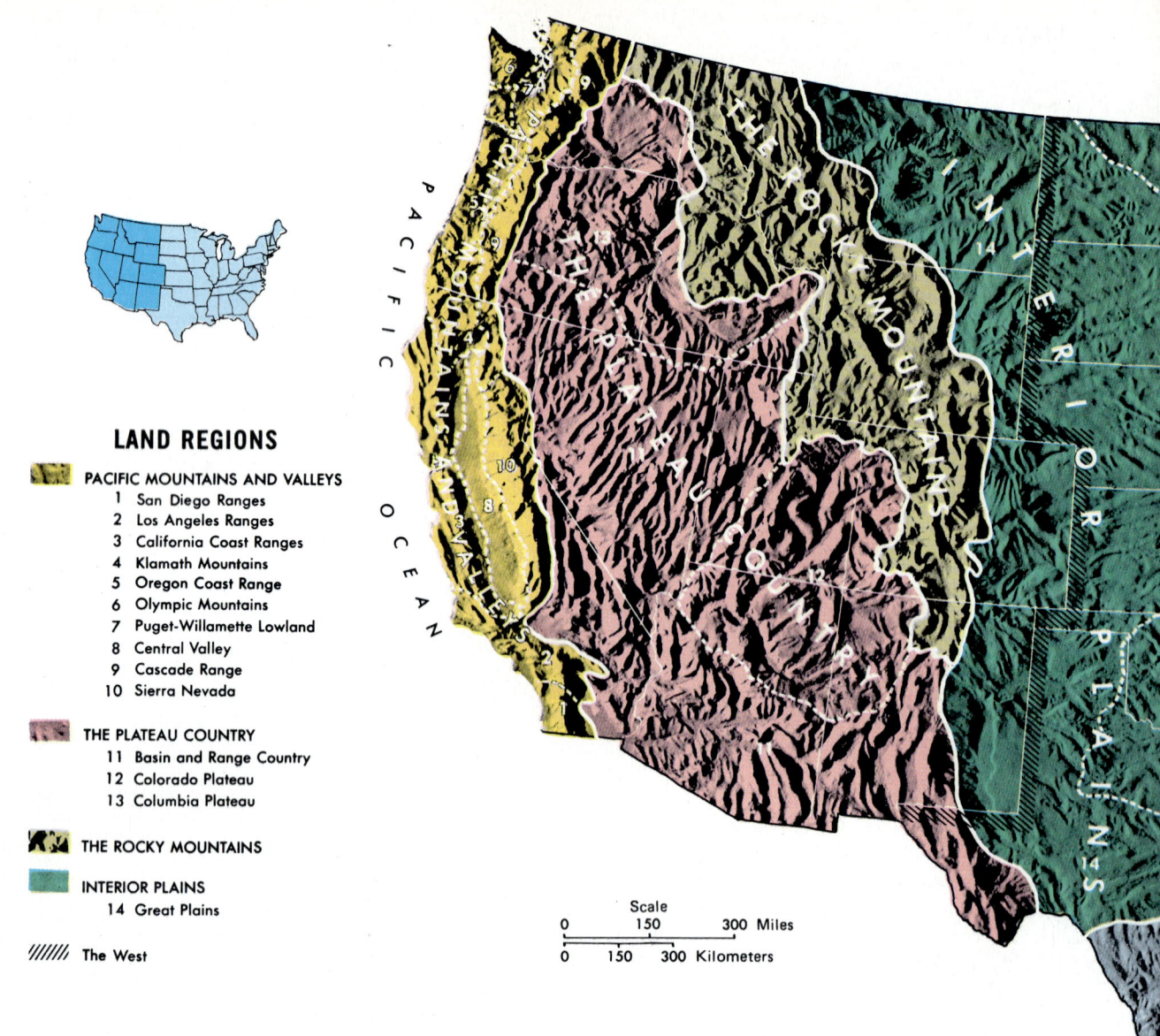

LAND REGIONS

PACIFIC MOUNTAINS AND VALLEYS
1 San Diego Ranges
2 Los Angeles Ranges
3 California Coast Ranges
4 Klamath Mountains
5 Oregon Coast Range
6 Olympic Mountains
7 Puget-Willamette Lowland
8 Central Valley
9 Cascade Range
10 Sierra Nevada

THE PLATEAU COUNTRY
11 Basin and Range Country
12 Colorado Plateau
13 Columbia Plateau

THE ROCKY MOUNTAINS

INTERIOR PLAINS
14 Great Plains

The West

are much lower than the Sierra Nevada or the Cascade Range. In some places, however, they are very steep sided. Rocky cliffs rise above the ocean in many places.

The long mountain chain along the coast is made up of several groups of mountains. (See map above.) In these mountains, much of the land is too steep and the soil is too poor for farming. Dense forests of firs, spruces, and other evergreen trees cover the mountains along the coast in Washington, Oregon, and northern California. Farther south, the forests give way to grasses and low, bushy plants.

Between the mountain ranges in southern California are several lowland areas. Although they are not very large, they are densely populated. In one lowland is Los Angeles, the largest city in the West.

Making Discoveries

In this book and in other books look for information about one of the subjects below. Then write a short report about it. Use the questions given under each subject as a guide. Suggestions in the Skills Manual will help you find information and write a good report.

A. <u>The Rocky Mountains</u>
 1. How were the Rocky Mountains formed?
 2. About how old are the Rockies?
 3. What kinds of plants and animals are found in these mountains?
 4. How have the Rockies affected our country's history?
 5. What is the Continental Divide? (You may wish to draw a map showing the Continental Divide.)

B. <u>The Grand Canyon</u>
 1. How was the Grand Canyon formed?
 2. What kinds of plants and animals are found in the Grand Canyon?

Along the coast of California. Mountain ranges extend from north to south along our country's Pacific coast. These mountains are much lower than the Sierra Nevada or the Cascade Range.

Monument Valley, in Arizona. Much of the land in the West is too dry for growing crops. The land in these areas is used for grazing livestock such as cattle, sheep, and goats.

3 Climate

A visit to the dry lands of the West

It is a July afternoon, and we are riding in a car through the northern part of Nevada. (See map on page 8.) The land here is dry. Much of it is covered with sagebrush* or with clumps of grass that have turned yellow under the hot summer sun. The only trees we see are growing along the banks of streams.

By the next afternoon, we have reached southern Nevada. The sky is bright blue, and the sun is very hot. Our lips feel dry, and we are thirsty. The land here is even drier than the land we rode through before. We do not see any grass or sagebrush. Instead, we see cactus and other strange-looking desert plants. We drive many miles without seeing a river or a lake.

At last we come to a tiny town in the desert. Here we can buy gasoline and get water to drink. A thermometer in the gas station shows that the temperature is 110° F. (43° C.).† We are glad when evening comes. As we watch a beautiful red-and-gold sunset over the desert, we notice that the air is growing cooler.

†F. means Fahrenheit scale
C. means Celsius scale
*See Glossary

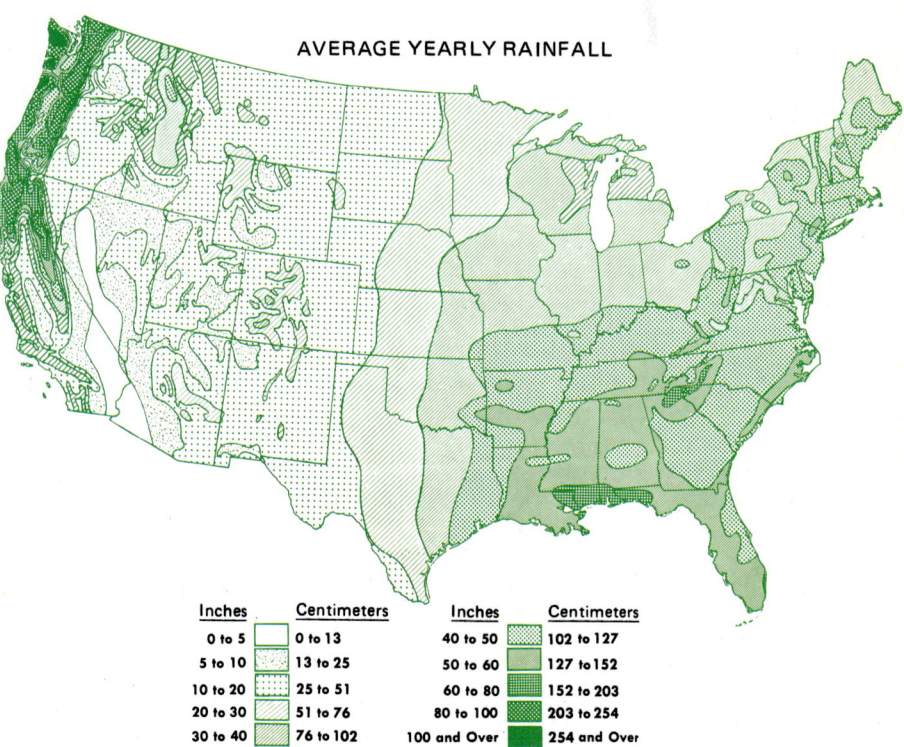

The West 27

Areas of little rainfall

If we could travel all over the West, we would find many places that are like the ones we have just visited. Most parts of the West are very dry. The map on page 27 shows how much rain usually falls each year in different parts of the United States. Notice that most parts of the West receive less than 20 inches (51 cm.)† of rainfall a year. This is not enough rainfall for most trees to grow. Much of the land in these areas is covered with grass or sagebrush. These plants do not need as much water to grow as trees do.

Because the West is so dry, much of the land here is used for raising cattle, sheep, and goats. These animals can feed on the grass that grows in dry places. Most kinds of farm crops do not grow well where rainfall is less than 20 inches (51 cm.) a year. Farmers who want to grow crops in these dry lands must bring water from other places to moisten the soil. This is called irrigation. (See Chapter 9.)

Some parts of the West are so dry that they are called deserts. Here, there is too little rainfall for grass, or even sagebrush, to grow. The land is dotted with cactus, yucca,* and other desert plants.

In the desert lands of the West, weeks, or months often pass without a drop of rain. Then there will be a sudden shower that lasts only a few minutes. After the shower, bright desert flowers burst into bloom. For a short time, they make the barren desert seem like a garden.

Areas of heavy rainfall

Not all of the West is dry. In fact, one small area in the state of Washing-

ton gets more rain than any other place in the conterminous* United States. We can learn more about the wet lands of the West by driving through the mountains of the Cascade Range in Washington.

A light, gentle rain is falling as we drive along a twisting road through the

† cm. means centimeter

Dense forests grow in the coastal mountains of California, where the rainfall is heavy. What are some of the facts that help to explain why the rainiest parts of the West are in the mountains?

mountains. On each side of the road are thick forests of firs, spruces, and other evergreen trees. Sometimes we catch a glimpse of bright-green fields and pastures in a valley far below. Because everything looks so fresh and green, we know that much rain falls in this area. Farmers in the valley do not usually have to irrigate their fields, because there is enough rain for most crops to grow.

Why rainfall is heavy in some areas

Rainfall is heaviest in parts of the West where there are mountains. All year long, moist winds from the Pacific

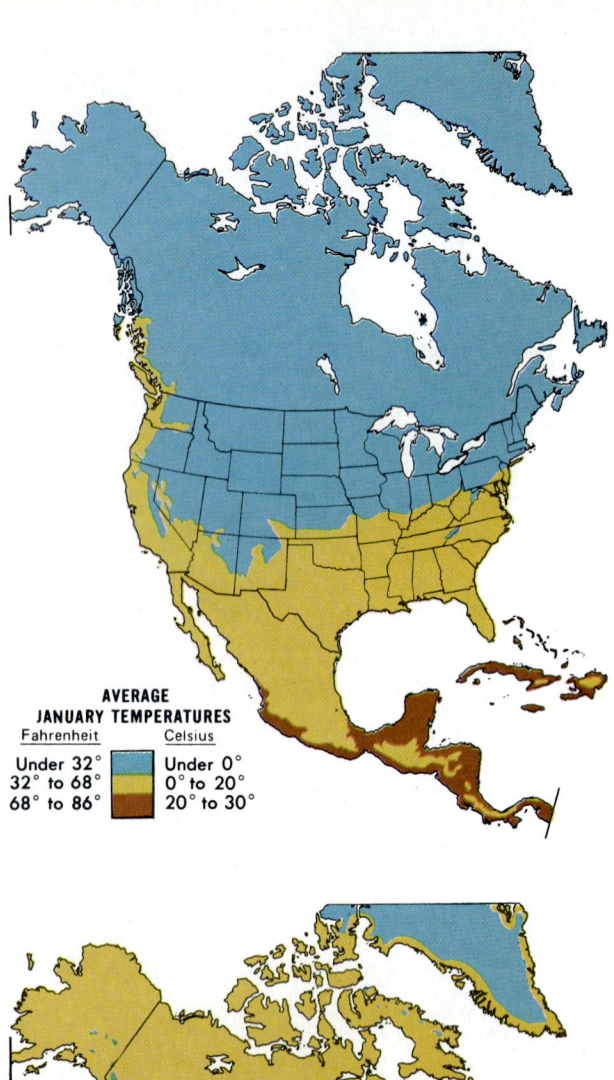

AVERAGE JANUARY TEMPERATURES

Fahrenheit	Celsius
Under 32°	Under 0°
32° to 68°	0° to 20°
68° to 86°	20° to 30°

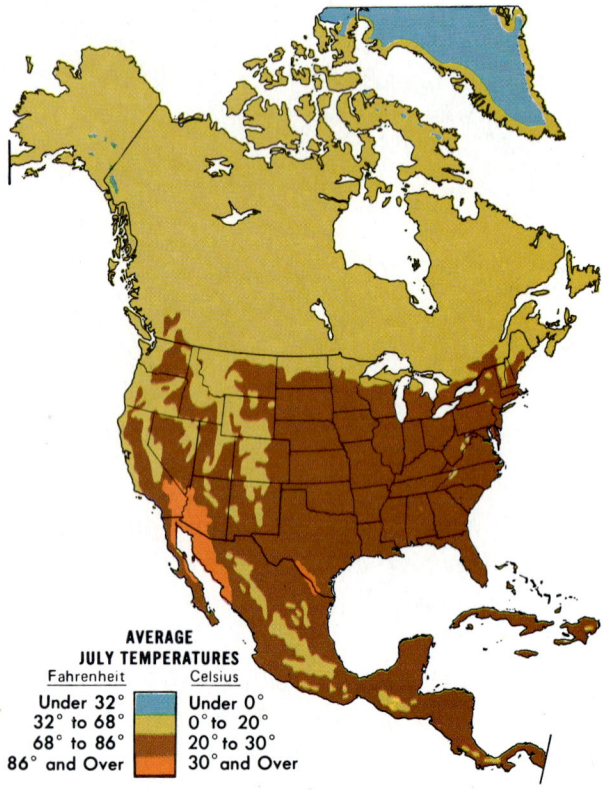

AVERAGE JULY TEMPERATURES

Fahrenheit	Celsius
Under 32°	Under 0°
32° to 68°	0° to 20°
68° to 86°	20° to 30°
86° and Over	30° and Over

Ocean blow toward the western coast of the United States. These winds contain much water that has evaporated* from the ocean. As the moist winds reach the mountains, they are forced to rise. The higher they rise above the level of the sea, the cooler they become. Cool air cannot hold as much moisture as warmer air, so part of the moisture falls to earth in the form of rain or snow. For this reason, rainfall is heavy on the mountains along the Pacific coast and on the western slopes of the Sierra Nevada and the Cascade Range. It is very heavy in the western parts of Washington and Oregon. Here, the yearly rainfall may be more than 100 inches (254 cm.).

By the time the winds blowing from the west have crossed the mountains, they have lost much of their moisture. As they move down the eastern slopes of the mountains, the winds become warmer. Instead of giving off moisture, they take up moisture from the land. This is one reason why the land to the east of the mountains is so dry. We say that it lies in the "rain shadow" of the mountains.

The winds continue to blow eastward until they reach the Rocky Mountains. Again they are forced to rise and give off some of their moisture. But this time the winds do not contain as much moisture as they did when they blew in from the ocean. For this reason, the Rocky Mountains do not receive as much rainfall as the mountains that lie farther to the west.

During the winter, most of the moisture in the air falls on the mountains in the form of snow. In the high Sierra Nevada and in the Cascade Range, the snow is often very deep. The railroads that cross these mountains must use giant snowplows to clear the tracks so that the trains can get through. In the spring, the melting snow helps to fill the rivers of the West with fresh water.

Differences in temperature

In the West, there are great differences in temperature from one place to another. You can see this if you study the two maps on the opposite page. These maps show average temperatures

Hikers near Mount Rainier, in Washington's Cascade Range. Mount Rainier is one of the highest peaks in the West. Summer weather is cooler in the mountains than it is in the lowlands. Why is this so?

Winter in Montana. Winters in the northern parts of the Great Plains and the Plateau Country are generally very cold, while summers are often quite hot. What facts help to explain why this is so?

in North America during the months of January and July.

On the January temperature map, find the part of the West where the average temperatures are below 32° F. (0° C.). You can tell that winters are cold in this area, because 32° F. is the temperature at which water freezes. In the rest of the West, the average temperatures during the month of January are between 32° and 68° F. (0° and 20° C.). This is neither very hot nor

either warm or hot during the summer. In other parts of the West, summers are mild. You will find out some of the reasons for these differences as you study about the climate in different parts of the West.

Climate of the plains and plateaus

In the northern parts of the Great Plains and the Plateau Country, winters are cold and summers are very warm. For example, in eastern Montana the temperature sometimes drops to -30° F. (-34° C.) on winter nights. But on a summer afternoon the temperature here may rise to more than 100° F. (38° C.).

Why are winters so cold and summers so warm in these parts of the West? First, these areas are shut off from the Pacific Ocean by high mountains. Also, they are far from any other large body of water. So they are not cooled in summer or warmed in winter by mild ocean breezes.

Farther south in the Great Plains and the Plateau Country, winters are milder and summers are warmer than they are in the north. Usually the southern part of our country has higher temperatures than the northern part. The reasons for this are explained in "The Seasons of the Year," on pages 34 and 35.

Climate of the high mountains

Winters are cold in the Rocky Mountains, the Sierra Nevada, and other high mountains of the West. For several months each year, the ground is buried under a deep blanket of snow. Some peaks are covered with snow the year around.

During the summer, the weather in the mountains is seldom very warm.

very cold, so we can say that winters are mild in this part of the West.

Now look at the July temperature map. You can see that in some parts of the West, the average temperatures are above 68° F. Here the weather is

SUMMER IN THE NORTHERN HEMISPHERE

The chart above shows how the earth is lighted by the sun at noon on June 21, the first day of summer in the Northern Hemisphere.

THE SEASONS

The year is divided into four natural periods, or seasons. We call them summer, autumn, winter, and spring. Each season is marked by changes in the length of day and night and by changes in temperature.

The seasons are caused by the tilt of the earth's axis and the revolution of the earth around the sun. It takes one year for the earth to revolve around the sun. On this trip, the earth remains tilted at the same angle to the path along which it travels. The chart below shows how this causes the Northern Hemisphere to be tilted toward the sun on June 21 and away from the sun on December 22. On March 21 and September 22, the Northern Hemisphere is tilted neither toward the sun nor away from it.

The chart on the left shows that on June 21 the sun shines directly on the Tropic of Cancer.* This is the northernmost point ever reached by the sun's direct rays. In the Northern Hemisphere, June 21 is the first day of summer and the longest day of the year.

The chart on the right shows that on December 22 the sun shines directly on the Tropic of Capricorn.* This is the southernmost point ever reached by the sun's direct

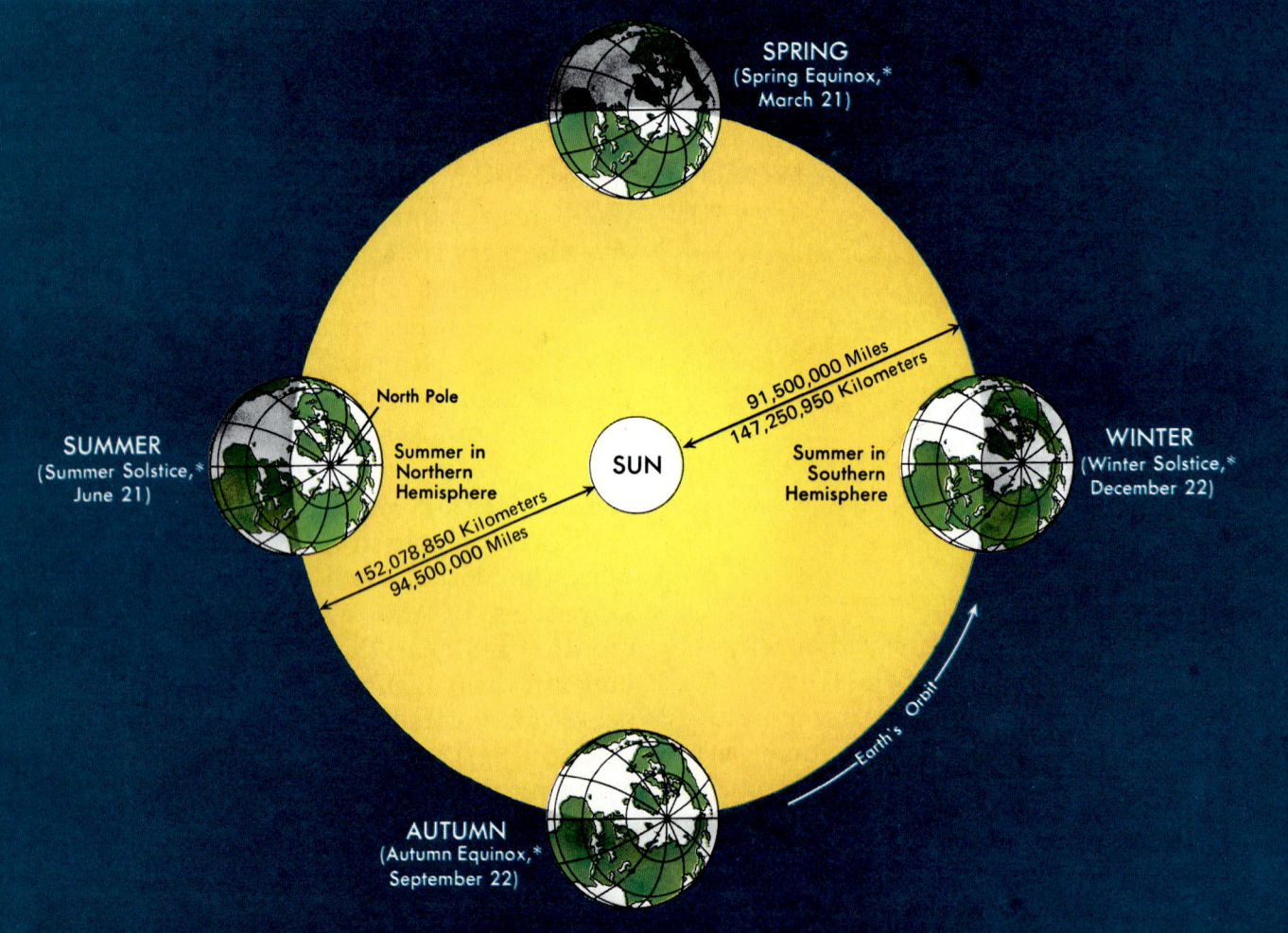

OF THE YEAR

rays. In the Northern Hemisphere, December 22 is the first day of winter and the shortest day of the year.

When one hemisphere is tilted toward the sun, the other is tilted away from the sun. For this reason, the seasons in the Southern Hemisphere are just the opposite of those in the Northern Hemisphere. Summer in the Southern Hemisphere begins on December 22, and winter begins on June 21.

Temperatures are affected by the slant of the sun's rays as they strike the surface of the earth. Study the chart below, and the picture of San Diego, California, to help you understand why this is true.

Near the equator, the sun is almost directly overhead throughout the year. For this reason, the weather near the equator is always hot, except in the mountains. In areas farther away from the equator, the sun's rays are more slanted. Therefore, the weather is usually cooler.

The southern part of the United States is nearer the equator than the northern part. This helps to explain why the weather is generally warmer in the southern part of our country than it is in the northern part.

*See Glossary

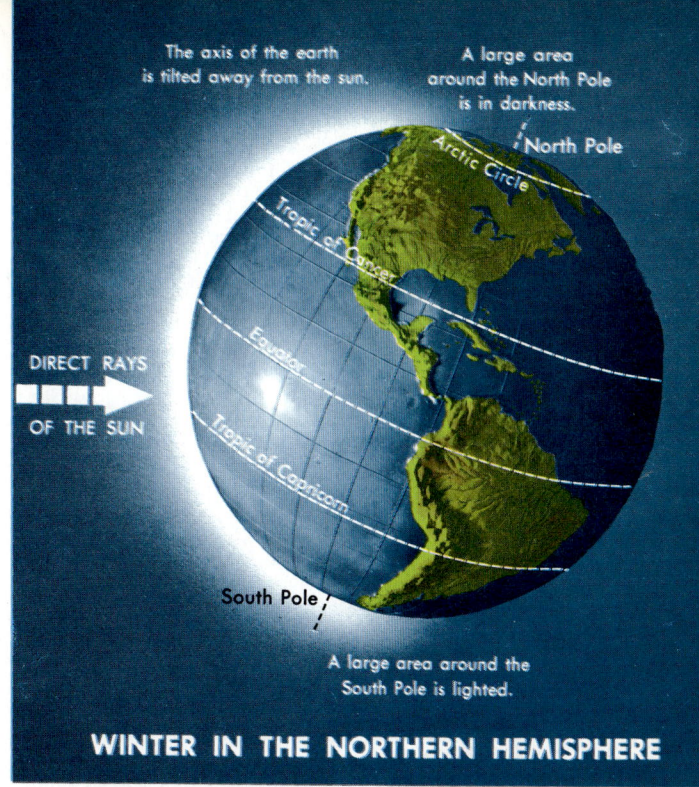

WINTER IN THE NORTHERN HEMISPHERE

The chart above shows how the earth is lighted by the sun at noon on December 22, the first day of winter in the Northern Hemisphere.

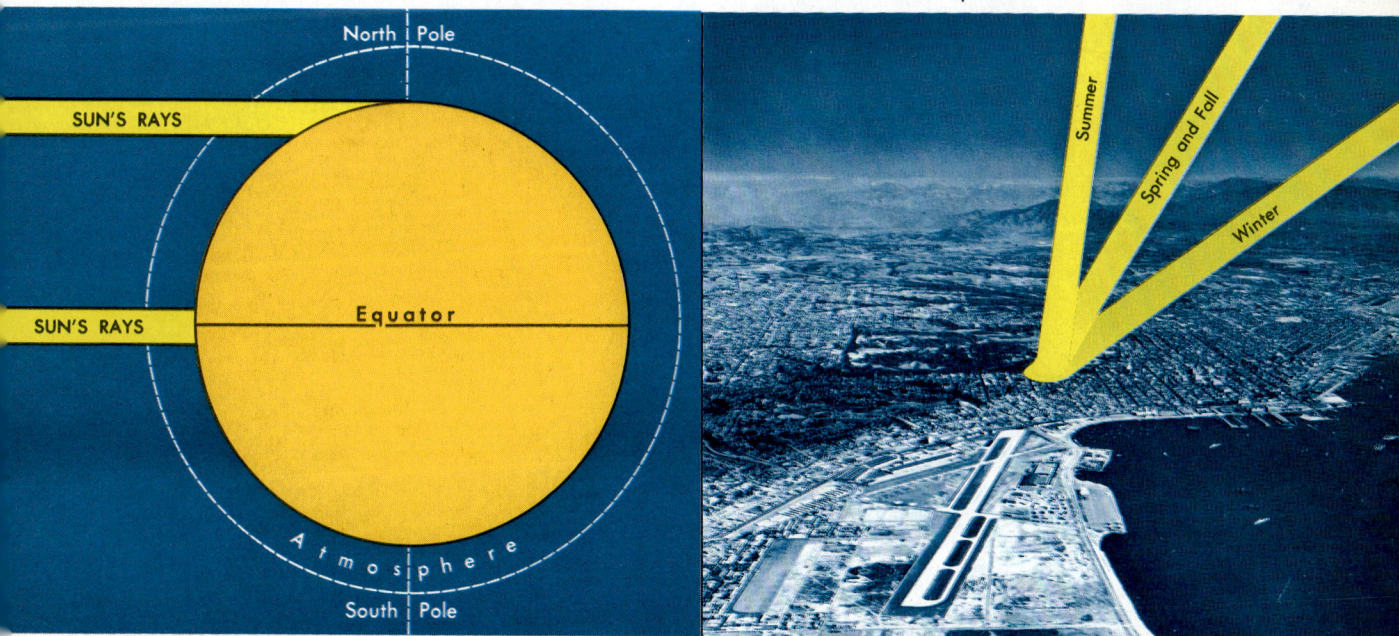

The chart above shows that when the sun's rays strike the earth at a slant, they must travel through more atmosphere, or air, than when they strike it directly. This affects temperatures because the air soaks up heat from the sun's rays. The more air the rays must pass through, the less heat they hold to warm the earth. This is one reason why temperatures are higher if the sun is directly overhead than they are if the sun is low in the sky.

This picture also helps to explain how changes in temperature are caused by the different angles at which the sun's rays strike the earth. During the summer, the noon sun is high in the sky. The rays of the sun are concentrated into small areas. For this reason, they give large amounts of heat. During the winter, the noon sun is lower in the sky. The slanting rays of the sun are spread over much wider areas, so they give less heat.

The West 35

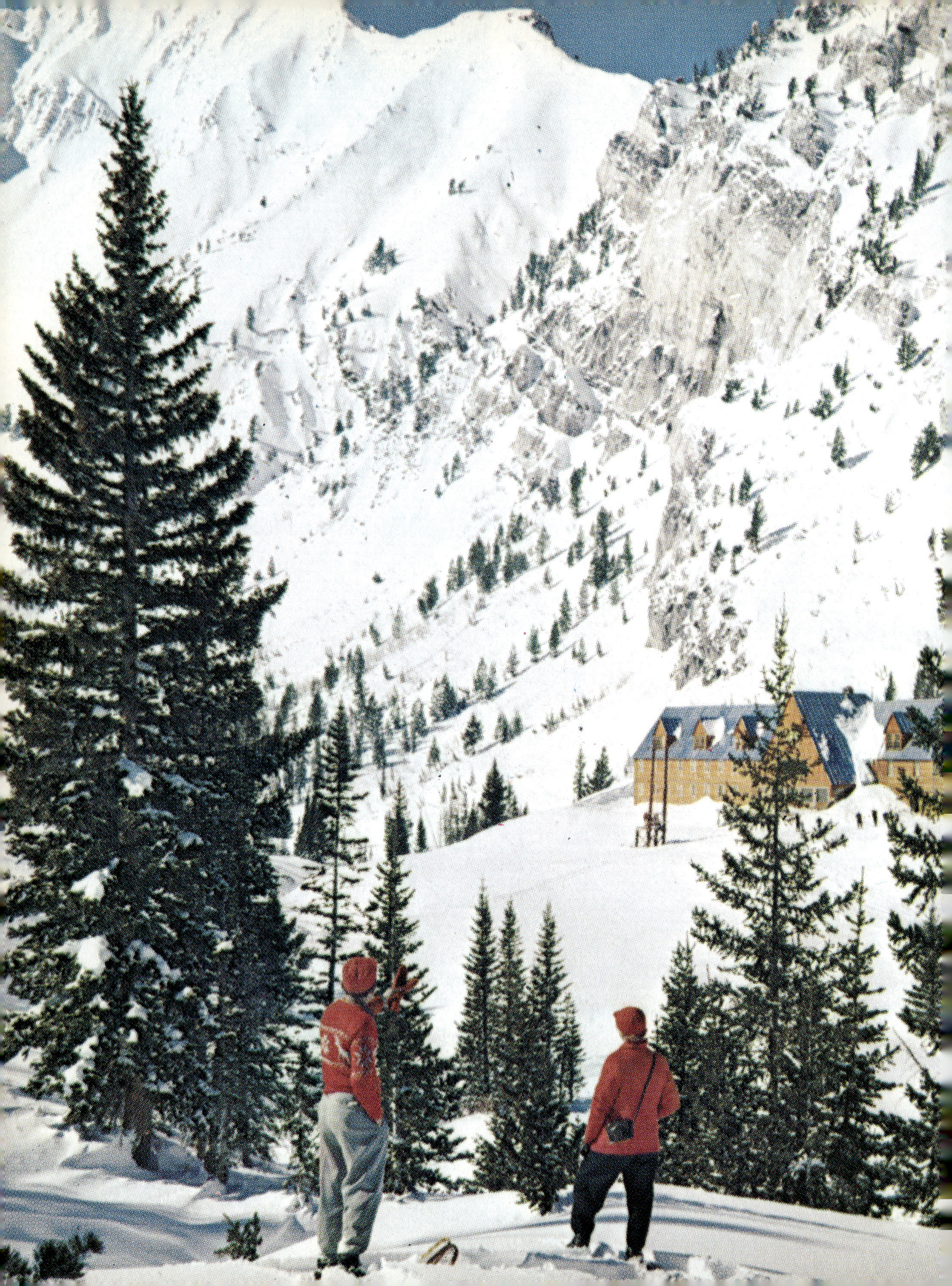

Many people come to the mountains in the summertime to enjoy the cool, refreshing air.

The mountains of the West are usually cooler than nearby lowlands because they are so much higher above the level of the sea. The higher you go above sea level, the cooler the air becomes.

As you may have learned in your science class, the earth gives off heat that it has received from the sun. Near sea level, much of this heat is held by tiny bits of dust and moisture in the air. High above sea level, the air is much cleaner and drier. It cannot hold as much heat. For this reason, the temperature is usually cooler at high altitudes* than it is at low altitudes.

In the high mountains, the growing season is less than four months long. (See map on page 38.) The growing season is the time when crops can be grown outdoors without danger of being killed by frost. Farmers cannot grow crops when the temperature is below freezing. They must plant their crops after the last heavy frost in the spring, and harvest them before the first heavy frost in the fall. Because the growing season is so short in the mountains, farmers must grow crops that do not take a long time to ripen. Among these crops are potatoes and barley.

Climate in the southern part of the West

Winters are mild all the way across the southern part of the West except in the high mountains. (See the top map on page 30.) In southern California, Arizona, and New Mexico, winter days are often warm and sunny. Snow seldom falls in these areas.

The people who live in the southernmost part of the West are able to work and play outdoors all year long. They enjoy the mild

Physical Needs

See Needs of People

In the high mountains of the West, winters are long and cold. For several months each year, the ground is buried under a deep blanket of snow. In fact, some of the highest peaks are covered with snow even in summer. As a class, discuss the following questions. Information in this book and other books will help you prepare for your discussion.

1. Do you think the people in this picture have the same physical needs that you do? Do they need food? Clothing? Exercise?
2. In what ways does the climate of the West's high mountains affect the ways in which people meet their physical needs in the winter? In the summer?
3. At what time of the year would you most like to visit the high mountains of the West? Why do you feel this way?

winters. When they go outside, they do not have to wear heavy clothing. Many bright flowers bloom even during the winter. Thousands of people from the northern part of our country come here for winter vacations.

During the summer, the weather in the southern part of the West is usually warm or hot. There are many summer days when the temperature in the deserts rises above 100° F. (38° C.).

In some places in the southern part of the West, the growing season lasts more than eight months. (See map below.) Here, farmers can grow cotton and other crops that ripen slowly.

Crops can be grown all year long in some parts of southern California and southern Arizona. In these areas, there is seldom a frost. Farmers can grow such warm-weather crops as oranges and lemons. They can also grow vegetables outdoors during the wintertime. Some of these vegetables are sold to people in colder parts of our country.

Climate along the Pacific coast

In most places along the Pacific coast of the West, the weather is mild the year around. (See maps on page 30.) Snow usually falls only on the mountains. The growing season is longer here than in places farther inland.

This part of the West has mild weather all year long because it lies near the Pacific Ocean. Like all large bodies of water, the ocean is warmer than the land in winter and cooler than the land in summer. All year, winds that blow eastward from the ocean bring mild weather to the lands along the coast.

The growing season is the period of time during which crops can be grown outdoors without danger of being killed by frost. In the West, there are great differences in the length of the growing season.

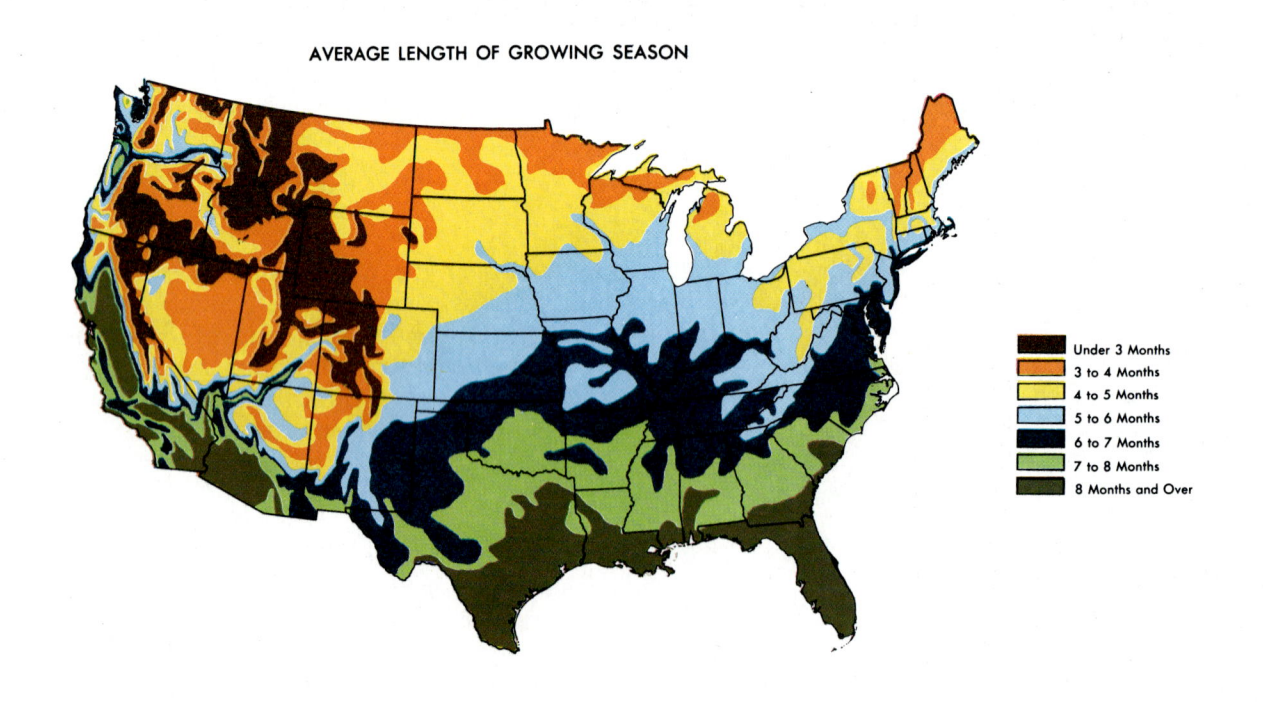

AVERAGE LENGTH OF GROWING SEASON

- Under 3 Months
- 3 to 4 Months
- 4 to 5 Months
- 5 to 6 Months
- 6 to 7 Months
- 7 to 8 Months
- 8 Months and Over

Surfers riding a wave in the Pacific Ocean, along the coast of southern California. The climate here is mild enough for people to enjoy summer sports for many months of the year. Do you think these surfers have a feeling of freedom? What makes you think this? Have there been times in your own life when you felt completely free? When were those times? Do any persons ever have the freedom to do just as they please, or are there always limits on freedom? Think carefully about this question before giving your answer.

Freedom

See Great Ideas

Problems To Solve

1. Winter weather varies from place to place in the West. Winters are cold in some areas and mild in others. Why is this so? In making hypotheses* to solve this problem you will need to consider how temperatures in different parts of the West are affected by the following:
   a. distance from the equator
   b. height above sea level
   c. distance from large bodies of water

2. How does the climate in different parts of the West affect farming? To solve this problem, you will need to consider facts about each of the following:
   a. the length of the growing season in different parts of the West
   b. the amount of rainfall in these areas
   c. the kinds of crops that are grown
   d. the kinds of livestock that are raised
   Chapter 8 contains information that will be helpful in solving this problem.

   See Skills Manual, "Thinking and Solving Problems"

The West 39

Part 2
People

Many different groups of people make their homes in the West. As you do research about the people of the West, you will discover why so many different groups live in this part of our country. You may also wish to find answers to the following questions.
- Why have so many people come to the West to live during the last one hundred years?
- Why does much of the West have few people? Why do some areas have many people?
- What are some of the largest cities in the West? Why did these cities grow up where they did?
- How are the communities in our country governed?
- What makes a successful community? Why are some communities in our country unsuccessful?
- What important artists have lived and worked in the West?

The chapters in Part 2 will help you answer these questions. Use maps, charts, and pictures, as well as text, to get the information you need.

A computer center in California. Do you think the people in this picture have the same needs as you do? Do you think they meet their needs in the same way? Explain your answers.

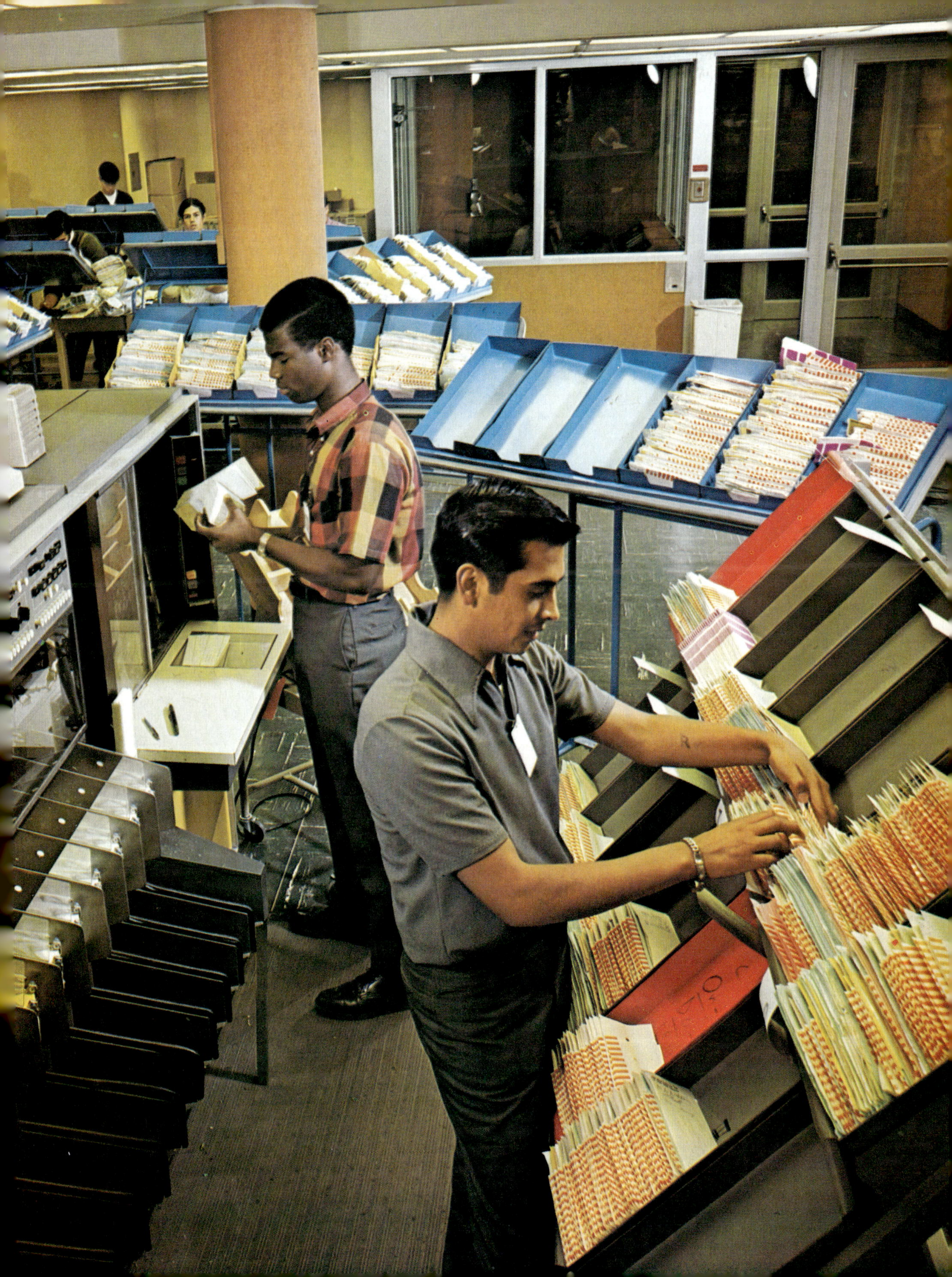

POWELL
AND
MARKET
FISHERMAN'S WHARF
3 BLOCKS
FROM TERMINAL
BAY
AND
TAYLOR
501
RICE A RONI
San Francisco treat

4 People

A growing region

In the 1840's, pioneers began moving to the West over the Oregon Trail.* Ever since then, large numbers of people have been moving to the West. Some of these people have come from other countries. But most of them have come from different parts of the United States.

Today, the population of the West is still growing rapidly. More than 38 million people now make their homes in the West. Even though so many people live in the West, this region is still not crowded. The West makes up almost one third of the area of the United States. But only about one sixth of our country's people live here.

Migration

People in San Francisco, California. For more than one hundred years, large numbers of people have been moving to the West. This movement of people out of one region or country into another is known as migration. Do research in this chapter. Then answer the following questions about migration and population density in the West.

1. In what parts of the West do large numbers of people live?
2. What are some of the reasons why people may have settled in these parts of the West?
3. What part of the West would you most like to live in? Give reasons for your answer.

The West 43

Much of the West has few people

In much of the West there are few people. (See map on page 46.) In some places, a traveler can drive for many miles across lonely plains without seeing another person.

Several facts help to explain why so much of the West has so few people. As Chapter 2 explained, water is scarce in many places. People cannot live without a steady supply of fresh water. Also, farmers need water in order to grow crops.

There are some other reasons why much of the West has few people. Many areas of the West do not have railroads or paved highways. Mountains and canyons* make it hard to build them. Also, in much of the West there is very little industry to provide jobs. (See Chapter 10.)

Many people live in California

More people live in the state of California than in the other ten states of the West together.

California is now the home of about 22 million people. It has a larger population than any other state in the United States. Many Californians live in the southern part of the state. Here are the great cities of Los Angeles and San Diego. (See map on page 8.) Many people also live farther north, in an area around San Francisco Bay. The cities of San Francisco and Oakland are located here. There are also large numbers of people in the Central Valley.

Why many people live in California

There are several reasons why California has so many people. In many parts of the state, the weather is mild most of the time. Many people who used to live in places where winter is cold have moved to California. Here they enjoy pleasant weather during most of the year. People also move to California because there are many interesting places to visit. There are sandy beaches and high mountains. There are dense forests and sparkling lakes. California also has five national parks.

Many of the people in California came here to find work. In the 1940's, many huge factories were built in this state. These factories make airplanes, automobiles, clothing, and many other kinds of goods. Today, millions of people work in these factories and in other businesses.

As more people moved to California, still more jobs were created. The families that arrived each year needed homes. In order to meet this need, new houses and apartment buildings were built. This provided many jobs for builders. The newcomers also needed food, furniture, and other goods. New factories were built to make these goods. Also, new stores and shopping centers were opened. As a result, more workers were needed in factories, stores, and offices. As California's population continued to grow, more people were also needed to provide different kinds of services. These people included doctors, teachers, and police officers.

People in other parts of the West

Outside of California, there are only a few areas in the West where large numbers of people live. One of these is the Puget-Willamette Lowland in Washington and Oregon. Many cities, towns, and farms are located in this lowland. The two largest cities—Seattle,

Portland, Oregon, and **Seattle, Washington,** are in the Puget-Willamette Lowland. This is one of the few parts of the West where large numbers of people live. As you can see by the map on page 46, most of the West's densely populated areas are in California.

Washington, and Portland, Oregon—are busy seaports. Factories and offices in these cities provide jobs for many thousands of people.

Most of the other people in the West live in or near a few large cities. (Compare the map below with the map on page 61.) These cities are located along main transportation routes. They are served by good highways, railroads, and airlines. Farmers and ranchers come from many miles away to buy the goods they need. Many people in these cities work in stores and offices. Others have factory jobs. Thousands of retired workers and other people have moved to Arizona and New Mexico. They like the warm, sunny climate there.

Many groups of people

Through the years, people have come to the West from many parts of the world. Today, people of many different races and national* origins make their homes in this part of the United States.

People of European descent

More than three fourths of the people in the West are descended from people who came to North America from Europe. Our country was settled mainly by people from the British Isles. These people brought the English language and many customs to the colonies.* It is not surprising that many people in the West are of English, Scotch, or Irish descent.

There are also many people in the West whose ancestors* came from other parts of Europe. For example, many of the people in Colorado, Washington, and Oregon are of German descent.

Mexican-Americans

More than two million Mexican-Americans live in the West. About four fifths of these people were born in the

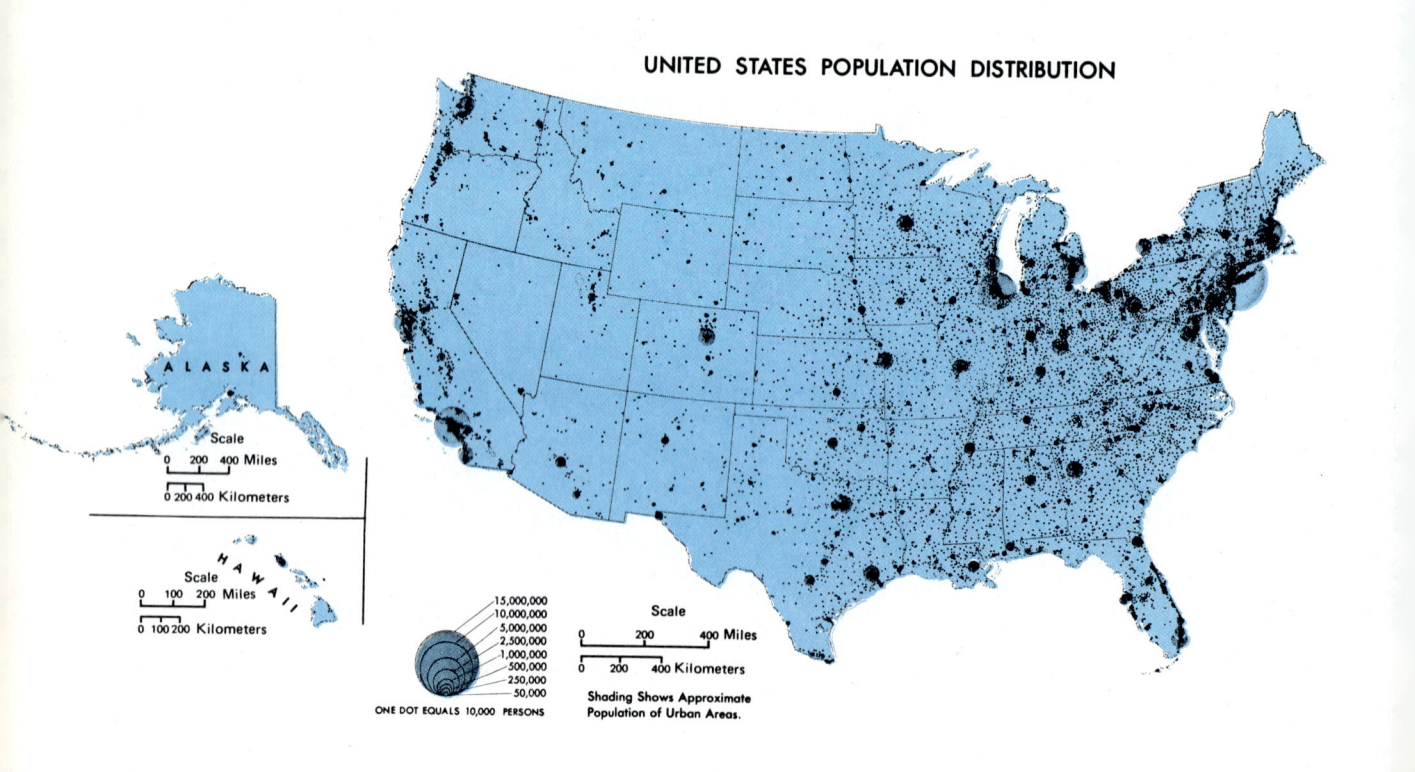

UNITED STATES POPULATION DISTRIBUTION

Language

See Great Ideas

Mexican-Americans in San Francisco. More than two million Mexican-Americans make their homes in the West. In the past, many of these people were thought of as "outsiders." This was partly because they spoke Spanish instead of English. Today, more and more Mexican-Americans are using the English language. Do you think it is important for people in our country to speak English? Why do you think this? Do you think it would be a good thing to speak both Spanish and English? Explain.

United States. The others have come here from Mexico. Some Mexican-Americans earn their living as farmers. Most of them live and work in or near Los Angeles and other large cities.

People from Mexico were coming to the West even before the Pilgrims came to America. Some of the early Mexican settlements were in areas that are now part of New Mexico or California.

Until recent years, people of Mexican descent* were often thought of as "outsiders." They spoke Spanish instead of English, and many of them dropped out of school at an early age.

Today, more Mexican-Americans are getting the education they need to hold well-paying jobs. Some are doctors, lawyers, or teachers. Others work in stores, factories, or government offices. Many of these people live in comfortable, modern homes. They enjoy the same conveniences as most other Americans.

The West 47

Fishermen in the West. Nearly two million people of African descent make their homes in the West. Many of them live in Los Angeles, San Francisco, and the other large cities of California.

Many Mexican-Americans are also taking an active role in government. During the 1960's, thousands of Mexican-Americans registered to vote for the first time. A number of political groups have been formed by Mexican-Americans. These groups support candidates who have promised to help Mexican-Americans meet their needs and solve their problems.

People of African descent

Nearly two million people of African descent live in the West. They live mainly in the large cities of California. Many of them have moved to the West from other parts of our country.

For many years, black Americans did not enjoy the same freedoms as most other citizens. For example, some business people refused to hire black workers. Some apartment owners refused to rent to black families.

Today, laws have been passed to prevent discrimination.* Under these laws, black people have an equal opportunity with all other citizens to get good jobs. There are also laws that forbid discrimination in housing. Black people enjoy other rights and freedoms as well. As a result, more black people now have good jobs in business and industry. Some of them work in medicine, education, and other fields. Others are

48 The West

lawyers or government leaders. More black Americans now have the opportunities they need in order to live happy and successful lives.

People of Asian descent

Many people in the West are of Asian descent. Almost all of them are Japanese, Chinese, or Filipino. Thousands of these people live in the West's large cities. For example, there is a section called "Chinatown" in San Francisco. Large numbers of people of Chinese descent live and work in this section.

Like Mexican-Americans and blacks, people of Asian descent have often been denied rights and freedoms that other Americans enjoy. For example, during World War II,* many loyal Americans suffered from discrimination. This was because their ancestors came from Japan. When Japan became our enemy, it was feared that these people might be disloyal to our country. Because of this fear, our government moved more than 100,000 of these Japanese-Americans away from their homes on the Pacific coast. They were kept in camps that were located far inland. They were not permitted to return to their homes until the war was nearly over.

Today, the people of Asian descent in the West enjoy the same rights and

People of Japanese descent at a festival in Seattle. Thousands of people who live in the West's large cities are of Asian descent. Many of them are Japanese. Others are Chinese or Filipino.

freedoms that other Americans do. They vote and hold government offices. They have an opportunity to get a good education. They also have many opportunities to hold well-paying jobs. Some are doctors or teachers. Others have their own businesses. Still others work in stores or factories.

Native Americans

Nearly 400,000 Indians, or Native Americans, live in the West. About half of these people make their homes in California and Arizona. Other states in the West with large populations of Native Americans are New Mexico and Washington.

Like the other minority* peoples in our country, Native Americans have suffered from discrimination. During the last half of the 1800's, most of the Indian tribes in the West were forced to move onto reservations.*

Life was not easy for the people who lived on Indian reservations. In many cases, the only way to make a living was by farming. But much of the land on the reservations was not good for

A Navaho Indian woman. Nearly 400,000 Indians, or Native Americans, make their homes in the West.

Education

See Great Ideas

The picture above shows a classroom on an Indian reservation in New Mexico. Do you think going to school is a good way of getting an education? Why do you think this? The picture on the opposite page shows a Navaho Indian woman weaving. How do you suppose she learned this skill? Do you think learning in this way can also be called education? What are some of the skills you have learned? How did you learn them?

growing crops. Also, many Indians had little interest in farming.

To add to their problems, the Indians on reservations were not allowed to govern themselves. The United States government treated them like children who had to be kept out of trouble. It gave the Indians few chances to decide things for themselves.

In recent years, the federal government has done a number of things to help the Indians on reservations. Many groups of Indians now make some of their own laws. They can also set up courts to judge Indians accused of crimes that are not very serious. The federal government has also helped to create new job opportunities for Indians. A number of factories have been built on or near the reservations. With the help of money loaned by the government, many groups of Indians have started businesses.

Work as a Social* Scientist

The picture on pages 42-43 shows people in a large city in the West. Think and work with this picture as a social scientist does. Study the picture and record your findings.
1. Where do you think this picture was taken? Why do you think this?
2. Do you think the people in this picture are similar to the people where you live? Explain your answer.
3. What does this picture tell you about ways in which the people of this city meet their needs? (See "Needs of People" at the back of this book.)
4. What does this picture tell you about ways in which people earn their living in this city?

5 Cities

A Problem To Solve

The West is a very rapidly growing region. It has a population of more than 38 million. Yet many parts of the West are very thinly populated. For example, Wyoming is the ninth largest state in our country. It has an area as large as the states of New York and Pennsylvania together. Even so, Wyoming has a smaller population than any other state.

Almost half of the people of the West live in or near a few large cities such as Los Angeles, San Francisco, Seattle, and Denver. Why is this so? In forming hypotheses* to solve this problem, think about how the population distribution of the West is affected by the following:
1. climate
2. transportation routes
3. ways of earning a living in the West

See Skills Manual, "Thinking and Solving Problems"
*See Glossary

Rules and Government

See Great Ideas

Los Angeles is the largest city in the West and the third largest in our country. More than two and a half million people live here. Do you think so many people could live together in one city if they didn't follow certain rules? Why? Why not? What are some of the rules people must follow to live and work together successfully in large cities? Are rules also needed by people who live in small towns? Explain your answer.

About five out of every six people in the West live in cities or large towns. Most of the large cities here are on or near the Pacific coast. In two western states, Montana and Wyoming, there are no cities with more than 100,000 people.

In recent years, metropolitan* areas in the West have been growing rapidly in population. (See chart at right.) Today, some metropolitan areas have more than twice as many people as they did twenty years ago.

Los Angeles

The largest city in the West is Los Angeles, California. Except for New York and Chicago, Los Angeles is larger than any other city in the United States. It spreads across a lowland in the southern part of California. To the north and east of Los Angeles are ranges of rugged mountains. The Pacific Ocean lies to the west and south.

Los Angeles and its neighboring cities have grown so close together that it is difficult to tell where one ends and another begins. Altogether, there are more than seventy-five cities in the huge metropolitan area that includes Los Angeles. The largest of these cities, except for Los Angeles, is Long Beach. South and east of Los Angeles are other metropolitan areas.

If you were to fly over the Los Angeles-Long Beach metropolitan area, you would see large groups of one-story houses. You would see schools and shopping centers. Most of the buildings you would see are low. However, in some places, there are groups of tall office buildings and hotels. Many freeways* pass through Los Angeles and its neighboring cities. They make it easier for people to travel from one place to another in this huge metropolitan area.

SIX METROPOLITAN AREAS

Metropolitan Area	Population of Entire Area	Population of Central City (or Cities)
Los Angeles-Long Beach	7,004,400	2,737,000 343,000
San Francisco-Oakland	3,158,900	660,000 338,000
Anaheim-Santa Ana-Garden Grove	1,755,600	202,000 181,000 120,000
San Diego	1,623,400	805,000
Denver-Boulder	1,442,500	502,000 84,400
Seattle-Everett	1,421,700	505,000 52,800

The six largest metropolitan* areas in the West are listed above. Their populations are given in the middle column. For each of these areas, the population of the central city or cities is also given.

*See Glossary

Industry

There are thousands of factories in and near Los Angeles. Some of them make airplanes or electronic* equipment. Other factories assemble automobiles or make tires and other automobile parts. Many factories in the Los Angeles area process* oranges, vegetables, and other crops. These crops are raised on the rich farmlands of southern California. Los Angeles is a leading producer of sports clothing, dresses, and furniture. The television and motion picture industries are also important here.

A leading seaport

Los Angeles is the most important seaport in the West. This city has one of the world's largest artificial harbors. To form this harbor, a breakwater* had to be built. Then channels were dug into the land. Along the channels, piers were built where ships could dock. Each year millions of tons of goods are loaded and unloaded at the port of Los Angeles.

History

Less than 150 years ago, Los Angeles was a little Mexican town. After California became a part of the United States, more people came to the Los Angeles area. They found a pleasant, sunny climate and fertile soil. There was plenty of space for homes and factories. Also, a valuable resource—oil—was found under the ground. All these things brought more people. As railroads and highways were built, people came to Los Angeles from many parts of the United States. The city grew rapidly. Today the Los Angeles metropolitan area is still growing.

San Francisco

The map on page 8 shows a large inlet of the Pacific Ocean that goes through the coastal mountains of California. This is San Francisco Bay. It looks somewhat like a lake. This is because it is almost separated from the ocean by two arms of land. The southern arm is called the San Francisco Peninsula. At the end of this peninsula* is San Francisco.

Around San Francisco Bay are many other cities and towns. The largest is Oakland. Together, San Francisco and its neighbors make up a metropolitan area of more than three million people.

To the north of the city of San Francisco is a narrow water passage called the Golden Gate. It connects the ocean with San Francisco Bay. Two great

The great city of San Francisco is bordered on the west by the Pacific Ocean and on the east by San Francisco Bay. How has San Francisco's location affected its growth?

The West 55

bridges connect San Francisco with neighboring cities and towns. One is the Golden Gate Bridge, which runs north and south across the Golden Gate. It is one of the longest suspension* bridges in the world. The San Francisco-Oakland Bay Bridge joins San Francisco with the city of Oakland. It goes across San Francisco Bay.

A fine natural harbor

The location of San Francisco has helped to make it an important seaport. San Francisco Bay is one of the world's best natural harbors. Together with the Golden Gate, it forms the only natural passageway through the mountains along the coast of California. From San Francisco, goods can easily be shipped to inland cities or to ports in other countries. Four main railroads carry goods to and from San Francisco. Ships from many different parts of the world dock at piers along the waterfront.

Industry

Many factories have been built in the San Francisco metropolitan area. Most of them are outside the city of San Francisco. In neighboring towns and cities there is more room for growth. Among the products made in the San Francisco area are automobiles, chemicals,* paper, clothing, and frozen foods. There are large shipyards on San Francisco Bay.

History

San Francisco began as a small Spanish fort and mission in 1776. About seventy years later, gold was discovered in California. Thousands of people came to San Francisco on their way to the goldfields. The city grew rapidly. In 1906, an earthquake started a fire that destroyed most of San Francisco. After the fire, the people worked together to rebuild their city. They made it more beautiful than it had been before. Today, San Francisco is considered one of the most beautiful cities in the United States.

Much of San Francisco is very hilly. Small streetcars called cable cars go up and down the hilly streets. They are pulled by long cables set in slots in the streets. San Francisco is also famous for a section called Chinatown. Here there are many shops and restaurants. Thousands of people of Chinese descent live and work in this part of San Francisco.

San Diego

The city of San Diego, California, is on the Pacific coast. It is near the border between the United States and Mexico. The city lies on a lowland along San Diego Bay. It stretches inland toward the peaks of the San Diego Ranges.

An important seaport

San Diego Bay is long and narrow. It is protected from the ocean by two long peninsulas. These form an excellent harbor for oceangoing ships. This fine harbor has helped to make San Diego an important seaport. Ships from many different countries load and unload their goods here. Also, one of the United States Navy's largest bases is at San Diego. Many people in San Diego serve in the navy or work at the naval base.

San Diego is also an important fishing port. Large catches of tuna, anchovies,* and other fish are brought to San Diego. Some of these fish are canned in plants in the city.

Industry

There are many other kinds of industry in San Diego. Large factories here make airplanes and airplane parts. Other factories make electronic equipment, plastics, and boat motors. At the edge of San Diego Bay are great salt flats where ocean water is evaporated* by the sun, leaving salt. The salt is gathered by bulldozers and power shovels

San Diego lies on the Pacific coast of southern California. It is a major seaport and an important manufacturing city. Why do many retired people and tourists come to San Diego?

Seattle is Washington's largest city and most important seaport. It is located on hilly land along the shores of Puget Sound. What important industry provides jobs for many people in Seattle?

and taken to factories where it is prepared for sale.

In San Diego, the weather is mild and sunny the year around. The pleasant climate is why many retired people have chosen to make their homes in this area. Each year, large numbers of tourists come to San Diego. Here, they enjoy warm weather, beautiful scenery, and many outdoor sports.

Seattle

The largest city in the northwestern part of our country is Seattle, Washington. Seattle is on hilly land along the shores of Puget Sound, a long arm of the Pacific Ocean. East of the city is Lake Washington.

Seattle began in the 1850's as a small lumbering town. Logs were brought here from nearby forests to be sawed into lumber. The lumber was shipped to other cities along the Pacific coast. During the 1880's and 1890's, railroads were built connecting Seattle with cities in the eastern part of our country. A few years later, gold was discovered in northern Canada and Alaska. Thousands of gold-seekers stopped in Seattle to buy their supplies. The city began to grow rapidly.

A major seaport

Seattle is one of the leading seaports along the Pacific coast. Many ships from around the world dock in Seattle's fine harbor along Puget Sound. Ships also travel between Puget Sound and Lake Washington through a canal and locks.* From Seattle, fishing boats journey out to sea to find halibut and other fish.

Industry

Manufacturing is also important in the Seattle area. The leading industry is the manufacture of aircraft. Many of the jet passenger planes that streak across our skies were made in plants near Seattle. Shipyards along Puget Sound build fishing boats, navy ships, barges, and pleasure boats. Some factories in the Seattle area process farm crops, timber, and minerals produced in the state. For example, there are flour and grain mills, sawmills, plywood* factories, and plants that can or freeze salmon. Hydroelectric* plants located on mountain streams near Seattle provide large amounts of electric power for industry.

Each year, Seattle attracts thousands of tourists. People come to Seattle in the summer for sports such as fishing and boating. In winter there is skiing on nearby mountains.

Denver

The capital and largest city of Colorado is Denver. Denver is located along the South Platte River, near the western edge of the Great Plains. To the west of the city rise the snowcapped peaks of the Rocky Mountains. Denver is sometimes called the "Mile High City." This is because a marker on the steps of the capitol building is exactly one mile above sea level.

History

Denver was founded by settlers who came to Colorado during a gold rush in the late 1850's. The storekeepers in Denver grew rich selling supplies to miners. The miners were seeking gold, silver, and other metals in the Rocky Mountains. After railroads were built to Denver, it became an important shipping point for farm products. In recent years, many new industries have been built in or near Denver. The population has grown rapidly.

A trading city

Denver is an important trading city for many people who live on the Great Plains or in the Rocky Mountains. A number of large manufacturing firms, banks, and insurance companies have offices here. Many ranchers bring their cattle and sheep to Denver's huge stockyards to be sold. People come from many miles away to shop in Denver's fine stores.

The West 59

Government offices

Many United States government agencies have offices in Denver. In fact, there are more government offices in Denver than in any other city except Washington, D.C. The United States Mint in Denver makes millions of our country's coins each year.

Industry

Denver is also an important manufacturing city. Some factories here use Colorado's farm products and minerals as raw materials. For example, there are sugar refineries, meat-packing plants, and oil refineries in the Denver area. Other products manufactured here include missiles, aircraft parts, mining machinery, and luggage.

Phoenix

One of the fastest-growing cities in the United States is Phoenix. It is the capital and largest city of Arizona. In 1950, only about 107,000 people lived in Phoenix. Today, the city has a population of 709,000. More than one million people make their homes in the Phoenix metropolitan area.

Trade and industry

Phoenix is located along the Salt River, in a rich farming area. Irrigated farms in the Salt River Valley produce such crops as cotton, citrus fruits, vegetables, grain, and alfalfa. Most of these farm products are brought to Phoenix to be processed or shipped to other parts of the country. There are fruit

Phoenix is the capital and largest city in Arizona. It is located along the Salt River, in the middle of a rich farming area. What are some important industries found in the Phoenix area?

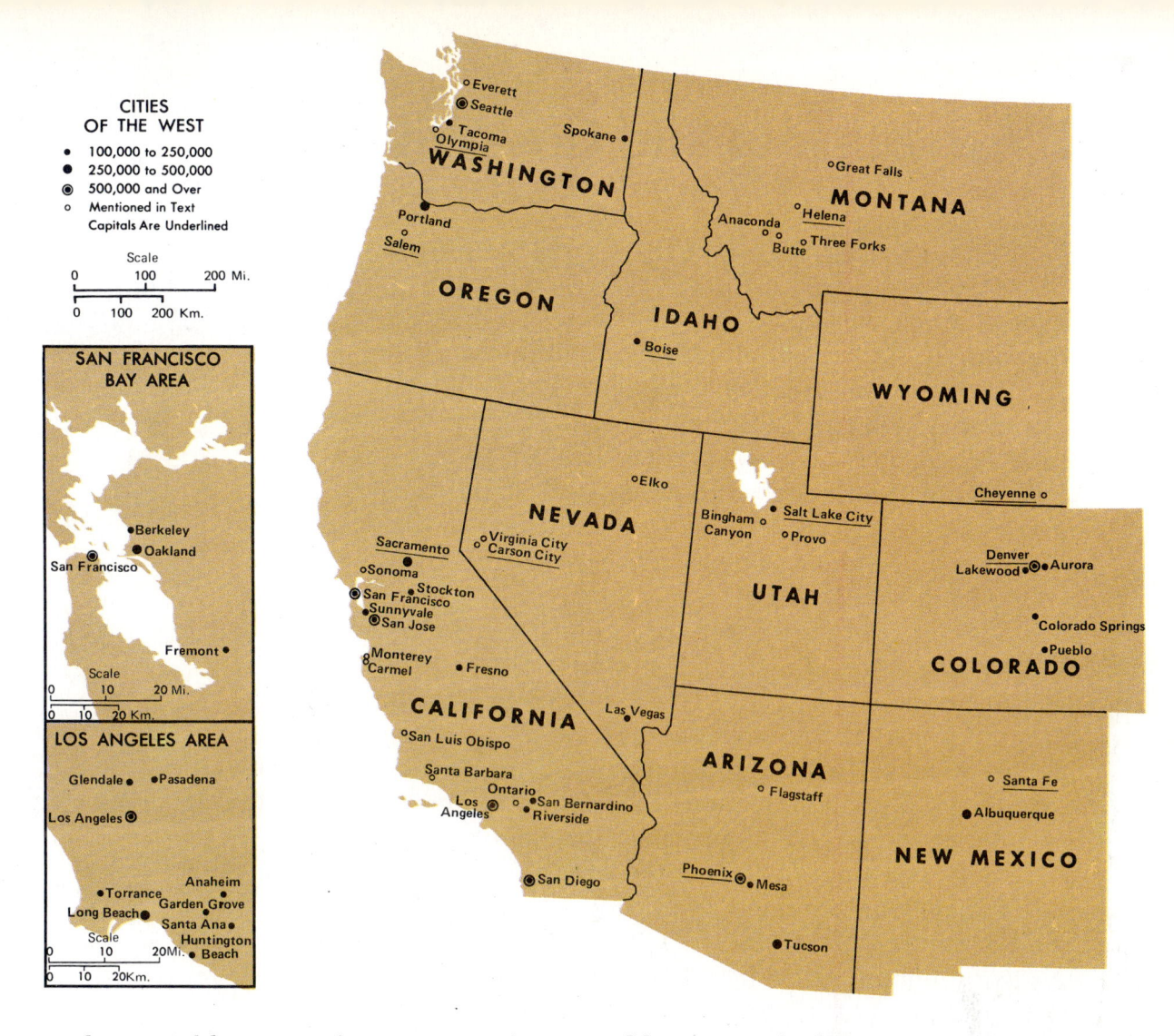

and vegetable canneries, cotton gins, grain mills, and meat-packing plants in the Phoenix area.

Phoenix has other industries as well. Factories here make aircraft parts out of aluminum. There are also factories that make electronic equipment.

Many people like to visit Phoenix. They enjoy the warm winter climate and the beautiful desert scenery nearby. There are many fine hotels, motels, and resorts in the Phoenix area. A number of people here earn their living by serving the needs of tourists.

Exploring Cities

1. Do research to discover how one of the cities described in this chapter began and how it has developed. Answer the following questions in a short report.
   a. Who were the first settlers?
   b. Why did they settle here?
   c. How has the city grown in size from the time it was founded until now?

2. Describe a visit to one of the cities discussed in this chapter. Present a short report to your class. Include the following in your report:
   a. how you traveled to the city
   b. the most interesting things you saw there
   c. your opinion of what the city's most serious problems might be

The West

6 Citizenship and Government

Government in Our Communities

A nation of strong communities

The United States is a nation of communities. As the map on pages 8-9 shows, our country stretches nearly 3,000 miles (4,827 km.)† from Maine to California. It also includes the far north state of Alaska and the island state of Hawaii. In this huge country, there are thousands of communities. Some are very large. For example, the cities of New York, Chicago, and Los Angeles have millions of people. Others are very small. Only a few families make their homes there.

Most of the communities in our country are good places in which to live. People in these communities are usually able to meet their basic needs. (See "Needs of People" in the Table of Contents.) For instance, most people have jobs that make it possible for them to earn a good living. Also, most people have a chance to get a good education. In these communities, most of the buildings and streets are clean and well kept. People are usually friendly and polite to one another. They enjoy working together and playing together. Most people have a feeling of pride in their community.

In strong communities like these, most of the people share certain ideas, or beliefs. Seven of these beliefs are described on page 64. Study these beliefs carefully. Do you agree with all of them? Do you think these beliefs are important in building a strong community? Explain your answers.

Government by the people

All of the communities in our nation are alike in certain ways. For example, they all need rules, or laws, for people to live by. Of course, there must be someone to make the laws and to see that they are carried out. This means that all communities need some kind of government.

In the United States, the citizens of each community have a share in the government. They choose the people who make the laws. They also choose some of the people who carry out the laws.

In most of our communities, the government is divided into three branches. One branch makes the laws. Another carries them out. The third branch explains, or <u>interprets</u>, the laws.

† km. means kilometer

Members of the Seattle City Council at work. What does the city council do? How are its members chosen? Do all communities have a group of men and women like this one? Explain.

Making the Laws

To see how the laws of a community are made, let's visit a large city in the West. We will go to Seattle, Washington. (See map on page 61.)

The city council

When we arrive in Seattle, we go to a large building in the downtown area where the Seattle City Council has its meetings. The city council makes the laws for Seattle. It also decides how the money collected in city taxes should be spent. There are nine members of the city council. They are elected by the voters of Seattle for terms of four years each.

Right now, the members of the city council are talking about a law that one of them has introduced. This law would forbid people to smoke in restaurants and other public places. A number of citizens have come to the meeting to say how they feel about the law. Some are in favor of it. Others are against it. The council members will listen to all points of view and then make their decision.

Other communities in our country also have groups of people who are elected to make the laws. These lawmaking bodies have different names, such as "city commission" or "board of aldermen." They differ from one another in a number of ways. For instance, some of them have more members than the Seattle City Council. Others have fewer members. In some communities, the lawmakers serve for less than four years at a time.

The West 63

SEVEN IMPORTANT BELIEFS THAT BUILD STRONG COMMUNITIES

1. Every person is important.

Most Americans believe that every person is important. It does not matter if you are young or old, a man or a woman. You are just as important as every other person. You are important whether your skin is black, white, or some other color. You are important no matter what religion you follow or what country your grandparents came from.

2. People have the right to govern themselves.

Americans believe the citizens of a country have the right to govern themselves. We think every person should be able to have some part in running our government.

3. Decisions should be made by majority* vote.

In the United States, all citizens have a chance to help choose the people who run the government. They do this by voting in elections. The candidate* with the most votes is elected. This is known as majority vote. Most Americans believe the fairest way for people to govern themselves is by majority vote.

4. All citizens should have a chance to get a good education.

Education is very important in a democracy. To have good government, citizens must be able to vote wisely for the people who make and carry out the laws. Most Americans believe that all young people should have a chance for a good education.

5. Laws should be the same for all citizens.

Most Americans believe all citizens should be treated the same by their government. Everyone should be required to obey the same laws. People should never gain or lose any rights because of such things as the color of their skin, or how much money they have.

6. All people have certain rights that no one can take away from them.

Most Americans believe that every person has a number of important rights and freedoms. Among these are freedom of speech and freedom of religion. Also every person has the right to a fair trial in a court of law. We believe that these rights cannot be taken away from any person, even by a majority vote. In a democracy, the government is expected to protect the rights of all citizens.

7. Citizens have responsibilities as well as rights.

For a democracy to work, all citizens must be willing to do their part. In other words, citizens have responsibilities as well as rights. Among these responsibilities are obeying the laws of the community, taking part in the government, and doing useful work.

*See Glossary

Carrying Out the Laws

To see how the laws of a community are carried out, we will visit another large city in the West. This time we will go to Los Angeles, California.

The mayor

We arrive by plane at the Los Angeles' airport and take a taxi to the City Hall. This is a tall building in the heart of the city. The mayor of Los Angeles has his office here.

We go to the mayor's office, where we meet one of his aides. This young woman tells us that the people of Los Angeles elect a mayor every four years. The mayor is in charge of carrying out the laws the city council has made. He chooses the members of about forty different commissions. Each commission has a certain job to do in the city government. For example, one commission runs the police force. Another is in charge of the city's harbor.

In Los Angeles, the mayor has a great deal of power. But this is not true in all communities. Sometimes the mayor's only duties are to lead city council meetings and to take part in public ceremonies, such as parades. In some cities, the mayor is a member of the city council.

Many communities have a city manager instead of a mayor to run the government. The city manager is not elected by the voters. Instead, he or she is chosen by the city council.

Workers for the community

The mayor's aide tells us that about forty thousand people work for the city government of Los Angeles. These people do many different jobs. Some are police officers or fire fighters. Others are street cleaners or garbage collectors. Still others take care of the city's parks and playgrounds. There are workers who inspect houses and apartments to make sure they are safe to live in. Other people run the city's water system.

Freedom
See Great Ideas

The picture below shows Mayor Thomas Bradley of Los Angeles. During the last fifteen years, black persons have become mayors of several large American cities. In earlier times, black Americans were seldom chosen for important government jobs. What do you think were the reasons for this? Why do you suppose there has been such a change during recent years? Do you think that black Americans today have more freedom than they did in the past? Explain.

We ask the mayor's aide where the city gets the money to pay all these people. She says the money comes from taxes that people pay to the city government.

Other communities have the same kinds of government workers that Los Angeles does. But in smaller communities, fewer workers are needed.

The city's schools

Like other communities, Los Angeles has a system of public schools. There are more than 600 schools in the Los Angeles school district. About 580,000 students attend these schools.

The public schools are run by a group of men and women called the Board of Education. This board is made up of seven members, who are elected to four-year terms. The Board of Education chooses a person called a superintendent to be in charge of running the schools. Most other communities in our country also have a board of education and a superintendent of schools.

In the United States, public high schools and grade schools are free to all students. The money to run these schools comes mostly from taxes that people pay to their school districts. Some money also comes from the state and federal* governments.

Interpreting the Laws

There are law courts in most of our larger cities and towns. These courts try* people who are accused of breaking the law. They deal with crimes such as driving too fast and littering the streets. People who are arrested for more serious crimes, such as robbery, are usually tried in other courts.

Citizenship in a Strong Community

Opportunities for citizens

As you have seen, the United States is a nation of strong communities. The people in these communities have many opportunities to live a happy, satisfying life.

In a strong community, most people have steady jobs. They can do useful work and earn a good living for themselves and their families. Most people also have a chance to get a good education. This helps them to develop their talents and to accomplish goals that are important to them.

In a strong community, life is usually safe and pleasant. People can go about their business without fear of being attacked or robbed. Most of the homes are neat and well kept. The streets are clean and free of rubbish. There are parks and playgrounds where people can spend their leisure time.

In a strong community, people are friendly and helpful to one another. They have a feeling that they can trust one another. People are willing to work together on projects that will make their community a better place to live.

What makes a strong community?

A successful community does not just "happen." Every citizen must do his or her part to make the community strong. As you know, most people in a strong community follow the seven beliefs shown on page 64. For example, they believe that every person is important. They believe that all people should have the same rights and freedoms. In addition, they believe that

*See Glossary

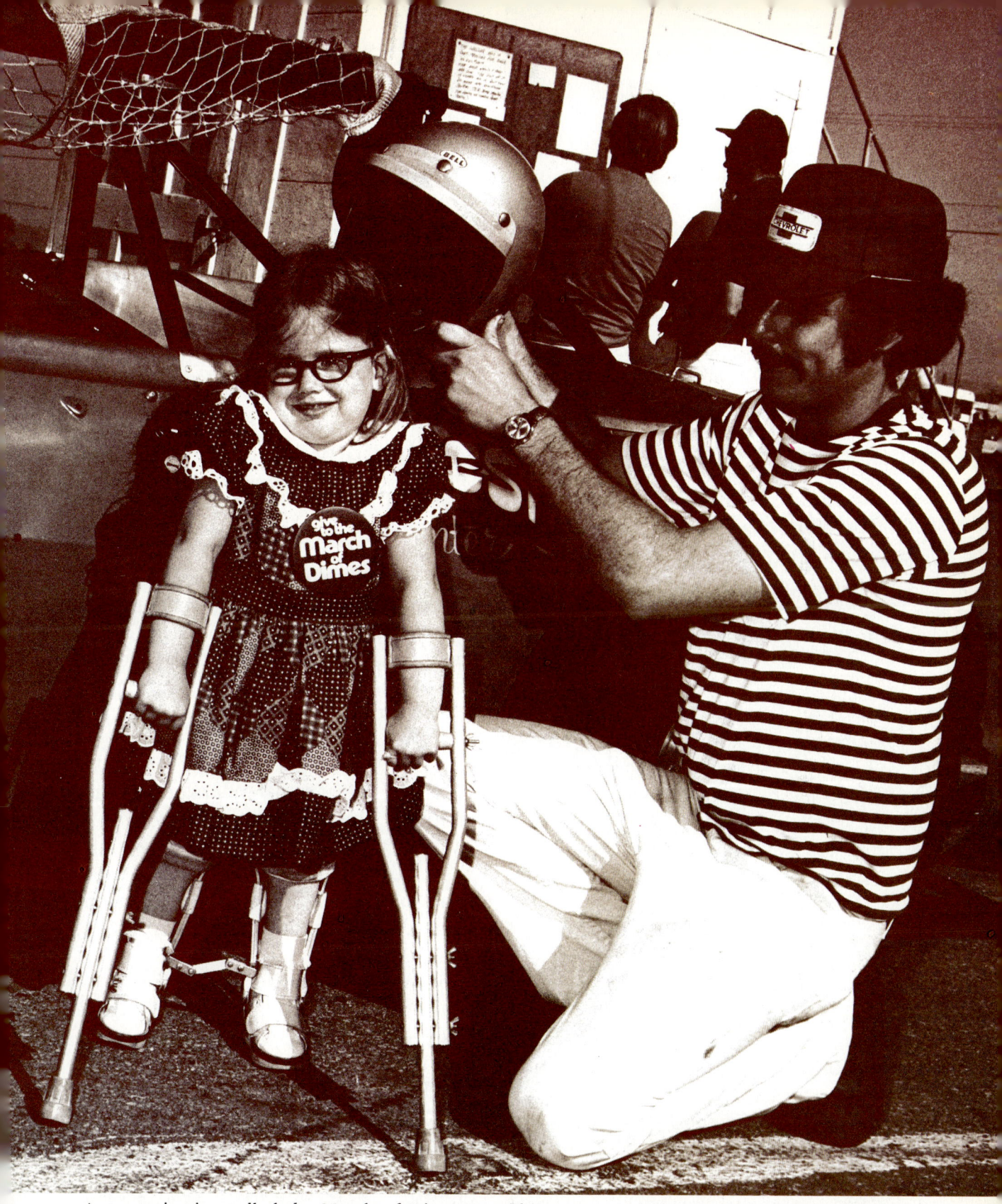

An organization called the March of Dimes provides money to help crippled children. This picture shows a race-car driver who is helping to raise money for this organization. Good citizens are willing to help out on community projects. What are some other responsibilities of a citizen?

The West 67

RESPONSIBILITIES OF CITIZENS IN A STRONG COMMUNITY

Obeying the laws

Good citizens obey the laws of their community, state, and country. Even if they think a law is unfair, they will not disobey it. Instead, they will work in a peaceful way to get the law changed.

Treating other people with respect

Good citizens treat other people the same way they would like to be treated. They try to be friendly and polite to everyone. This is because they truly believe that every person is important.

Getting a good education

In the United States, most people have an opportunity for an education. Young people are responsible for making good use of this opportunity. By learning as much as they can, they are preparing to become useful citizens when they grow up.

Doing useful work

Most Americans feel they are responsible for doing useful work. When they become adults they do not expect other people to take care of them. Instead, they expect to work hard and do their job well.

Taking part in the government

In the United States, it is important for every citizen to take part in the government. People who are over eighteen can do this by voting in all elections. Also they can work for candidates* they think would do a good job. Young people have a responsibility to learn as much as they can about their government. This will help prepare them to make wise decisions when they are older.

Cooperating with other people

Many jobs in a community cannot be done well by persons working alone. Instead, there must be cooperation among many people. Citizens of a community have a responsibility to work together. In this way, they can make their community a better place to live.

all citizens should take part in the government.

In a strong community, most people realize that they have responsibilities* as well as rights. Some of these responsibilities are shown at left. Study the list carefully. Do you agree that all citizens of a community have these responsibilities? Why? Why not? Can you think of any other responsibilities that citizens of a community have? If so, what are they?

Community Problems

Today, communities in the United States face a number of important problems. Some of these problems keep large numbers of people from meeting their basic needs. They are known as social problems. Seven of the most important social problems are shown on page 70. Let us examine one of these problems more closely.

Unsuccessful Communities

In our country, there are some communities that are not as successful as others. Many of the people who make their homes there find it hard to meet their basic needs. We will visit one of these communities to see what it is like.

A visit to an unsuccessful community

We are taking a taxi ride through a large city in the United States. Our taxicab turns down a narrow street lined with tall apartment buildings. All of the buildings on this street are run-down and shabby. Paint is peeling from the walls. Many buildings appear to be empty. Their windows are broken, and the doors are hanging loose from the hinges. Some of the buildings are streaked with black soot. It looks as though the insides of these buildings have been destroyed by fire.

We notice that the street and the sidewalks are littered with bottles and other rubbish. Someone has written all over the sidewalks and the buildings with paint. In a nearby alley, large rats are scurrying between overflowing garbage cans.

Our cab driver tells us that there is a great deal of crime in this part of the city. A person walking down the street is in danger of being robbed or beaten.

We ask the cab driver why so many buildings on this street are empty. He says that most of the people who once lived here have moved away. Many left because they could not find any good jobs. Some left because they felt their children were not getting a good education. Other people left because they wanted to find better housing. Still others left because they were tired of living where there was so much crime. They wanted to move to a community where life was safer and more pleasant.

A street in a large American city. The insides of some of these apartment buildings have been destroyed by fire. Do you think this picture shows a successful community? Explain your answer. Why are some communities unsuccessful? What can be done to help build stronger communities?

SEVEN SOCIAL PROBLEMS

In our country, a number of serious problems prevent people from meeting their needs. These are called social problems. The government and the people of our country have been working hard to solve these problems. As we make progress toward this goal, more Americans will have happier and more successful lives. Our country's social problems include:

1. **The need for more jobs.** At the present time, about six out of every hundred workers in the United States are unable to find jobs.
2. **The high cost of living.** In recent years, the high cost of goods and services has kept many people from meeting their needs. This continuing rise in prices is called inflation.
3. **The need for better education.** Many people in our country are not getting a good education. They are not gaining the knowledge they need for good citizenship.
4. **Illness and handicaps.** Americans are among the healthiest people in the world. However, millions of people in our country suffer from serious illnesses and handicaps.
5. **Lack of freedom for certain groups.** In the past, some groups of people in our country did not have the same freedoms as other people. Today, our laws give every person the right to fair treatment and equal opportunity. Even so, some Americans still do not have all the rights and freedoms promised by our laws.
6. **Crime.** Over the years, there has been a great increase in the number of major crimes in our country. In many areas, people live in fear for their lives.
7. **Unsuccessful communities.** In many parts of the United States there are unsuccessful communities. Many of the people in these communities are not doing useful work. They are not getting the education they need to get jobs or to be good citizens. The crime rate in these communities is very high.

Why some communities are not successful

If we could travel through the United States, we would find other communities like the one we have just visited. There are many reasons why these communities are not successful. Let us explore just two of the reasons.

Communities are sometimes unsuccessful because the people there have been treated unfairly by other Americans. Often the people who live in these communities are members of minority* groups. Some are blacks or Indians. Others are Latinos* or people of Asian descent.

In the past, members of minority groups were often the victims of discrimination.* Many companies would not hire them. Or they would only give them jobs that took little skill and did not pay very much money. Often these people could not get good housing, because other Americans would not sell houses or rent apartments to them.

Sometimes members of minority groups were not given a chance to get a good education. They were not allowed to go to the same schools as other children. Often the schools they did attend were not as good as those for other children. As a result, they often grew up without the knowledge or skills they needed to earn a good living.

Today there is much less discrimination against minority groups than there used to be. But even today the members of these groups often lack many of the opportunities that other Americans have. They were treated unfairly for so long that they have not yet "caught up" with the rest of our citizens.

What do you think about people who discriminate against other persons? Are these people living up to the seven beliefs that build strong communities? Are they meeting their responsibilities as citizens? Give reasons for your answers.

There is another important reason why communities are unsuccessful. Some of the people who live there do not meet their responsibilities. For example, some people are not willing to do any kind of useful work. Instead, they expect other people to support them. They do not try to get a good education so that they can become useful citizens. Some of them drop out of school as soon as they are old enough to do so.

In some communities, there are people who break the laws whenever they feel like it. They may rob other people or hurt them in some way. They may break windows or start fires just for fun. These people are not treating others as they would like to be treated themselves.

Usually there are only a small number of people in a community who act in this way. But even a few of these people can cause great harm to a community. They make it hard for all the other citizens to meet their needs.

Building stronger communities

Today, many Americans are trying to solve the problem of unsuccessful communities. For instance, our federal and state governments have passed laws against discrimination. Many companies have started programs to hire members of minority groups and train them for well-paying jobs. In many communities, there are special classes for people who have not finished high school. Here, people can gain the knowledge and skills they need to earn a good living.

The federal government has spent large amounts of money to improve our nation's cities. Some of this money is being used to find jobs for people who are out of work. Some is being used to get rid of slums.* Cities are tearing down entire blocks of run-down apartment buildings and stores. In their place, they are putting up rows of modern apartment buildings where people can live without paying high rents.

All of these things can help to build stronger communities. But something more is needed also. Today, most people realize that they cannot depend on the government or on other people to solve all their problems. They must be willing to help themselves. By working together and having faith in their own abilities, they can build a better way of life. For an example of this, let us see what happened in a section of Los Angeles known as Watts.

The story of Watts

In the past, the people of Watts faced serious problems. Many of these people had been the victims of discrimination. They had settled in Watts because they could not buy houses or rent apartments in other parts of the city. In Watts there were few stores or factories that hired large numbers of workers. Most people in Watts had to go to other parts of Los Angeles to find work. But bus service between Watts and other sections was poor. Also, many families in Watts did not own

Cooperation

See Great Ideas

In the city of Los Angeles is a section known as Watts. A riot caused great damage to Watts in 1965. After the riot, the people of Watts began working together to build a stronger community. The picture above shows some citizens of Watts helping their community by painting a house. Do you think it is important for the people of Watts to work together? Why? Why not? Is it important for the members of any community to work together? Explain.

cars. Partly for this reason, a large number of people in Watts did not have steady jobs.

There were other problems also. Many of the houses in Watts were old and run-down. There was a great deal of crime in the area. Many people in Watts felt there was little they could do about these problems. As a result, they had given up trying.

In the summer of 1965, a riot broke out in Watts. Mobs of angry people fought with the police. They destroyed cars, broke store windows, and set fire to buildings. Thirty-four people were killed in this riot, and hundreds of others were injured.

After the riot, people in Watts began taking steps to build a stronger community. A number of citizen's groups were started for this purpose. Thousands of young people went to work repairing houses, cleaning up streets, and planting gardens. Special classes were started for people who lacked a high-school education. Jobs were found for thousands of people who had been out of work.

Today the people of Watts still lack some of the opportunities that people in other parts of Los Angeles have. But they are making steady progress toward a better way of life. The changes that have taken place in Watts show what can be done when people work together to solve their problems.

Your opportunity as a citizen

You are a citizen of a community. This is true even though you are not old enough to vote. As a citizen, you have a chance to help build a stronger community. You can do this by:

. . . obeying the laws.

. . . treating other people as you would like to be treated.

. . . doing useful work at home.

. . . trying to get a good education.

. . . learning as much as you can about your community, so you will be able to vote wisely when you are older.

If you do all of these things, you will be meeting your responsibilities as a citizen. You will also be helping to make your community a better place in which to live.

Find Out How Your Government Works

This chapter has provided certain facts about the way communities are governed. Now you may want to find out how the government of your own community works. Do research to answer the following questions.
1. Who makes the laws for your community? How are these people chosen?
2. Who is in charge of carrying out the laws for your community? How is this person or persons chosen?
3. About how many people work for your community's government? What kinds of jobs do they do?
4. What courts do you have in your community? What kinds of cases do they deal with? How do the judges in these courts get their jobs? How long do they serve?
5. Where does your community get the money it needs to run the government? Who decides how this money will be spent?

There are several ways of getting this information. Some communities put out booklets that explain how the government works. Perhaps you could get one of these booklets. Or you might plan a field trip to the offices of your community government. You might also invite someone who knows about the government of your community to speak to the class.

7 The Arts

Painters

One of the first western painters was George Catlin. His paintings and books about Indians give us valuable information about their lives and customs. *The White Cloud, Head Chief of the Iowas* is one of his most famous paintings.

Perhaps the greatest western painter was Frederic Remington. He painted or drew nearly 2,800 pictures of the West. Soldiers, Indians, and cowboys are shown in many of Remington's paintings. Some of his best-known works are *Flight of Geronimo, A Dash for Timber,* and *Dismounted, the Fourth Troopers Moving.*

Another important artist of the West was Charles M. Russell. Russell traveled through the West looking for adventure and freedom. He painted pictures and made sculptures.* One of his sculptures is called *Where the Best of Riders Quit.* It shows a rider being thrown from a bucking horse.

Artists Albert Bierstadt and Thomas Moran painted pictures of the West during the 1800's. Bierstadt traveled through the Rocky Mountains and northern California. Many of his paintings show the beauty of the western mountains. Among his paintings are *The Rocky Mountains* and *In the Yosemite Valley.* Moran is perhaps best known for his *Grand Canyon of the Yellowstone River.*

Georgia O'Keeffe and Mark Tobey are recent painters who have lived and worked in the West. O'Keeffe has painted many desert scenes. She has also painted pictures of such things as bones and flowers in new and different ways. One of her best-known paintings is called *Cow's Skull with Calico Roses.* During the 1920's, Tobey painted true-to-life pictures of loggers

*See Glossary

A painting by Frederic Remington called *Dismounted, the Fourth Troopers Moving*. Remington's true-to-life paintings and sculptures provide valuable information about life in the early West.

and sailors. His later pictures, such as *Written Over the Plains*, were painted in a more abstract* style.

Writers

During the 1800's, many poets, novelists,* and short-story writers wrote about the lives of pioneer families in the West. They also wrote about miners and cowboys. The poet Joaquin Miller lived with the Indians in California. He also lived in mining camps in the West. His most famous work is *Songs of the Sierras*.

Two important writers during the late 1800's and early 1900's were Bret Harte and Jack London. Harte was known for his poems and stories about California. Two of his best-known short stories are "The Luck of Roaring

Camp" and "The Outcasts of Poker Flat."

London wrote many novels and stories. His best-known novel is *The Call of the Wild*. This book tells about the adventures of a dog that was taken from California to northern Canada.

More recent writers include John Steinbeck, William Saroyan, and Phyllis McGinley. One of Steinbeck's best-known novels is *The Grapes of Wrath*. It tells about the hardships of a family that moved from Oklahoma to California. Other well-known works by Steinbeck are *Of Mice and Men, East of Eden,* and *The Red Pony*. Among Saroyan's best-known works are his novel *The Human Comedy,* and a play called *The Time of Your Life*. McGinley wrote humorous poems about everyday life. In 1961, she won the Pulitzer* prize for poetry.

Music

Western composers* have given us many famous songs. These include "The Lone Prairie," "Streets of Laredo," and "The Chisholm Trail." Early cowboys sang these songs to help quiet their cattle and to fill the lonely hours.

Composers have also given us serious music about the West. These include

Arts These pictures show two of the West's best-known artists. Georgia O'Keeffe (left) has painted many pictures of Western scenes. John Steinbeck (right) has written stories and novels about the people of the West. Who are some of the other painters and writers who have lived and worked in the West? What are some ways in which arts such as painting and writing can help us understand the history of a region?

Antonia Brico conducting the Los Angeles Philharmonic Orchestra in a rehearsal. Brico, who lives in Denver, Colorado, is well known as an orchestra conductor. Many people in the West enjoy listening to the fine symphony orchestras in this part of our country.

Ferde Grofé's *Grand Canyon Suite* and Hershey Kay's ballet *Western Symphony*. Aaron Copland's ballets *Billy the Kid* and *Rodeo* are other musical works about the West.

Many people also enjoy listening to the fine symphony orchestras in the West. One of our country's greatest orchestra conductors is Zubin Mehta. He conducts the Los Angeles Philharmonic Orchestra. Other well-known conductors include Edo de Waart and Antonia Brico.

Gain an Understanding

In order to gain a greater understanding of western painting, literature, or music, do one of the following:

1. Borrow a library book that shows paintings by an artist mentioned in this chapter. Choose the painting you like best. Explain to your class why you like it.
2. Read a novel by Jack London, such as *The Call of the Wild* or *White Fang*.
3. Play a recording of the *Grand Canyon Suite*. As you listen to the music, write a few sentences describing how it makes you feel.

The West 77

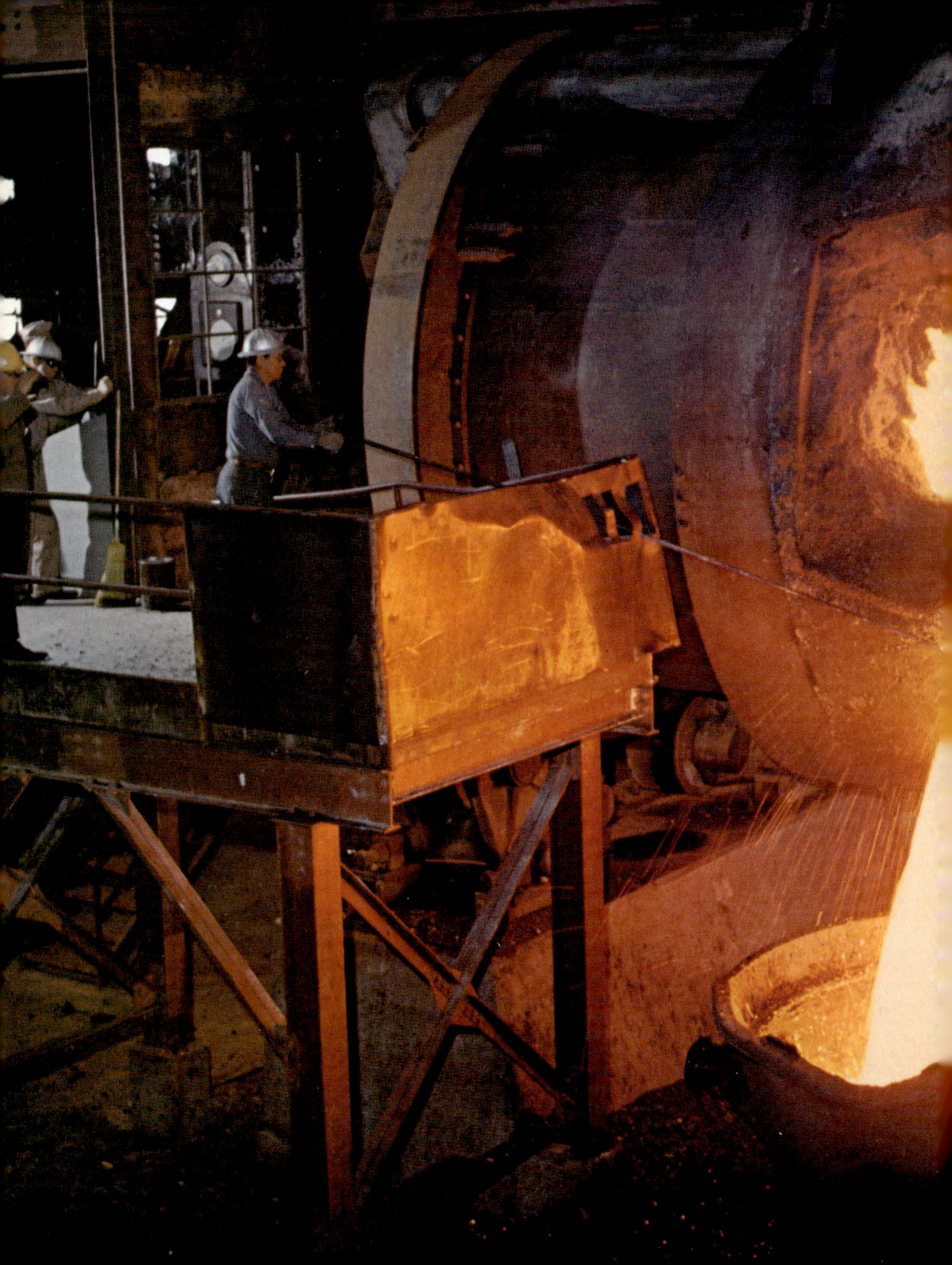

Part 3

Earning a Living

Industry provides many jobs for people in the West. Some people work in factories where airplanes are built. Others work in plants where food is frozen or canned. In what other ways do you think people in the West earn their living? As you do research in Part 3, you may wish to discover answers to the following questions:

- What natural* resources would you find in the West? In what ways do people in the West use these resources?
- What is dry farming? What is the most important crop grown by dry farming in the West? What other crops are raised here?
- What are the West's leading industrial cities? What are some of the products made in these cities?

*See Glossary

Pouring hot, melted copper at a smelter* in Arizona. More copper is produced in Arizona than in any other state in our country.

The West 79

8 Farming

A Problem To Solve

<u>Farmers in different parts of the West raise different kinds of crops and livestock. Why is this true?</u> In making hypotheses* to solve this problem, you need to know what crops and livestock are raised in different parts of the West. Then you need to think about how raising these crops and livestock is affected by:
1. the amount of water available
2. the length of the growing season
3. the kind of land available

Chapters 2, 3, and 9 also contain information that will be helpful in solving this problem.

See Skills Manual, "Thinking and Solving Problems"

Imagine that it is more than one hundred years ago, and we are pioneers. We are making a trip across the West in a covered wagon. We plan to stop and make our home wherever we can find land that is good for farming. When we find just the right land, we will plow the soil and begin to raise crops.

The land we choose for our farm must not be too hilly or too rocky. Where hills are steep, it is hard to plant crops and to take care of them. Crops do not grow well on rocky ground.

In order to grow good crops, our farm must have fertile soil. It must also have plenty of water and sunshine. We say that soil is fertile if plants can grow well in it. If our land is in an area where rainfall is light, we must be able to get water from other places to moisten, or irrigate,* our fields. Some crops need many hours of sunshine each day and a long growing* season.

Land for raising livestock

The pioneers who came to the West many years ago found only a small amount of land that was good for growing crops. Nearly two thirds of the land is too rugged. Also, most of the West does not have enough water. In some places, the soil is not fertile. It may contain minerals that are harmful to plants. In the high mountains, the growing season is too short for most kinds of crops.

Today, just as in pioneer days, much of the land in the West is used only for raising cattle, sheep, and other livestock. These animals feed on grass,

*See Glossary

Harvesting lettuce in California. Farming is very important to the states of the West. Why is this so? Which western state earns the most money from farm products?

which will grow where the land is too dry or too steep for crops to be grown.

Land for growing crops

A few parts of the West are very good for growing crops. These areas have fertile soil, plenty of water, and land that is fairly level. The lowlands in the southern part of the West have a warm, sunny climate and a long growing season. (Compare maps on pages 8 and 38.) Here farmers can raise many kinds of crops that cannot be grown in the northern part of our country.

Although these rich farmlands cover only a small area, the West is an important farming region. It produces more than half of the fruits and nuts and about half of the vegetables grown in the United States. Sugar beets, wheat, and cotton are other important farm products of the West. Almost two thirds of our sugar beets and more than one fourth of our wheat are grown in

The West 81

the West. Nearly one third of our cotton comes from this region. Some of the West's farm products are used by the people here. The rest are sold to people in other states and countries.

The most important farming state in the West is California. In fact, this state leads our entire country in the value of farm products. California produces more than two hundred different kinds of crops. In this chapter, we will learn about farming in California and in other parts of the West.

How important is farming to the West?

The jobs of many people in the West depend upon farming. Farmers grow crops or raise animals to sell. Other people work in factories where farm products are processed.* Still others sell farm products to stores or directly to the people who use these products. To learn more about farming in the West, let's visit an irrigated farm in the valley of the Salt River in Arizona. (See map on page 94.)

Farming on Irrigated Land

The weather is hot and sunny as we drive through the Salt River Valley. Here the land is very flat. We see green fields of cotton plants on both sides of the road. Between the fields are ditches filled with water. Some of the water from the ditches is flowing between the rows of plants. Nearby, a large stream of water from an electric pump is pouring into a ditch. This pump lifts the water from the bottom of a deep well.

We stop to watch a tractor dragging a huge scraping machine across a field. This machine is used to make the field

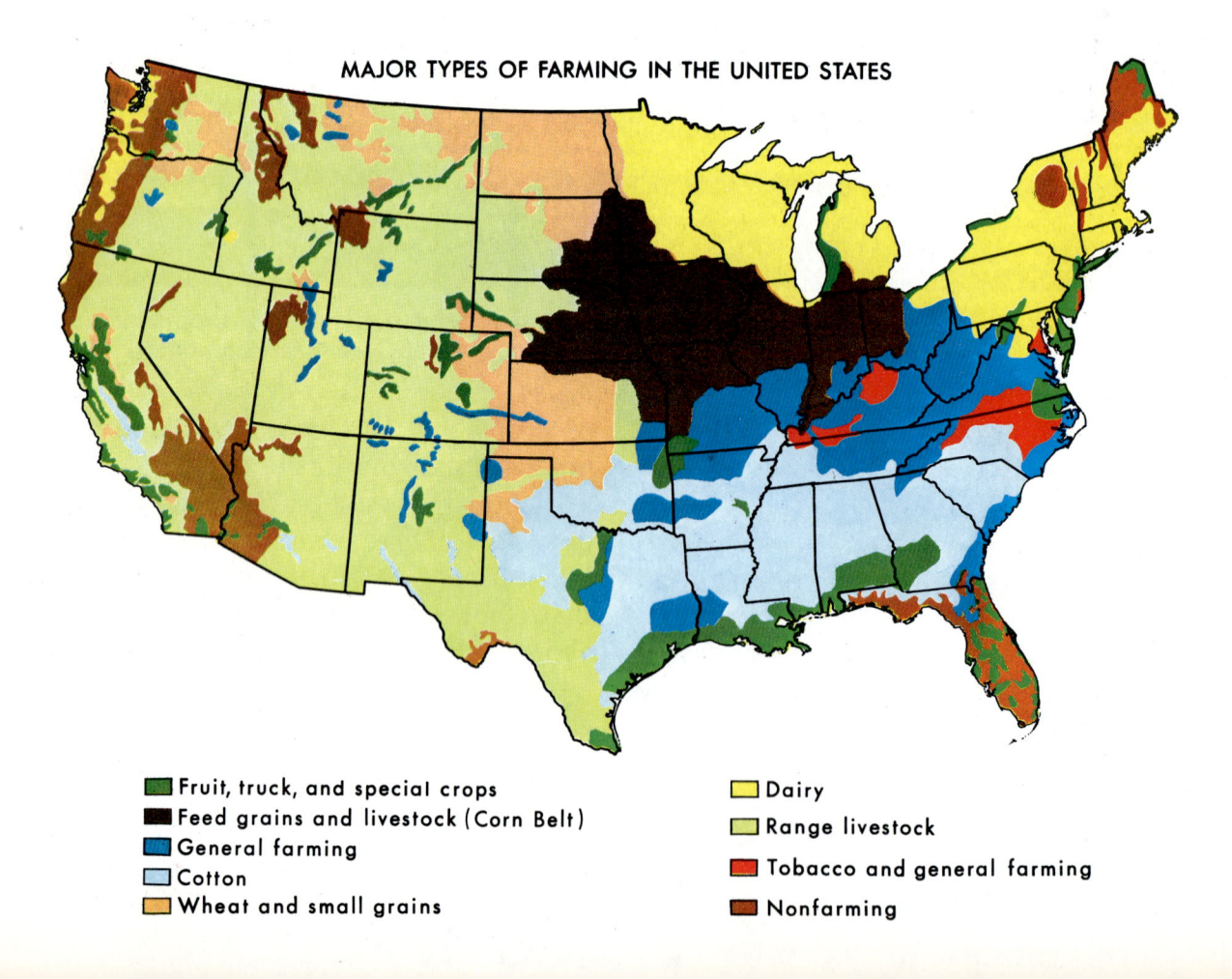

MAJOR TYPES OF FARMING IN THE UNITED STATES

- Fruit, truck, and special crops
- Feed grains and livestock (Corn Belt)
- General farming
- Cotton
- Wheat and small grains
- Dairy
- Range livestock
- Tobacco and general farming
- Nonfarming

level. Then water from the irrigation ditches can flow across it evenly.

The farmer stops his tractor and comes over to talk with us. He says that his farm is not very large—it covers only 40 acres (16 ha.).† "I like irrigation farming," he says. "I never have to worry about rainfall. When my crops need water, I pump it from under the ground. In this warm, sunny climate, I can grow crops nearly all year long."

Irrigation farming is hard work, however. First the farmer must level the land. Then he must drill a well, put in a pump, and dig irrigation ditches. Farmers who get water from reservoirs* instead of pumping it from the ground must pay for the water they receive.

Irrigated land in the West costs more money than the best farmland in other parts of the United States. This helps to explain why many irrigated farms are small. To earn a good living on these small but costly plots of land, farmers must grow crops that sell for high prices. Among the crops that are most often grown on irrigated land in the West are cotton, fruits, vegetables, and sugar beets.

Crop rotation

Like most other farmers, irrigation farmers cannot grow the same crop on the same land year after year. If they did, the soil would soon become less fertile. To keep the soil fertile, farmers must rotate their crops. In other words, they must plant different crops on the same land in different years. Many farmers rotate their other crops with a hay crop called alfalfa.* The tops of the alfalfa plant are used as feed for cattle. If the alfalfa roots and stalks are plowed into the ground, they help to put back some of the food materials that other plants take out of the soil. Alfalfa is grown on irrigated land in nearly all parts of the West.

Most crops grown on irrigated land must be planted, hoed, weeded, and harvested. In the past, these hard jobs were done mostly by people who moved from one farm to another to help with the crops. These people are called migrant workers. Today, there are still many migrant workers in the West. However, many farmers with irrigated land now use large, costly machines to do most of their planting, weeding, and harvesting.

Farmers with irrigated land sell their crops to people in many parts of the United States. Some of these products, such as fresh fruits and vegetables, must be used quickly. Otherwise, they will spoil. Such farm products are sent to other parts of the country in refrigerated cars on fast trains, or on large cargo planes.

There are irrigated farmlands in every state of the West. The map on page 94 shows us where the irrigated areas are located. These areas are often called oases.

The Central Valley

The largest oasis in the West lies in the Central Valley of California. Here the land is almost flat, and the soil is fertile. Most of the Central Valley receives very little rainfall in the summer. The fields there must be irrigated with water from reservoirs or wells.

One of the leading crops in the Central Valley is cotton. The long, hot summers here are good for raising this crop. When the cotton is ripe, the fluffy bolls* are picked by huge machines.

† ha. means hectare

There are seeds in the cotton that must be taken out. This is done by a machine called a cotton gin.

When the seeds have been removed, the cotton is pressed into big bundles called bales. Some of these are sent to factories in the eastern part of the United States. There the cotton is spun into thread. This thread is used in weaving cloth. Some of the cotton produced in California is sent to other countries.

The Central Valley is one of the leading producers of fruits and nuts in the United States. Many grapes are grown in the Central Valley. Almost half of these grapes are dried in the sun to make raisins. Some of the grapes are made into wine. Others are sold fresh in grocery stores and fruit markets. The Central Valley has many orchards where peaches, pears, plums, figs, or olives are grown. Orange and lemon groves are located in sheltered places. The leading nut crops in the Central Valley are almonds and walnuts.

Many other crops are grown in the Central Valley. This area produces

Harvesting cotton in Arizona. Large amounts of cotton are grown on irrigated land in parts of the West where there is a long growing season. Name two important cotton-growing areas in the West.

more than twenty-five kinds of vegetables. Among the most important kinds are potatoes, tomatoes, and asparagus. Some farmers grow barley, oats, rice, or other grains.

Orange groves in southern California

Neat rows of dark-green orange trees cover much farmland near the cities of Los Angeles and Santa Barbara in southern California. (See map on page 61.) Here the climate is mild or warm the year round. California produces more oranges than any other state except Florida.

The Imperial Valley

Another important area of irrigated farmland is the Imperial Valley of southern California. This valley is in a desert near the Mexican border. Water for the farms here is brought by canals from the Colorado River. In the Imperial Valley, winter days are warm and sunny. Vegetables grown during the winter are sold to people who live in the cold parts of our country.

Other oases in the West

In the oases of Washington and Oregon, there are many fruit orchards. The climate here is just right for growing large, bright-red apples. Washington produces more apples than any other state in the United States. Other fruits grown here include pears, peaches, and cherries.

Sugar beets are grown in oases in Colorado, Idaho, and other western states. They sell for a high price, and they do not need a long growing season. The roots of the plants are used to make sugar. The stems are fed to cattle and other livestock.

Potatoes are grown throughout the northern part of the West. Like sugar beets, they can be raised where the growing season is short. They are especially important in the oases along the Snake River in Idaho. (See map on page 94.) Idaho produces more potatoes than any other state.

Many other kinds of vegetables are also grown in oases in the West. Among these vegetables are peas, beans, lettuce, carrots, and onions.

In the oases of Arizona and New Mexico, many farmers grow crops that need a long growing season. The most important is cotton. Grapefruit, dates,

VALUE OF FRUITS AND NUTS SOLD

Each Dot Represents $2,000,000

ALL WHEAT HARVESTED

Each Dot Represents 10,000 Acres

VALUE OF VEGETABLES HARVESTED FOR SALE

Each Dot Represents $2,000,000

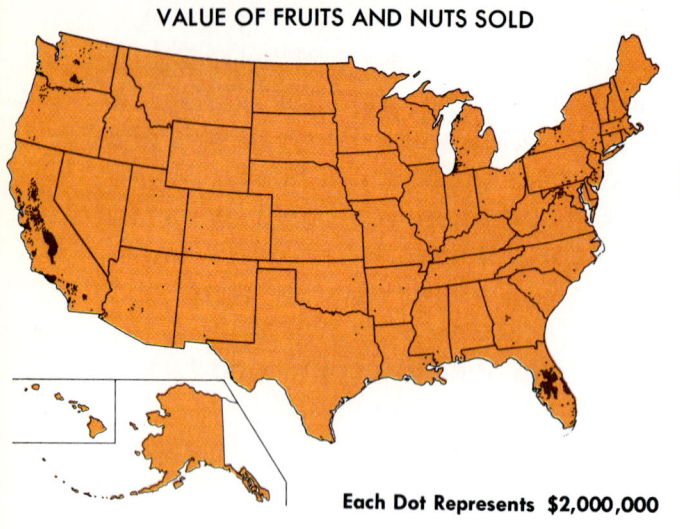

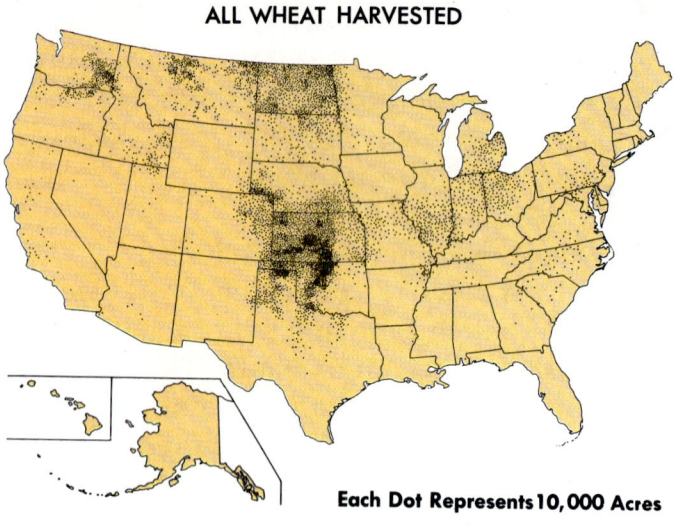

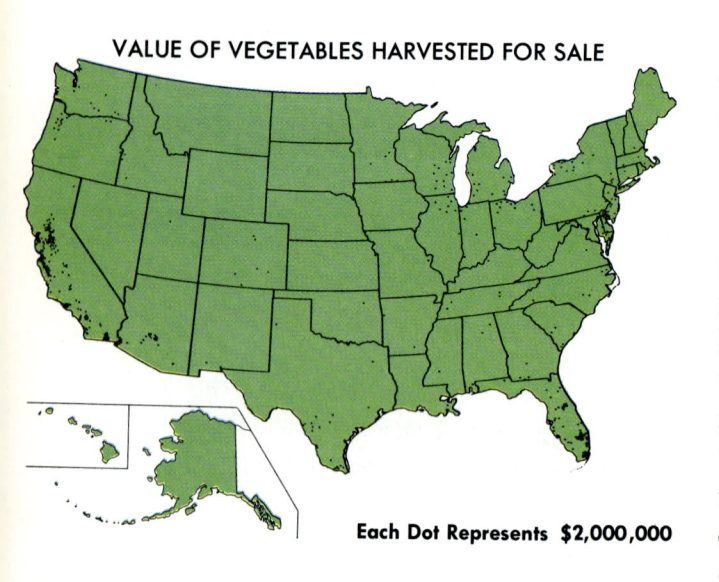

SUGAR BEETS HARVESTED FOR SUGAR

Each Dot Represents 2,000 Acres

oranges, and other fruits that need a warm climate are grown in Arizona.

Dry Farming

Now we are visiting a wheat farm on the Great Plains in central Montana. (Compare maps on pages 8 and 24.) It is an afternoon in late summer. We are watching a huge machine move slowly across a field of ripe, golden wheat. This machine is a combine, which cuts, threshes,* and cleans the grain. With a combine, one person working alone can harvest many acres of wheat. Driving a combine is a hot, dusty job. The farmer is glad to have a chance to stop and talk with us.

Between the golden wheat fields we notice wide patches of brown earth on which no crops are being grown. We ask the farmer why the land is not being used. The farmer says that he plants wheat on only part of his land at one time. He leaves the rest of the land unplanted, or fallow.* "It's because the climate here is so dry," he explains. "We seldom get more than 15 inches (38 cm.)† of rainfall a year. To grow

† cm. means centimeter

86 The West

CATTLE AND CALVES

Each Dot Represents 5,000 Head

SHEEP AND LAMBS

Each Dot Represents 10,000 Head

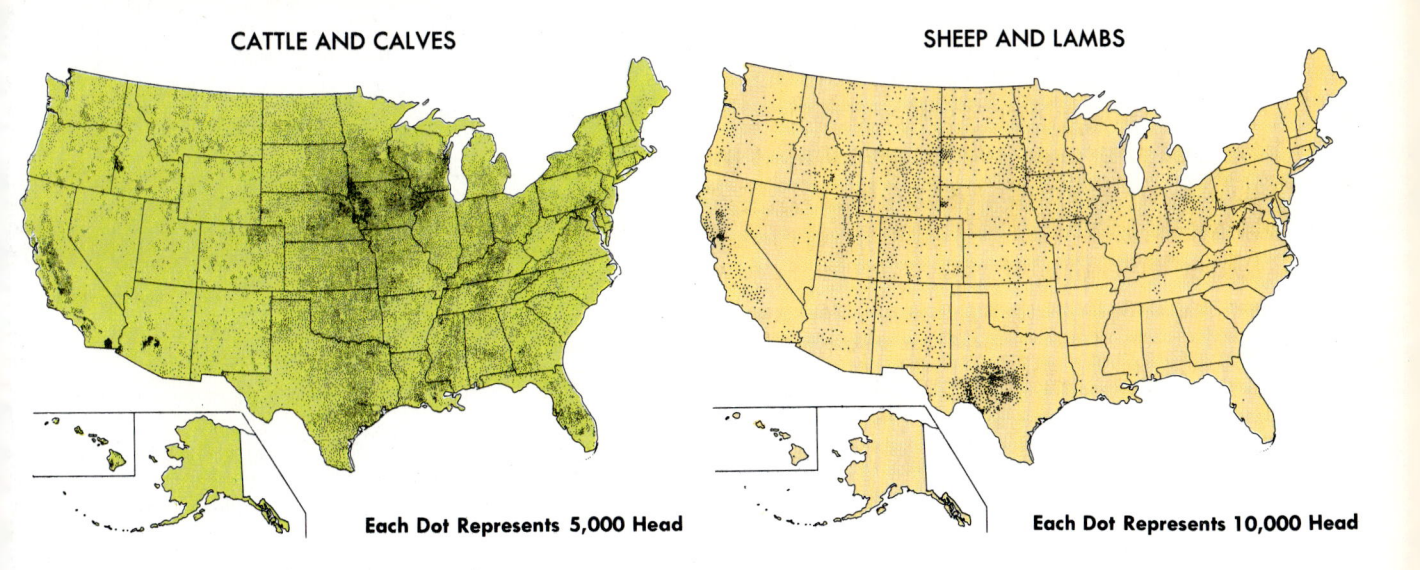

good crops, we must use rainfall from two years instead of one."

Rain that falls on fallow land is stored in the soil. Later, when crops are grown on this land, they can use the stored moisture. They will not need so much rainfall. The fallow fields must be cultivated* several times each summer to keep weeds from growing. Weeds would use some of the precious moisture in the soil.

When land is left fallow, strong winds may blow away much soil. To prevent wind erosion,* some farmers plant their wheat in strips between the fallow fields. This is called "strip-cropping." The wheat stalks slow down the wind so that it does not strike the bare soil with its full force.

The farmer tells us that his farm covers 2,000 acres (809 ha.). He needs such a large farm because he can use only about half of it each year. Because the climate is so dry, he does not get a large harvest of wheat from each acre. Therefore, he must plant many acres of wheat to pay for the combines and other expensive machines that he uses.

The farmer says he bought all this land at a much lower price than he would have had to pay for irrigated farmland.

We ask the farmer where he lives, because we can see no farmhouse. "I live in a town 10 miles (16 km.)† from here," he says. "I'm what they call a 'sidewalk farmer.' I have to be here on the farm for only a few weeks each year. During those weeks I plant and harvest my wheat. Our family would be lonely, living way out here."

The farmer tells us that the kind of farming he does is called "dry farming." This means farming without irrigation, in areas of light rainfall. Dry farming is carried on in every state in the West. However, some parts of the West are too dry even for this kind of farming.

Wheat is the most important crop grown by dry farming in the West. The top right-hand map on the opposite page shows us where the main wheat-farming areas are located. Huge amounts of wheat are raised on the Great Plains of Montana and eastern Colorado. In Montana, farmers plant their wheat in the spring. They harvest

† km. means kilometer

The West 87

it late in summer. This is called spring wheat. In eastern Colorado, winters are not so cold as they are in Montana. Farmers plant their wheat in the fall and harvest it early in the summer. This is called winter wheat.

Large amounts of wheat are also grown on the fertile Columbia Plateau in eastern Washington. Here farmers plant both winter wheat and spring wheat.

Food that is made from the West's wheat is eaten by people throughout the United States and in other countries. When the wheat is harvested, it is taken to the nearest town. There it is stored in tall buildings called grain elevators. Later it is loaded into railroad cars and taken to flour mills in the cities.

Wheat is not the only crop grown by dry farming. Barley is an important crop in some of the dry areas of California, Montana, and other states of the West. Peas, rye, and alfalfa are also grown by dry-farming methods.

Grazing

We have learned that much of the land in the West is used for raising cattle and sheep. These animals feed on grass that grows where the land is too dry or too steep for raising crops. Feeding on grass is called grazing. More than half of all the grazing lands in the United States are in the West.

To learn more about grazing in the West, let's visit a cattle ranch in Wyoming. It is late September, which is roundup time at the ranch. All summer long, the cattle have been grazing on green pastures high in the mountains. Now the cowhands are bringing them back to a corral at the ranch headquarters. A corral is a pen where animals are kept.

The cattle that are a year old are called yearlings. They are being separated from the other animals. The yearlings have been sold to a corn farmer in the Midwest. They will be taken to a nearby town and loaded into railroad cars for their journey to the Midwest.

We ask the rancher why he sells his cattle to a midwestern corn farmer. The rancher says that the cattle he raises are very lean. This is because they feed

Using Natural Resources

See Great Ideas

The farmer shown in the picture above raises barley by using dry-farming methods. These methods make it possible to grow crops in areas that receive only 10 to 20 inches (25 to 51 cm.) of rainfall a year. Dry-farming methods provide a good example of the careful use of natural resources. Besides water, what other important resource must farmers try to save? How is this resource sometimes lost? Do you think it can ever be replaced? Why? Why not?

The West 89

mainly on grass. The corn farmer in the Midwest is glad to buy these lean yearlings in the fall, after he has harvested his crops. He will feed the yearlings some of his corn to fatten them. Then he will sell them for meat.

The rancher also tells us what happens to the cattle that are not sold at roundup time. These animals will be taken to nearby pastures. There they will graze until January. Then the rancher will bring them to sheds at the ranch headquarters. The cattle must be protected from the bitterly cold winter weather in this area.

During the rest of the winter, the rancher must supply his cattle with food. He has worked all summer growing alfalfa. Now he will have enough hay to feed the animals. He grows the alfalfa on a small plot of irrigated land along the banks of a stream that runs through the ranch.

Until recently, ranchers in Wyoming sent most of their cattle to farms in the Midwest to be fattened. Now, many ranchers sell large numbers of cattle to farmers who own irrigated farms in the West. The irrigation farmers fatten the cattle on farm products such as sugar beet pulp and pea vines. Many cattle are being fattened on irrigated lands in California in order to help feed the large number of people there.

In the southern part of the West, winters are warmer. Cattle can graze all year round on the same land. But the climate is so dry that cattle sometimes cannot find enough grass to eat or water to drink.

Cattle on a western ranch. Much of the land in the West is used for raising cattle and other animals. Cattle and calves are the West's leading farm product. Why do so many western farmers raise cattle?

Many ranchers in the West raise sheep instead of cattle. Sheep do not need so much water or such rich grass as cattle do. Sheep can graze in very dry areas and in mountain pastures that are too rugged for cattle. Some ranchers take their sheep to the mountains during the summer to graze on grass that grows on the mountain slopes. During the winter, the sheep graze on plateaus or in sheltered mountain valleys.

Farming Where Rain Is Plentiful

To grow most crops without using irrigation or dry-farming methods, farmers need at least 20 inches (51 cm.) of rainfall a year. The map on page 27 shows that only a small part of the West receives this much rainfall. Most of the farmlands in the West that get more than 20 inches (51 cm.) of rain a year are located in the Puget-Willamette Lowland of Washington and Oregon.

In the Puget-Willamette Lowland, there are many dairy farms. The mild, rainy climate of this area is good for growing grass needed by dairy cows. Some of the milk from these cows is sold to people in nearby cities and towns. However, much of it is made into butter or cheese and sent to other parts of the West.

Many different kinds of crops are grown in the Puget-Willamette Lowland. Some farmers raise wheat or barley. Others grow such vegetables as beans and cabbages. There are many orchards where cherries, pears, and other kinds of fruit are grown. Berry farming is also important here. Some farmers raise flower bulbs, such as tulips, daffodils, and iris to sell to people for their gardens.

A sheep ranch in Montana. Many ranchers in the West raise sheep instead of cattle. What facts explain why this is so?

Investigate an Interesting Topic
Wheat is an important farm product of the West. Do research about wheat. Then write a report about it to share with your class. You may wish to use the questions below as a guide.
1. What are the parts of the wheat plant and the wheat kernel? (You may want to draw a diagram.)
2. How is wheat planted?
3. How is wheat harvested?
4. What is the difference between winter wheat and spring wheat?
5. What are some of the uses of wheat?

See "Learning Social Studies Skills" in the Skills Manual for help in finding information and in preparing your report.

Grand Coulee Dam on the Columbia River in Washington. The lake behind this dam supplies water to nearby areas that receive little rain. What are some ways in which people use water?

9 Natural Resources and Energy

A Problem To Solve

Why are natural resources important to the people of the West? In making hypotheses* to solve this problem, you will need to think about how the natural resources of the West have affected the following:

a. the location of towns and cities here
b. the growth of industry
c. the ways in which some of the people here earn their living

Information in Chapters 5, 8, and 10 will help you solve this problem.

See Skills Manual, "Thinking and Solving Problems"
*See Glossary

Natural resources are gifts of nature that people use to meet their needs. The part of our country we call the West is rich in natural resources. In some places, the soil is fertile and there is plenty of warm sunshine. Farmers use these natural resources in growing their crops. Rainfall is light in many parts of the West. But there are rivers and lakes that help to supply the water people need. Under the surface of the earth are large deposits of copper, oil, and other useful minerals. In some parts of the West, there are valuable forests. Also, the waters of the Pacific Ocean are rich in fish.

Water Resources

Water is one of our most important resources. People drink water. They use it to wash dishes, clothing, and other things. Factories use water in making many products. Farmers use water to raise crops and animals. Water is also used to produce electricity for homes and factories. Boats travel on waterways such as rivers and lakes. These bodies of water are also used for swimming and other sports.

Not enough water in the right places

The water that we use comes to the earth in the form of rain or snow. As you discovered in Chapter 3, rainfall is very light in most parts of the West. It is heavier in the mountains. But in these rugged areas there are few people to use the water. We can say that the West does not have enough water in the right places.

If people are to live and work in the dry parts of the West, they must get water from places where there is more rainfall. One way to do this is by building dams. To learn how dams can help supply water to dry areas, let's take a trip to the state of Washington.

A visit to Grand Coulee Dam

We are camping on a hill high above the Columbia River. When we look at the bare, brown land around us, we can tell that this area receives little rain. In the distance we see what appears to be a huge wall that stretches across the river. This is Grand Coulee Dam.

We drive down to the dam for a closer look. There we meet a guide who explains why Grand Coulee Dam was built. She says it is like a wall that holds back the

The West 93

water of the Columbia River. Behind the dam, the water has formed a huge lake, or reservoir.*

Irrigation.* Some of the water in the lake is used for farming. This part of Washington is so dry that farmers must irrigate their land to grow most crops. Water for irrigation is pumped from this lake into another reservoir nearby. From there it flows through canals, ditches, and large pipes to the farms where it is needed.

Flood Control. In the past, the Columbia River sometimes rose so high that it flooded the land. Floods destroyed houses and crops. Today the dam helps to prevent floods. When the river is high, some of the water is stored in the lake behind the dam so that it will not flood the land. When the river is low, some water from the lake is allowed to flow through pipes in the dam to the river far below.

Waterpower. The dam has another important use. Water from the lake is allowed to flow through the large pipes inside the dam. The rushing water turns huge engines called turbines. These are located in two buildings called powerhouses, at the foot of the dam. The turbines run machines that produce electricity. Wires carry the electricity to many homes and factories in Washington, Oregon, and Idaho.

Water Resources

This map shows some of the most important rivers and dams in the West. It also shows areas of irrigated land.
1. What are three different purposes for which dams have been built in the West?
2. Compare this map with the map on page 46. What relationship do you see between the location of irrigated lands and population distribution in the West? Why do you think this relationship exists?

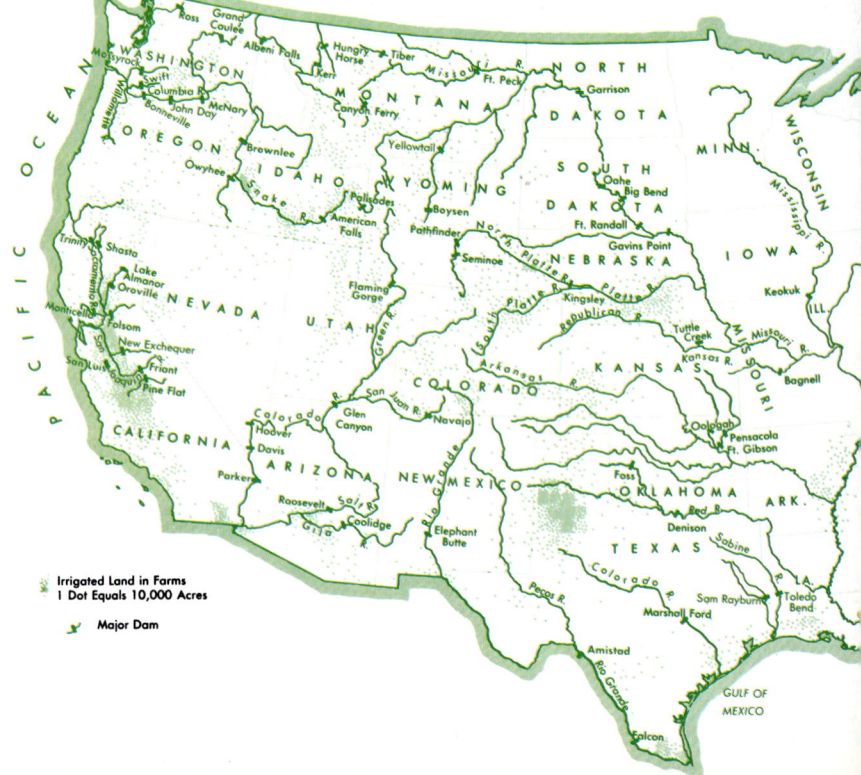

94 The West

Irrigating a farm field in Colorado. Irrigation is an example of the wise use of water. Do you think there will always be enough water to meet people's needs? Why do you think this?

Sports. Our guide tells us that Grand Coulee Dam helps the people of this area in still another way. The lake behind the dam can be used for swimming, fishing, and other sports.

Many dams in the West

There are many other dams besides Grand Coulee in the West. Some are built of concrete.* Others are made of many layers of earth packed tightly together. The map on page 94 shows the most important of these dams.

Like Grand Coulee, these dams are useful in different ways. Many are used to store water for irrigation. Some are used mostly to prevent floods or to provide waterpower for making electricity. Still others are used to store the water needed by people who live in cities.

Pumping water from wells

Not all of the water used in the West comes from rivers and lakes. There is more water under the ground than there is in all the rivers and lakes of the West. Most of this water comes from rain and snow that fall on the mountains.

Some of the water on the mountain slopes soaks into the ground. It goes down into layers of rock beneath the soil. Because these layers are full of

The West 95

Copper Deposits

Lead Deposits

Uranium Deposits

Oil Fields

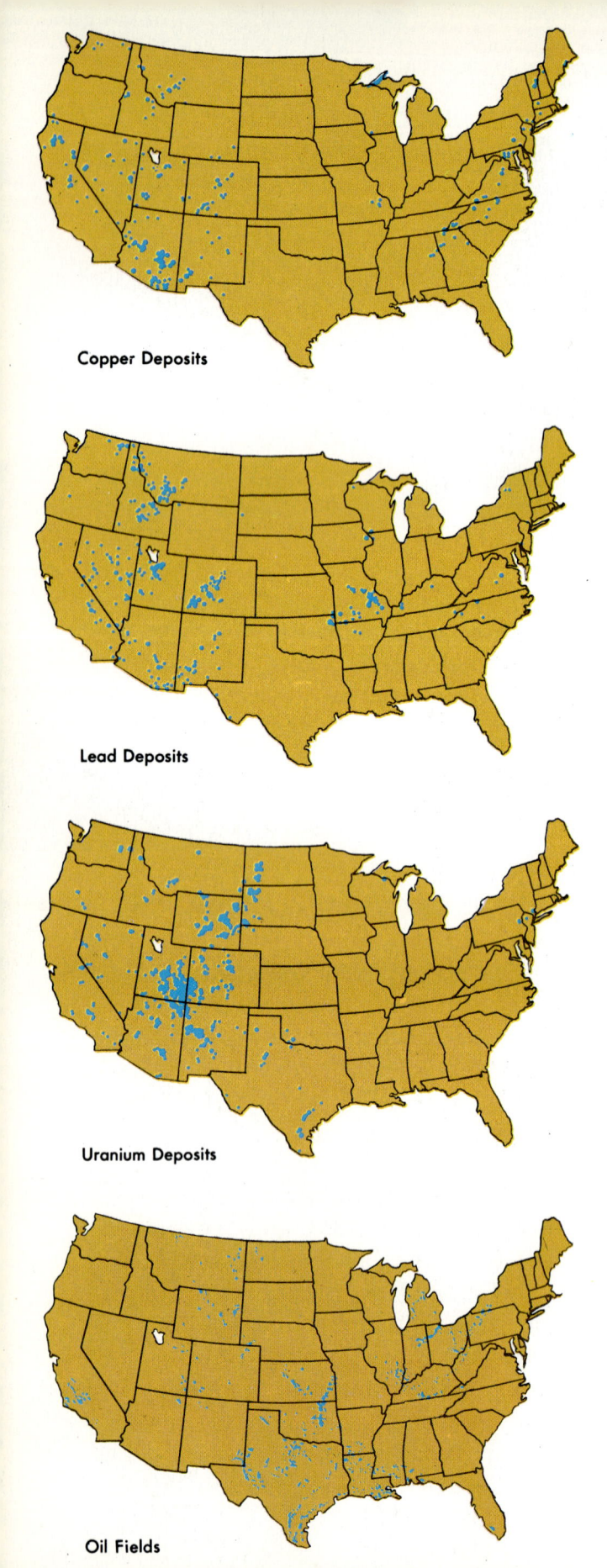

tiny holes and cracks, they can hold large amounts of water, just as a sponge does. The water that remains in the soil and rock is called groundwater. Layers of rock and soil that contain groundwater often extend from mountains into nearby valleys.

When people want to get water from beneath the ground, they drill wells. Then they use pumps to bring the water to the surface. In parts of Arizona and in the Central Valley of California, farmers use large amounts of groundwater to irrigate their fields.

Why much land is not irrigated

Irrigation has helped many western farmers to grow crops in dry places. But irrigated lands cover only a very small part of the West.

It will probably never be possible to irrigate all the dry lands of the West. The main reason is that there is not enough water. The West is already using most of the water that it receives every year from rain and snow.

Many places in the West are far from rivers or lakes that could supply water for irrigation. Water would have to be brought long distances through aqueducts.* Farmers would have to pay so much for this water that they would not be able to make a profit from growing crops.

Even where there is plenty of water, it cannot always be used for irrigation. Some water contains salt or other minerals* that are harmful to crops. Often the water cannot be used because it is full of waste materials from homes and factories. Today our government is working to clean up the water in rivers and lakes.

Mineral Resources

Perhaps you have seen a movie or a television show about prospectors in the West. A prospector is a person who goes from place to place hunting for gold, silver, or other minerals.

There were many prospectors in the West during the 1800's. Rich deposits of gold and silver were found in California, Nevada, and other western states. Many cities and towns in the West were started by people who were looking for these valuable minerals.

Minerals are still important to people of the West. Some people work in mines or oil fields where minerals are taken from the ground. Others work in factories where these minerals are made into hundreds of products.

Energy Fuels

Three of the most valuable minerals found in the West are oil, natural gas, and coal. These are known as energy fuels, because they can be burned to produce energy. We need energy to give us heat and light. We also need energy to run all the machines we use in our everyday lives. (See "Meeting Our Need for Energy" at right.)

Oil

Oil, or petroleum, is a dark-colored liquid that is found in layers of rock deep in the earth. To learn how people get oil, imagine that we are driving along the Pacific coast near Long Beach, California. (See map on page 8.) From our car, we can see a group of tall steel towers. These are oil derricks. They support the long pipes and other equipment needed in drilling for oil.

Meeting Our Need for Energy

In the United States today, people get energy from a number of different sources. The chart below shows the main sources of energy in our country.

Notice that about ninety-three percent of all the energy we use comes from oil, natural gas, and coal. These energy fuels are found in deposits under the earth. They were all formed from the remains of plants and animals that lived on the earth millions of years ago.

Today the United States does not have enough oil and natural gas. New deposits of these fuels are becoming harder to find. Some experts believe we will run out of oil and natural gas by about the year 2000.

We still have enough coal under the ground to meet all our energy needs for several hundred years. But coal cannot be used as a fuel to run cars and airplanes. Also, the burning of coal causes serious air pollution. Scientists are looking for ways to change coal into liquid or a gas. They want to develop a new kind of fuel that will be cleaner and more useful than coal.

Today people are trying to make use of new sources of energy. One of these is solar energy—the energy that comes to the earth in the form of sunlight. Another is nuclear* energy. However, many problems must be solved before these new sources of energy can take the place of oil and natural gas.

*See Glossary

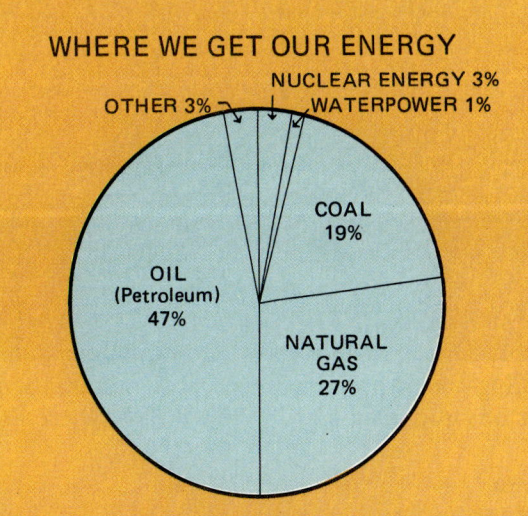

WHERE WE GET OUR ENERGY

- OTHER 3%
- NUCLEAR ENERGY 3%
- WATERPOWER 1%
- COAL 19%
- OIL (Petroleum) 47%
- NATURAL GAS 27%

Drilling for oil. The most valuable mineral product of the West is oil. Which is the most important oil-producing state in the West? Where are some of the other oil fields in the West located?

After a well has been drilled, the derrick is taken down. It is later used at a different place. Near the derricks are several oil pumps. Long arms on the pumps rock slowly up and down as the oil is brought from the earth. The oil is sent through large pipes to factories called refineries. There it is used to make gasoline and other products.

The oil field that we see here is only one of many oil-producing areas in California. This state produces more oil than any other state in the West. Most of California's oil fields are located along the Pacific coast in the southern part of the state, or in the Central Valley.

If we could travel through other states of the West, we would see many other oil fields. Some of the largest are in the state of Wyoming. Others are in eastern Montana, northern Colorado, and southeastern New Mexico.

Oil shale

In Colorado, Utah, and Wyoming, there are huge deposits of rock called oil shale. A form of oil can be obtained from this rock by heating it. In the past, very little oil shale was mined. The reason was that it cost much more to produce oil in this way than it did to pump oil from the ground.

Today, our country is beginning to run out of oil that can be pumped from the ground cheaply. (See "Meeting Our Need for Energy" on page 97.) Also, scientists are finding less costly ways of getting oil from oil shale. In the future, it may be possible to obtain large amounts of oil from the deposits of oil shale in the West.

Natural gas

Many people in the West use natural gas for heating, cooking, and other purposes. Natural gas is found wherever there is oil. Sometimes it is also found in places under the ground where there is no oil. New Mexico and California produce more natural gas than any other states in the West. Large pipes carry the natural gas to cities and towns where it is needed.

Coal

There are vast deposits of coal in the West, especially in the states of Wyoming, Utah, Colorado, and Montana. Until a few years ago, people did not bother to mine very much coal in the West. Most of this coal was thought to be of poor quality. Also, it was far from large cities where it could be used. Sending the coal for long distances by train was expensive.

The West

Today, all this is changing. Coal is becoming more important as a source of energy. Some of the coal in the West is now known to be of high quality. Also, people are finding cheaper ways of moving the coal to places where it is needed. Several new coal mines have been opened in the West, and others will be opened in the future.

Most of the coal mined in the West today is used as a fuel in electric power plants. Some coal is made into a fuel called coke,* which is used in making iron and steel.

Metals

It is hard to imagine what our lives would be like without metals such as iron and copper. Metals are used in making cars, stoves, television sets, and hundreds of other products.

The West is an important producer of metals. For example, it produces more than nine tenths of all the copper and silver mined in the United States. It also supplies about two thirds of the gold and more than one fourth of the zinc mined in our country.

The map on page 24 helps explain why the West is so rich in metals. Most of this area is made up of mountains or high plateaus. Metal ores* are likely to be found in places where there are mountains.

Millions of years ago, rocks containing metal ores were buried deep under the ground. Then movements within the earth pushed masses of rock upward to form mountains. Over many thousands of years, water and ice wore away some of the rock on the mountainsides. Layers of rock that contained metal ores were uncovered in places where people could find them.

Copper

One of the most useful metals found in the West is copper. Electricity passes through this metal easily. For this reason, copper wires are used to carry electricity into homes and factories. Telephones and other appliances contain many copper wires. Because copper does not rust, it is used to make pipes that carry water. Copper is also used in making pennies and other coins.

To learn about copper mining in the West, let's visit the city of Butte, Montana. (See map on page 8.) The hill on which this city was built has been called "the richest hill on earth" because it contains so much valuable ore.

On the edge of Butte, we see a huge pit in the earth like the one shown on the opposite page. The sides of this pit have been dug out to form terraces that look like stairsteps. On some of the terraces we can see giant electric shovels scooping up loads of rock. The rock is being dumped into trucks that will carry it out of the mine.

A miner tells us that the rock will be taken to a factory nearby. There, large machines crush the rock into tiny bits. Some of these are bits of copper ore. The rest are waste materials. The ore is taken in railroad cars to a plant called a smelter. This plant is in the town of Anaconda, twenty-five miles away. In the smelter, the ore is heated in large furnaces. This separates the copper from other materials in the ore.

The copper produced at the smelter is not pure enough for some purposes. It contains small amounts of gold and other metals. Some of the copper is sent to a plant called a refinery, where most of these other metals are removed.

The pure copper is then sent to mills where it is made into sheets, tubes, and wires. Now it is ready to be used by other factories in making many different products.

In the West, there are many other open-pit copper mines like the one we have just visited. Some of the largest are in Arizona, Utah, and Nevada. Arizona produces more copper than any other state in our country.

Lead and zinc

Two other important metals found in the West are lead and zinc. Lead is used to make paint, car batteries, and many other products. Zinc is mixed with copper to make brass. Because zinc does not rust, it is also used as a coating for iron products such as pails. Idaho produces more lead than any other state in the West. Colorado leads the West in zinc mining.

Gold and silver

In the West today, there are very few gold miners like the prospectors of one hundred years ago. Today, nearly all of the gold and silver is mined by large companies.

An open-pit copper mine in Arizona. Copper ore is dug from open-pit mines in several states of the West. Arizona ranks first in our country in the production of this useful mineral.

Gold and silver are often found in the same ores that contain copper. Since Utah, Arizona, and Montana have large copper mines, it is not surprising that they also produce much gold and silver. Gold is also taken from a large open-pit mine near Elko, Nevada. (See map on page 61.) This is the second richest gold mine in North America.

There are large silver mines in the mountains of northern Idaho. This state produces more silver than any other state in our country.

Iron and other metals

Many other metal ores are found in the West today. One of the most important is iron ore. This ore is needed to make iron and steel. Large amounts of iron ore are mined in California, Utah, and Wyoming. Ore from these mines is sent to steel mills in California, Utah, and other states.

The West produces large amounts of uranium. This metal is used in producing nuclear* energy. There are many small uranium mines in the "Four Corners" area, where the states of Utah, Colorado, Arizona, and New Mexico come together. New Mexico is our country's leading producer of uranium.

Three other important metals found in the West are molybdenum, vanadium, and manganese. These metals are used with iron ore to make certain kinds of steel that are very hard and strong. Colorado produces over one half of the molybdenum in the United States. It is also a leading producer of vanadium. Manganese ore is mined in the states of Montana and New Mexico.

Other Minerals

The West has large deposits of other minerals besides energy fuels and metal ores. There are deposits of sand, gravel, and stone in every state of the West. Each year, people use millions of tons of these materials to build highways and buildings. Large amounts of limestone are used in making cement. California produces more cement than any other state except Texas.

Several kinds of valuable minerals are found in the Great Basin. (See page 20.) Among these minerals are salt, potash,* and borates.* Potash is also taken from underground mines in southeastern New Mexico. These are the largest deposits of potash in the United States.

Using Natural Resources

See Great Ideas

A gravel plant in California. Many different kinds of minerals are found in the West. Why do you think minerals are called "natural" resources? What are some other kinds of natural resources? With other members of your class, discuss ways in which people use and misuse natural resources. Some of the information you will need for your discussion may be found in this chapter. Suggestions in the Skills Manual at the back of the book will help you locate other information and hold a successful discussion.

The West 103

Forest Resources

In a western forest

We are watching the sun rise over a beautiful mountain lake in Idaho. Birds are singing above us in the tall pine trees. Near the shore of the lake, we can see a mound of twigs and branches that was built by a family of beavers. Suddenly we see a mother deer and a spotted fawn as they dart through the forest.

As we are cooking breakfast over our campfire, a smiling woman in a green uniform comes up to talk with us. She is a forest ranger. Her job is to take care of the forest.

Where the West's forests are located

The ranger tells us that we would see many forests like this one if we traveled through the West. Almost one third of the West is covered with forests. Although much of the West is too dry for trees to grow, there are large forests in the mountains. There the rainfall is heavier.

The largest forests in the West are in the Cascade Range and in the coastal mountains of Washington, Oregon, and northern California. Trees grow very well in the mild, wet climate of this area. Most of the trees are large evergreens, such as spruce, hemlock, cedar, and Douglas fir. Along the coast of northern California and southern

Cutting timber in a western forest. Forests cover almost one third of the West. Where are the largest forests located? Why are forests important to the people of the West?

Oregon are forests of coast redwoods. These are among the tallest trees in the world.

Dense forests also grow on the western slopes of the Sierra Nevada in California. Here most of the trees are also evergreens, mostly pines and firs. In some places, there are groves of giant sequoias. These huge trees have larger trunks than the coast redwoods but are not so tall.

Because the Rocky Mountains receive less rainfall than the mountains farther west, the forests in the Rockies are not so dense. Among the main kinds of trees that grow here are pines, firs, and spruces.

Why forests are important

The wood that comes from forests in the West is used in many different ways. Some of it is sawed into lumber It is used for building houses, making furniture, and for other purposes. Some of the wood is made into pulp.* Paper and other products are made from this material. Many people in the West have jobs in factories that make wood products.

Forests are also important for other reasons. For example, they help to store the water that falls on the mountains in the form of rain or snow. Under the trees, the winter snow melts slowly. Some of the water sinks into the soft forest soil and trickles down the mountains beneath the ground.

If there were no forests on the mountain slopes, the sun would melt the winter snow quickly. The water would have little chance to sink into the soil. It would pour into the rivers, causing many of them to rise and flood the

Loading logs in a western forest. Today, loggers are using our forests more wisely than they did in the past. What are some of the ways in which lumber companies are helping to conserve our forests?

land nearby. Most of the water would flow away so quickly it could not be used by the people of the West.

Trees also hold the soil. They keep it from being washed away, into rivers and streams. Without the forests, many reservoirs in the West would fill up with soil. Then these reservoirs could no longer be used to store water for irrigation.

National forests

Because forests are so valuable to everyone, they must be protected carefully. Many forests are owned by the national government. These are called national forests. (See map on page 107.) There are about one hundred national forests in the states of the West.

The national forests are used in many different ways. During the summer, ranch owners let their sheep and cattle graze on grassy meadows among the forests. They pay the government for the use of this land. Many kinds of wild animals make their homes in the forests. Here they can find food and shelter. The national forests are also used for recreation. Each year, millions of people camp, hunt and fish, or enjoy winter sports in these forests.

Some of the trees in the national forests are cut for lumber and other purposes. Each year, the rangers decide which trees are ready for cutting. Private companies pay the government for the right to cut these trees and use the wood. The rangers make sure that new trees will grow up to replace the ones that have been cut down.

Other forests

Not all the forests in the West are owned by the national government. Some are owned by states or cities. Many forests are owned by private companies. These companies cut down some of the trees to use in making lumber, paper, and other products.

Lumbering is an important industry in the West. The chart below shows us the five states of the West that produce the most lumber. More than half of all the lumber produced in our country comes from these five states.

NATIONAL FORESTS IN THE WEST

LUMBER PRODUCTION IN THE WEST
1976   Millions of Board Feet

	0	1000	2000	3000	4000	5000	6000	7000
OREGON								
CALIFORNIA								
WASHINGTON								
IDAHO								
MONTANA								

(Number of Board Feet Produced in the United States: About 36,905 Millions)

The chart above shows lumber production in the five main lumbering states of the West. More than half of all the lumber produced in our country comes from these five states.

The West 107

Fish Resources

Along the Pacific coast of the United States, fishing is an important industry. Many kinds of fish live in the waters of the Pacific Ocean. Each year millions of pounds of fish are brought to shore by fishers in California, Oregon, and Washington.

California is the most important fishing state in our country except for Alaska. About two thirds of all the fish that are caught by people in the West are brought to ports in California. To learn more about this state's fishing industry, let's visit Terminal Island in the harbor of Los Angeles.

A visit to a tuna fleet

We are standing on a long platform, called a pier. It extends into the harbor. Here the air smells of fish, salt water, and fuel oil. In the harbor, we can see the tall masts of many fishing boats. Some of these boats are large enough to hold a crew of fifteen persons.

A fisher standing on the pier tells us that the larger boats are used for tuna fishing. They have to be large and sturdy because they go far out to sea. These fishing trips may take several weeks. Sometimes the tuna fishers go all the way to South America looking for fish to catch.

We learn that the tuna swim around in the ocean in large groups called schools. When workers on a fishing boat find a school of tuna, they drop a huge net into the water. The fish are trapped by closing the net with a rope, in the same way a purse is closed with a drawstring. A powerful engine is used to pull in the net. The fish are then loaded into the boat.

Not all of California's tuna are caught with nets. On some boats, the fishers use bamboo poles. Each pole has a line and a hook hanging from the end. When a tuna is hooked, the fisher raises the pole quickly and flips the fish into the boat.

As soon as the fish are caught, they are chilled in icy salt water. Then they are put in large refrigerators so they will stay fresh. When the boat returns to port, the fish are taken to nearby factories called

In the picture above, tuna fish are being caught with poles and lines. Not all of the tuna brought to fishing ports in the West are caught in this way. Many are taken with nets. As the chart below shows, California is the West's leading fishing state. The only state in our country that earns more money from fishing is Alaska.

LEADING FISHING STATES IN THE WEST
1974 Value of Fish Caught (Millions of Dollars)

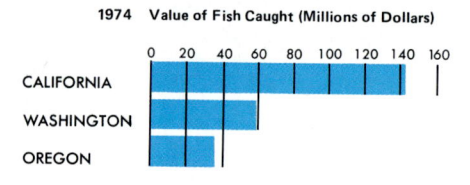

	0 20 40 60 80 100 120 140 160
CALIFORNIA	
WASHINGTON	
OREGON	

(Total Value of Fish Caught in the United States: $932,464,000)

108 The West

canneries. There they are cut in pieces, packed in cans, and cooked. The cans of tuna are sold in food stores all over the United States.

Los Angeles is not the only city in California with a tuna fleet. Many fishing boats dock at San Diego and other cities along the Pacific coast.

A visit to a "fish ladder"

Now we are driving eastward from Portland, Oregon, along the south bank of the Columbia River. (See map on page 8.) On both sides of the river are steep, wooded mountains. Ahead of us we see a large dam that has been built across the river. This is Bonneville Dam.

We notice what seem to be large stairsteps. They lead up around the end of the dam and into the lake beyond. But as we come closer, we see that this "stairway" is really a series of pools. They are like the ones in the picture on page 110. Each pool is one foot higher than the one below it. Water flows down from one pool to the next in a series of waterfalls.

Suddenly we see a large fish jump out of one pool into the pool above it. Then the fish leaps into the next pool, and then the next, until it reaches the lake behind the dam. This fish is a salmon. It has just climbed a fish ladder.

A guide at the dam tells us why the fish ladder was built. She says that the

The West 109

Rules and Government

See Great Ideas

A "fish ladder" at Bonneville Dam on the Columbia River. The federal* government built this fish ladder to help salmon get past the dam. How did building the fish ladder help protect the supply of salmon in the West? In what other ways are the fish in our country's lakes and rivers protected? Do you think private groups and individual citizens need to help in the conservation* of our fish supply? Give reasons for your answer.

salmon here are hatched in streams that may be more than 200 miles (322 km.)† from the sea. While they are young, they swim all the way to the ocean. There they live for two to six years. When the salmon are full grown, they return to the streams to lay their eggs.

On their long journey up the rivers, the salmon often leap high over rocks and waterfalls. But they cannot leap over dams. Fish ladders are built so the salmon can get past the dams to lay their eggs. Otherwise, there would soon be no more salmon.

In Washington, Oregon, and northern California, salmon fishing is a very important industry. Thousands of people earn their living by catching salmon or working in salmon canneries.

Unlike tuna fishers, people who catch salmon do not make long trips out to sea. Some of them sail along the coast in small boats. They catch the salmon as the fish are returning to the rivers to lay their eggs. Others spread nets across the rivers to catch the fish.

Most of the salmon are taken to canneries near the river mouths. Nearly all the work in the canneries is done by machines. First the heads, fins, and tails of the salmon are cut off. Then the fish are cleaned, cut into pieces, and sealed in cans. The salmon are cooked in the cans, then shipped to all parts of our country. Not all the salmon are canned. Some are smoked or frozen. Others are sold fresh in fish markets.

Other kinds of fish.

Off the coasts of Washington and Oregon, people also catch large numbers of halibut. Some of these fish weigh several hundred pounds. Most of the halibut are sold fresh or are frozen. They are shipped to other parts of the country on fast trains with refrigerated cars.

Mackerel is one of the leading kinds of fish caught in the ocean near the coast of southern California. Fishers catch the mackerel in large nets. Some of the mackerel are canned, and some are sold fresh in fish markets.

From the ocean, people in the West get many other kinds of seafood. Among these are sea herring, sole, and sea bass. Shellfish such as crabs, shrimp, and clams are also caught. People who live near the Pacific coast can buy fresh seafood at markets.

† km. means kilometer

Practice Using Your Map Skills
With the help of the map on page 8 and the maps and charts in this chapter, answer these questions.
1. Which state in the West has the most irrigated farmland?
2. Which state has the most copper?
3. Which is the leading fishing state in the West?

Use Your Creativity
Choose one of the following projects. You will find some of the information you need in this chapter. "Learning Social Studies Skills" in the Skills Manual will help you locate more information.
1. Write a report about a dam in the West that provides water both for irrigation and for making hydroelectricity. For example, you might write about Shasta Dam or Hoover Dam. You may wish to illustrate your report with diagrams or pictures.
2. Write a story about the life of a salmon. Tell where the salmon was hatched and where it spent most of its life. Also tell how it made its way upstream as a full-grown fish.

The West 111

A paper mill in Washington. Wood is the raw material used for making paper in this large factory.

10 Industry

A Visit to a Paper Mill

We are flying in a small plane over the western part of the state of Washington. On our left, we can see green forests and high mountains. On our right is a large body of water. This is Juan de Fuca Strait. It connects Puget Sound with the Pacific Ocean.

Along the shore of the strait, we see a large factory with tall smokestacks. Our pilot tells us that this is a paper mill. After our plane lands, we visit the mill to see how paper is made.

Wood for the paper mill

Our guide at the paper mill tells us that wood is the raw material used for making paper here. Each year, thousands of trees in the forests we saw from the airplane are cut down. The logs are sent to sawmills where they are made into lumber. When this is done, many tons of wood scrap are left over. This material used to be burned and wasted. Now it is used in making paper.

Large trucks and barges bring wood chips and sawdust from the sawmills to this paper mill.

Machines for making paper

Now our guide shows us what happens to the wood chips and sawdust after they arrive at the mill. We see the chips and sawdust being put into huge grinding machines.

Water is added to the ground-up material. This mixture is called pulp. The pulp now goes to the papermaking machines. There are three of these huge machines in this mill. The pulp is poured onto a screen that moves at a speed of thirteen to twenty miles an hour. (See the picture below.) As the screen moves along, much of the water is drained away. The wood fibers* in the pulp join together to form paper. Then the paper passes between heavy rollers. These rollers squeeze out the rest of the water and give the paper a smooth surface.

As the paper comes out of the machine, it is wound into huge rolls. Some of these rolls weigh more than eight tons. Next, the wide rolls are cut into narrower rolls. Now the paper is ready to be sent to customers.

*See Glossary

Part of a papermaking machine. To make paper, wood pulp is poured onto the moving screen shown below. As the screen moves along, most of the water is drained away. The wood fibers in the pulp join together to form paper.

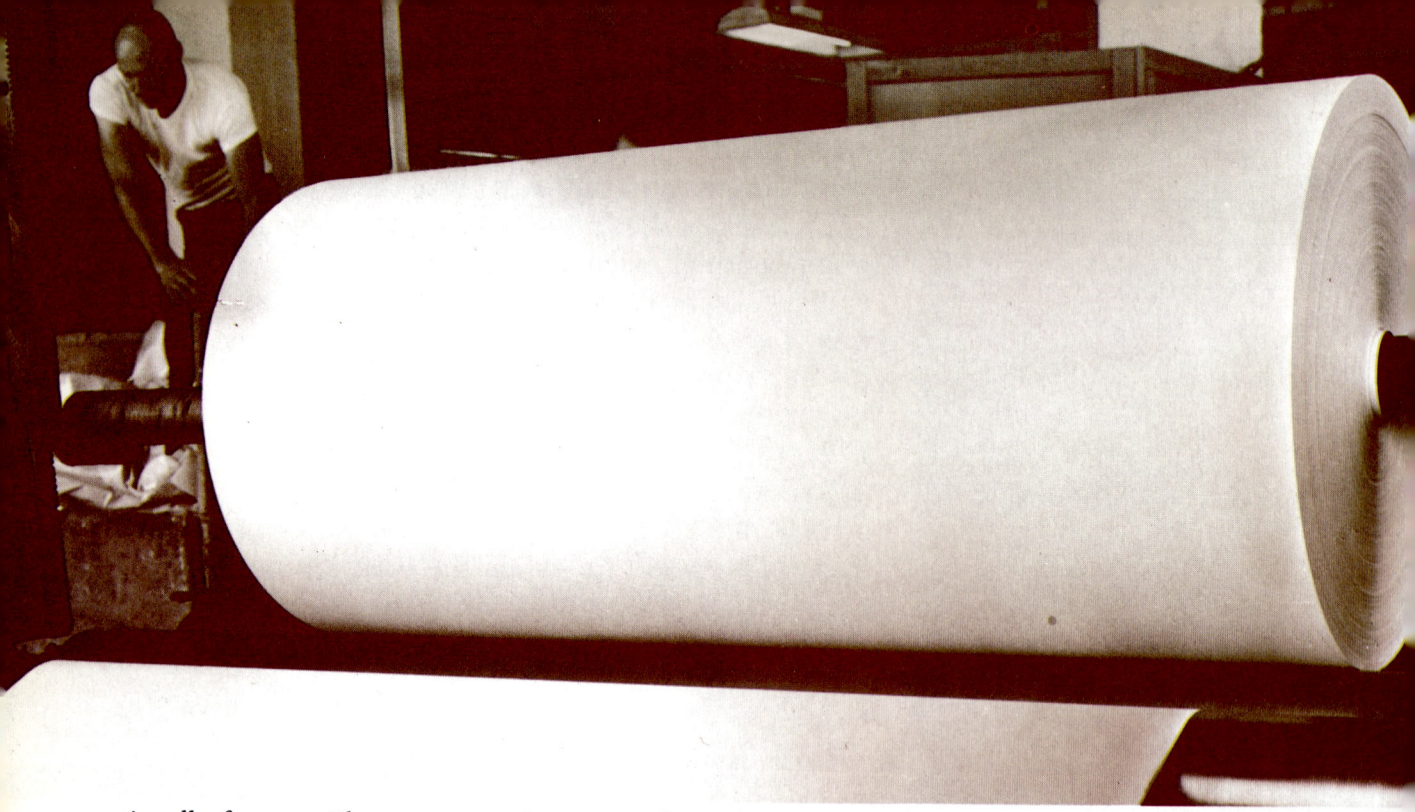

A roll of paper. The wet paper that comes from the screen (see picture on page 113) passes between heavy rollers. These rollers squeeze out the rest of the water and give the paper a smooth surface. As the paper comes out of the papermaking machine, it is wound into huge rolls.

Power for the paper mill

A large amount of electric power is needed to run the machines in this paper mill. The mill gets some of its power from a river that flows from the mountains nearby. Two power plants have been built on this river by the company that owns the paper mill. The mill also uses electric power produced at Bonneville Dam on the Columbia River.

Water for the paper mill

The nearby river supplies the paper mill with the water it needs. We learn that it takes 15,000 gallons of water to make one ton of paper. However, the mill is able to use much of this water over and over. The mill makes sure that the water is clean again before it is emptied into Juan de Fuca Strait. The plentiful supply of water here is one reason why the paper mill is located in this area.

Many workers are needed

Almost 350 people work at this mill. Some of them run the machines. Others are managers. They direct the other workers and see that everything runs smoothly. Most of the workers live in a town near the paper mill.

Owned by a large company

Our guide tells us that the paper mill is owned by a company that has offices in many parts of the United States. This company was started a long time ago by business people who provided the money to buy machines and to pay workers. Later, many other people paid money for shares of stock* in the company. Their money helped the company to grow. Today, more than thirty thousand people own stock in this company.

How the paper is used

Most of the paper made at this mill is called newsprint. It is the kind of paper used for newspapers. More than three hundred newspaper plants in the West buy paper from the company that owns this mill. Paper from this mill is also used for telephone books and catalogs. Some of the paper made here is loaded onto ships. They will carry it to cities and towns along the Pacific coast. The rest of the paper is carried from the mill on trains or in trucks.

Main Industrial Areas

The paper mill we just visited is only one of many thousands of factories in the West. Some of these factories, like the paper mill, make products from wood. Other factories refine petroleum* or produce metals from ores.* (See pages 97-102 of Chapter 9.) Still other factories in the West process* farm products such as fruits, vegetables, and meat. There are also factories that make airplanes, clothing, and many other products.

Industry is growing

Industry is growing in the West. Each year, new factories are built here. However, most of the factories in the West are in or near a few large cities, such as Los Angeles or San Francisco. (See the map below.) In many parts of the West, there is very little industry.

On our visit to the paper mill, we learned that a factory needs many things. Money is needed to start a factory and keep it operating. A factory

A Problem To Solve

This chapter has information about the main industrial areas of the West. <u>Why has industry developed in these areas?</u> In making your hypotheses* to solve this problem, you will need to think about how industry here has been affected by each of the following:

a. the supply of workers
b. the markets for manufactured goods
c. the supply of raw materials
d. nearness to transportation routes

Chapter 9 has information that will help you solve this problem.

See Skills Manual, "Thinking and Solving Problems"

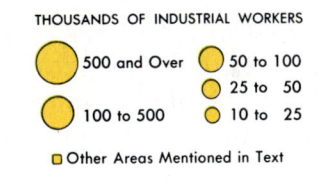

MAIN INDUSTRIAL AREAS OF THE WEST

THOUSANDS OF INDUSTRIAL WORKERS
- 500 and Over
- 100 to 500
- 50 to 100
- 25 to 50
- 10 to 25
- ▢ Other Areas Mentioned in Text

The West 115

must have raw materials. It must have machines to change the raw materials into manufactured goods. Power is needed to run the machines. A factory also needs skilled workers. Railroads and other kinds of transportation are needed to bring raw materials to factories. They are also needed to carry manufactured goods to customers. Most of these things can be found in the large industrial areas of the West.

Chapter 9 of this book tells about some of the raw materials produced in the West. Many different food products come from the farms and ranches here. In some parts of the West, there are large forests that supply factories with wood. The Pacific Ocean provides many kinds of fish. Factories get copper, lead, zinc, and other valuable minerals from the mines in the West.

The large industrial areas of the West are also well supplied with the electric power needed by factories. Power plants have been built on many rivers in the West. (See pages 94-95.) These plants use waterpower to produce large amounts of hydroelectricity.* In some parts of the West, oil and natural gas are found. These can also be used to produce electric power.

The number of people in the West is growing rapidly. Since 1950, the population of this region has increased from less than 20 million to more than 38 million. Many Americans are moving to the large cities of the West every year. Some of them are coming to these areas to get jobs in factories. For this reason, factories in or near large cities have plenty of workers. The people that arrive need such things as food, clothing, houses, and cars. They buy many of the goods made in the factories of the West.

The large industrial areas of the West have good transportation systems to serve their industries. There are many fine highways in this part of our country. New ones are being built every year. Railroads and airlines connect the cities of the West with each other and with other parts of our country. From seaports on the Pacific coast, ships carry goods to all parts of the world.

Southern California

The map on page 115 shows that there are several large industrial areas near the Pacific coast in southern California. The great city of Los Angeles is located here. There are also many other cities, such as San Diego, Long Beach, Anaheim, and San Bernardino. More than one million people work in the factories of southern California. The value of the goods made in these factories is about half the value of all goods made in the West.

There are several reasons why so many industries have come to southern California. The aircraft and motion-picture industries came here because of the

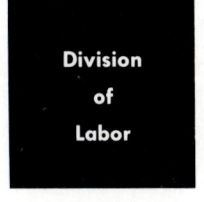

Division of Labor

See Great Ideas

What do you think would happen if the television stars in the picture at right traded jobs with the steelmakers in the picture above? Would the TV stars be very good at making steel? Would the steelmakers be able to present a good TV show? In most communities, all the work that must be done is divided into many different jobs that call for different kinds of skills. This is known as division of labor. How does division of labor help people meet their needs?

mild, sunny climate. Ranches in southern California furnish farm products for canneries and frozen-food plants. Southern California has large amounts of oil and natural gas. These are used to provide electric power for factories. As well as good land and air transportation, southern California has two large seaports. Ships from all over the world dock in the fine harbors at Los Angeles and San Diego. Some industries have come to southern California because of the large number of skilled workers. Also, products made in southern California are sold to the millions of people who live in this part of the West.

More than one third of all the factories in the West are in the Los Angeles-Long Beach industrial area. (See map on page 115.) They manufacture many different products. This area is one of the nation's leading producers of airplanes. It also has factories in which automobiles are put together. Television and motion-picture films made in the Los Angeles-Long Beach area are shown throughout the United States. Many factories in this area can or freeze fruits, vegetables, and seafood. There are also large oil refineries.* Other factories make machinery and electronic* products. The Los Angeles-Long Beach area is one of our country's leading producers of sports clothing.

Near Los Angeles are many smaller cities that make a wide variety of goods. For example, factories in Anaheim, Santa Ana, and Ontario make electronic equipment for the aircraft and space industries. Airplane engines and paint are made in Riverside. In several cities, there are plants that process fruits and vegetables from nearby farms. The Kaiser Steel plant near San Bernardino is one of the largest steel plants in the West.

Another leading industrial city of southern California is San Diego. Many people here work in large factories that make airplanes and airplane parts. Other people work in plants that make missiles* or electronic equipment. Fishing boats, tugs, and other kinds of

Workers in an airplane factory. The manufacture of airplanes is an important industry in the West.

boats are built at shipyards in San Diego. One of the nation's most important naval bases is located here. San Diego also has large canneries that process tuna and other seafood.

The San Francisco Bay area

Another part of California with many industries is the San Francisco Bay area. Among the cities here are San Francisco, Oakland, Berkeley, and San Jose. In recent years, the population of this area has been growing rapidly. There are many people to work in the factories and to buy some of the goods that are manufactured here. Factories near San Francisco Bay are served by one of the finest harbors in the world.

Thousands of factories are located in the San Francisco-Oakland industrial area. Many of these factories process

The West

fruits and vegetables grown in the Central Valley and other fertile valleys nearby. Several oil refineries and chemical* plants use oil from the Central Valley. Some factories in the San Francisco-Oakland area make tin cans, hardware, and other metal products. There are large shipyards on San Francisco Bay. Automobiles are made at several plants in the area. Other factories manufacture clothing and paper.

Several miles south of San Francisco Bay is the important manufacturing city of San Jose. One of the oldest industries in San Jose is food processing. Plums, apricots, and other kinds of fruit grown in the fertile Santa Clara Valley are brought to San Jose to be canned or frozen. There are more than sixty canneries and frozen-food plants in the San Jose area. Other factories package dried fruit.

In recent years, many new industries have come to San Jose. They have been attracted by the pleasant climate, the fine roads and railroads, and the large number of workers here. In the San Jose industrial area are an automobile plant and a missile factory. Other factories in the area make such items as electric motors, matches, carpets, and chemical sprays.

The Puget-Willamette Lowland

Outside of California, the part of the West that has the most industry is the Puget-Willamette Lowland. (Compare maps on pages 24 and 115.) Among the important manufacturing cities here are Seattle, Everett, and Tacoma in Washington, and Portland in Oregon.

Seattle and its neighboring cities, Everett and Tacoma, are all located along an arm of the Pacific Ocean known as Puget Sound. Here are deep harbors where ships can come to load and unload goods. The cities along Puget Sound are also served by fine highways and railroads. Nearby are large forests that provide wood for many different industries. Hydroelectricity is supplied by power plants that have been built on rivers in the Cascade Range.

Many factories in and near Seattle make transportation equipment. There are huge airplane plants here. Other plants make railroad cars or truck bodies. On Puget Sound, there are large shipyards.

If we were to visit the Puget Sound area, we would see many other factories. Plants that make aluminum are located here mainly because of the large supply of hydroelectric power. Large amounts of electricity are needed to produce aluminum. In Seattle there are factories in which fish are canned or frozen. Everett and Tacoma have factories that make lumber, paper, and other wood products. Wheat grown in eastern Washington is ground into flour in Seattle.

Portland, Oregon, is near the place where the Willamette River flows into the Columbia River. Ocean ships can sail up the Columbia and Willamette rivers and dock at this city. The rich farmlands of the Willamette Valley and the large forests in the mountains nearby provide raw materials for factories in the Portland area. Power plants on the Columbia and other rivers produce hydroelectricity.

Factories in Portland make many different products. Sawmills, paper

Exchange

See Great Ideas

A shipyard in Seattle. Shipbuilding is an important industry in Seattle. Some of the ships built here carry goods from our country to other parts of the world. They also bring goods back to the United States from other countries. Why do you suppose people in communities far away from each other would want to exchange goods? Do some communities have different natural resources than others? Do people in some communities have skills that are different from those of people in other communities? Explain.

mills, furniture factories, and other plants use wood from Oregon's forests. There are also plants that process fruits, vegetables, or dairy products. Some factories make bathing suits, sweaters, or other kinds of clothing. Machinery and chemicals are other important products of the Portland area.

Other industrial areas of the West

One of the largest industrial areas in the West that is not near the Pacific coast is Denver, Colorado. Denver is located in the Great Plains, a few miles east of the Rocky Mountains. It is a great transportation center. Fine highways, railroads, and airlines connect Denver with cities in other parts of our country. Food processing is the most important industry here. Many factories in the Denver area get their raw materials from farms and ranches nearby. Among these factories are meat-packing plants and sugar refineries. Electronic equipment and parts for airplanes and missiles are made here. Other factories in the Denver area make such products as mining machinery and rubber goods.

Several other cities in the West also have much industry. Many factories have been built in Phoenix and Tucson,

Working on a jet engine in Seattle, Washington. Seattle is the leading industrial city in the northwestern part of our country. Do research in this chapter and Chapter 5 to find out why Seattle is an important industrial city. What are some of the products that are made here?

The control panel in a steel plant. There are thousands of factories in the West. Most of these factories are in or near a few large cities. In much of the West, there is very little industry.

Arizona. Some of these factories make electrical equipment, chemicals, and parts for airplanes. Albuquerque, New Mexico, has meat-packing plants and lumber mills. Near Salt Lake City, Utah, there are refineries that make metals from ores that are mined nearby. Large iron and steel plants are located near Provo, Utah, and at Pueblo, Colorado. Making aluminum is important at Spokane, Washington. Aluminum plants here get the electricity they need from power plants at dams on the Columbia and other rivers.

Make Discoveries About Airplanes

Airplanes are made in several factories in the West. Do research about airplanes in other sources. Record your findings in a written report. Your report may include information about one or more of the following:
1. history and development of the airplane
2. the different kinds of airplanes
3. the parts of an airplane
4. how an airplane flies
5. how airplanes are built

"Learning Social Studies Skills" in the Skills Manual will help you find the information you need.

Farming near Anchorage. Farms in Alaska produce less than one tenth of the food needed by the people here. Large amounts of food must be shipped in from other parts of the United States.

Alaska and Hawaii

Two of our states are separated from the other forty-eight. These are Alaska and Hawaii. Alaska is the largest state in our country. It is in the far northwestern part of North America. Hawaii is an island state in the Pacific Ocean. It lies about 2,400 miles (3,862 km.)† west of California.

Alaska

Land and climate

Alaska may be divided into three regions. (See map on opposite page.) The largest is the Central Plateau. This is a region of low mountains and broad valleys. It covers over half of Alaska. Summer days in the Central Plateau are often hot. Winters here are bitterly cold.

North of the Central Plateau the land slopes gradually downward to a coastal plain along the Arctic Ocean. This region is the Arctic Slope. Much of this area is covered with ice and snow for eight or nine months each year. Summers are short and cool.

† km. means kilometer

South of Alaska's Central Plateau is the Pacific Mountains region. This region includes several high, rugged mountain ranges. In one of these is Mount McKinley. (See map below.) It is the highest mountain in North America. Between the mountain ranges and along the coast are several lowland areas. One of these is known as the Panhandle. It extends about 500 miles (805 km.) southeastward from the main part of Alaska. The Pacific Mountains region has milder winters than the rest of Alaska. Summers here are cool and rainy.

Alaska's people

Alaska is our largest state, but it has a very small population. Only about 407,000 people live here. About four fifths of the people are white. Most of the rest are Eskimos,* Aleuts,* and Indians.

Anchorage is Alaska's largest city. It is on Cook Inlet, an arm of the Pacific Ocean. About 161,000 people live in or near Anchorage. Alaska's other cities are very small. Fairbanks, on the Central Plateau, is the home of the University of Alaska. The port city of Juneau is Alaska's capital. A new capital city

*See Glossary

is being planned, however. It will be built about 35 miles (56 km.) north of Anchorage.

Many of Alaska's workers have government jobs. Others earn their living by working in hotels and other businesses that serve tourists. Some Alaskans earn their living by fishing.

Natural resources

Alaska's most valuable mineral resource is oil. There are huge deposits of oil on the Arctic Slope. Also there are large deposits of natural gas. Millions of tons of sand and gravel are mined in Alaska every year.

Alaska leads our country in the value of its fish catch. Many salmon and halibut are caught off the coast in the Pacific Ocean. Shellfish, such as crabs and shrimp, are also caught here.

Forests are another valuable resource in Alaska. Dense forests of hemlocks, spruces, and other evergreen trees cover much of the Panhandle. More than three fourths of the trees cut from Alaska's forests are made into wood pulp.* Others are cut into lumber.

Facts About Alaska	Number or Value	Rank
Area (square miles)	586,400	1
(square kilometers)	1,518,717	
Population	407,000	49
Capital — Juneau		
Admission Date: January 3, 1959		49
Colleges and Universities	3	44
Farm Products	$ 9,342,000	50
Dairy products	2,725,000	50
Greenhouse and nursery	2,000,000	45
Hay	1,794,000	46
Vegetables	1,064,000	50
Fish	$145,220,000	1
Timber Harvested (cubic feet)	118,995,000	23
Minerals	$448,437,000	23
Petroleum	347,408,000	9
Sand and gravel	52,788,000	6
Natural gas	21,919,000	16
Manufactures*	$179,700,000	49
Food and kindred products	57,000,000	47
Lumber and wood products	34,700,000	38
Printing and publishing	9,600,000	50

Building an Alaskan oil pipeline. Alaska has huge deposits of oil on its Arctic Slope. The pipeline shown below was built to carry oil from these deposits to a seaport on the southern coast of the state. From there, the oil is shipped to refineries in other parts of the United States.

Students at the University of Hawaii. The citizens of Hawaii are descended from people who came from many different lands. Who were the first people to live in Hawaii? Where did they come from?

Hawaii

Land and climate

Hawaii lies in the middle of the Pacific Ocean. It is made up of a long chain of islands. (See map on page 8.) These islands are the tops of a great mountain range that rises from the floor of the ocean. Volcanoes* formed this range millions of years ago.

If we were to fly over the Hawaiian Islands, we would see that parts of the main islands are high and mountainous. Between the mountains, we see many deep canyons. In some places, there are broad plateaus where cattle are grazing. Fields of sugarcane and pineapples are growing in the wide, rich valleys. On some of the islands, beautiful sandy beaches stretch along the coastline.

Hawaii is famous for its delightful climate. The weather here is pleasantly warm all year round. In most places, the temperature usually does not rise above 85° F. (29° C.)† or fall below 60° F. (16° C.). The only parts of Hawaii that ever have cold weather are the high mountains.

† F. means Fahrenheit scale
C. means Celsius scale

The West 127

A worker in a sugarcane field. The soil and climate of Hawaii are good for growing sugarcane, pineapples, coffee, and other valuable crops.

Facts About Hawaii		
	Number or Value	**Rank**
Area (square miles)	6,424	47
(square kilometers)	16,638	
Population	895,000	40
Capital — Honolulu		
Admission Date: August 21, 1959		50
Colleges and Universities	13	37
Farm Products	$323,257,000	41
Sugarcane	161,400,000	2
Fruits and nuts	70,793,000	7
Dairy products	21,943,000	45
Cattle and calves	18,511,000	42
Fish	$ 6,028,000	20
Timber Harvested (cubic feet)	605,000	49
Minerals	$ 42,042,000	44
Stone	21,370,000	32
Cement	17,111,000	15
Sand and gravel	2,379,000	50
Manufactures*	$412,300,000	44
Food and kindred products	206,700,000	35
Printing and publishing	53,100,000	39
Apparel and other textile products	31,000,000	36
Stone, glass, and clay products	29,400,000	42

People

The citizens of Hawaii are descended from people who came here from many different lands. The first people to live in Hawaii were Polynesians. They came here from other islands in the Pacific Ocean hundreds of years ago. Later, during the 1800's, large numbers of people began coming to Hawaii from the United States. They also came from various European countries. Others came from Japan, China, the Philippines, and other countries in Asia.

About four fifths of the people in Hawaii live on the island of Oahu. (See map on page 8.) On this island is Honolulu, the largest city in Hawaii. About 362,000 people live here. It is Hawaii's main seaport and trading city. Among the main industries in Honolulu are pineapple canning, sugar refining, and the manufacture of clothing.

Almost one fourth of all workers in Hawaii have jobs with the government. Many others earn their living by working for businesses that serve tourists. Others earn their living by growing or processing farm crops.

Natural resources

Hawaii's most important natural resources are its rich soil, its warm climate, and its beautiful scenery. The soil and climate of Hawaii are good for growing sugarcane, pineapples, coffee, and other valuable crops. Hawaii also has sandy beaches, steep mountains, and beautiful waterfalls. Many tourists come to Hawaii every year to enjoy the scenery and the climate.

The Pacific Ocean around Hawaii is a source of valuable seafood. Each year fishers bring millions of pounds of tuna and other fish to Hawaiian ports.

Index

Explanation of abbreviations used in this Index:

p — picture   *m* — map

Alaska, 124-126; *p* 124, 126; *m* 8, 125; *chart* 126
Albuquerque, New Mexico, 123; *p* 10-11; *m* 8, 61
Anchorage, Alaska, 125; *m* 125
Arizona, *p* 12-13, 78-79; *m* 8, 61, 115
  cities, *p* 60; *m* 61
  climate, 37; *p* 26-27
  farming, 82-83, 85-86; *p* 84-85
  industry, 122-123; *m* 115
  minerals, 101; *p* 101
  natural resources, 96
  people, 46, 50
arts, 74-77; *p* 74-77
  music, 76-77; *p* 77
  painters, 74-75; *p* 74-76
  writers, 75-76; *p* 76

Basin and Range Country, 20-21; *p* 20-21; *m* 24
Berkeley, California, 119; *m* 61
Bierstadt, Albert, 74
Bonneville Dam, 109-111; *p* 110; *m* 94
Bradley, Thomas, *p* 65
Brico, Antonia, 77; *p* 77
Butte, Montana, 100-101; *m* 61

California, *p* 1-5, 22-25, 28-29, 40-43, 47, 72; *m* 8, 61, 115; *chart* 107
  cities, 53-58; *p* 52, 54-57; *m* 61
  climate, 37
  farming, 82, 83-85, 88; *p* 80-81
  fishing, 108-109, 111; *chart* 108
  forests, 104; *m* 107
  growing season, 38
  industry, 117-120; *m* 115
  minerals, 97, 99; *p* 102-103
  natural resources, 96
  people, 44, 47, 48, 49, 50
Cascade Range, 21, 28-29, 30-31, 104; *p* 31; *m* 24
Catlin, George, 74
cattle, *see* farm products
Central Valley, 22-23, 44, 83-85, 96, 120; *m* 24
Chinese, *see* people, of Asian descent
cities, 52-61; *p* 12-13, 45, 52, 54-60; *m* 61
  history of, 54, 56, 58, 59
  industry, 53, 56, 57, 59, 60-61
  people, 44
  population, 53, 54, 60; *chart* 53
  See also names of cities
citizenship, 66-68, 73; *p* 67
citizenship and government, 62-73; *p* 62-63, 65, 67, 69, 72
climate, 26-39, 58, 83, 85, 87, 90, 118, 120, 124, 125, 127, 128; *p* 12-13, 26-29, 31-33, 36-37, 39; *m* 27, 30, 34-35, 38; *charts* 34-35
  in the dry lands, 27-28
  of the mountains, 33, 37
  along the Pacific coast, 38
  of the plains and plateaus, 33
  in the southern part of the West, 37-38
  in the wet lands, 28-31
  rainfall, 13-14, 17, 83, 86-87, 91; *p* 12-13; *m* 27
  seasons of the year, 34-35; *charts* 34-35
  summer, 33, 37, 38; *p* 31, 39
  temperature, 27, 31-33, 35, 37, 38; *m* 30
  winter, 32-33, 35, 37-38; *p* 32-33, 36-37
coal, *see* minerals
Colorado, *p* 14-15, 94-95; *m* 8, 61, 115
  farming, 85, 87, 88
  minerals, 101, 102
  people, 46
Colorado Plateau, 19-20; *p* 18-19; *m* 24
Colorado River, 85; *m* 94
Columbia Plateau, 18-19, 88; *p* 18; *m* 24
Columbia River, 21, 93-94, 109-111, 114, 120; *p* 92-93, 110; *m* 94
communities, 62-66, 68-73; *p* 69, 72
community problems, 68-73
continents, 5-6, 7; *p* 6; *m* 5
cooperation, *see* great ideas
Copland, Aaron, 77
copper, *see* minerals
cotton, *see* farm products
crime, *see* social problems

dams, 93-95; *p* 92-93; *m* 94
Denver, Colorado, 59-60, 122; *m* 61; *chart* 53
deserts, 28
deWaart, Edo, 77
discrimination, 48, 49, 50, 70. *See also* social problems
division of labor, *see* great ideas

earth, 4-7; *p* 6; *m* 5
Eastern Hemisphere (hem′ə sfir), 6; *m* 5
education, 66, 70, 71, 73. *See also* great ideas
electric power, 100, 114, 116, 118, 120
Elko, Nevada, 102; *m* 61
energy fuels, 97-100; *p* 98-99; *m* 96; *chart* 97
Eskimos, *see* people
Everett, Washington, 120; *m* 61; *chart* 53
exchange, *see* great ideas

Fairbanks, Alaska, 125; *m* 125
farming, 37, 80-91; *p* 14-16, 18, 23, 80-81, 84-85, 88-91, 124; *m* 82, 86, 87
farming methods,
  crop rotation, 83
  dry farming, 86-88; *p* 88-89
  irrigation, 82-83
  strip-cropping, 87
farmland, 28, 29; *p* 94-95
farm products,
  alfalfa, 60, 83, 88, 90
  barley, 37, 85, 88, 91; *p* 88-89
  cattle, 16, 19, 28, 80, 88, 91, 127; *p* 16, 90; *m* 87
  corn, *m* 82
  cotton, 38, 60, 81, 82, 83-84, 85; *p* 84-85; *m* 82
  dairy products, 91; *m* 82
  flowers, 91
  fruit, 38, 53, 60-61, 81, 83, 84, 85, 86, 91, 127, 128; *m* 82, 86
  nuts, 81, 84; *m* 86
  sheep, 28, 80, 88, 91; *p* 91; *m* 87
  sugar beets, 81, 83, 85, 90; *m* 86

PRONUNCIATION KEY: hat, āge, cãre, fär; let, ēqual, tėrm; it, īce; hot, ōpen, ôrder; oil, out; cup, pùt, rüle, ūse; child; long; thin; ᴛʜen; zh, measure; ə represents a in about, e in taken, i in pencil, o in lemon, u in circus.

sugarcane, 127, 128; *p* 128
vegetables, 38, 53, 60-61, 81, 83, 85, 88, 91; *p* 80-81; *m* 86
wheat, 16, 19, 81-82, 86-88, 91; *p* 14-15, 18; *m* 82, 86
fish, 108-111, 126, 128; *p* 108-110; *chart* 108
fishing, 57, 59, 126
forest products, 105, 120, 122
forests, 16, 24, 29, 104-107; *p* 104-107; *m* 107; *chart* 107
freedom, *see* great ideas
fruit, *see* farm products

global view, 4-11; *p* 4-6, 10-11; *m* 5, 7-10
Golden Gate Bridge, 56; *p* 1
government, 62-66; *p* 62-63, 65
    carrying out the laws, 64-66
    city council, 63, 65; *p* 62-63
    interpreting the laws, 66
    making the laws, 63
    mayor, 64-66; *p* 65
    See also great ideas, rules and government
Grand Canyon, *p* 18-19
Grand Coulee Dam, 93-95; *p* 92-93; *m* 94
Grand Teton Mountains, *p* 16-17
Great Basin, 20-21
great ideas,
    cooperation, *p* 72
    division of labor, *p* 116-117
    education, 61, 66, 68, 71, 73; *p* 51
    exchange, *p* 121
    freedom, 48, 50; *p* 39, 65
    language, 47; *p* 47
    rules and government, 48, 51; *p* 52, 110
    using natural resources, 92-111; *p* 18, 88-89, 102-103
Great Plains, 14-16, 33, 86-88; *p* 14-15; *m* 14, 24
Great Salt Lake, 21; *m* 8
Grofé, Ferde, 77
growing season, 37, 38, 85; *m* 38

Harte, Bret, 75-76
Hawaii, 127-128; *p* 127, 128; *m* 8; *chart* 128
Honolulu, Hawaii, 128; *m* 8
hydroelectricity, 59, 116, 120

Idaho, *m* 8, 61, 115; *chart* 107
    farming, 85
    forests, *m* 107
    minerals, 101
Imperial Valley, California, 85
Indians, *see* people
industry, 112-123; *p* 78-79, 112-114, 116-119, 121-123; *m* 115

aircraft, 115, 117-118, 122, 123; *p* 118-119, 122
automobile, 118, 120
chemical, 56, 120, 122, 123
clothing, 53, 115, 122, 128
electronic equipment, 53, 57, 61, 118, 122
food processing, 53, 56, 59, 60-61, 118, 119, 120, 122, 123, 128
iron and steel, 118, 123; *p* 116-117, 123
lumbering, 107, 122; *chart* 107
metal, 120, 123
motion picture, 53, 117-118
oil refining, 60
papermaking, 56, 112-115; *p* 112-114
plastics, 57
shipbuilding, 118-119; *p* 121
television, 53, 118; *p* 117
tourist, 126, 128
transportation equipment, 53, 56, 57, 59, 60, 61, 120
iron ore, *see* minerals
irrigation, 20, 28, 83. *See also* water

Japanese, *see* people, of Asian descent
Juneau, Alaska, 125; *m* 125

Kay, Hershey, 77

land, 2, 12-25; *p* 2-3, 12-23, 25
    farming, 80-81, 82-83, 85, 86, 87, 88, 90
land regions of the West, *m* 14, 16, 17, 21, 24
    Pacific Mountains and Valleys, 21-24; *p* 22-23, 25, 31; *m* 21, 24
    Plateau Country, 17-21, 33; *m* 17, 24
    Rocky Mountains, 16, 30, 33, 59; *p* 14-15, 16-17; *m* 16, 24
language, *see* great ideas
London, Jack, 75, 76
Long Beach, California, 53; *m* 61; *chart* 53
Los Angeles, California, 24, 44, 53-54, 64-65, 73, 118; *p* 52; *m* 61; *chart* 53
    government, 64-65
    Watts section, 71-73; *p* 72

McGinley, Phyllis, 76
Mehta, Zubin, 77
metals, 100-102; *p* 101
    brass, 101

copper, 100-101
gold and silver, 101-102
lead and zinc, 101
See also minerals
metropolitan areas, 53, 54; *chart* 53
Mexican-Americans, *see* people
migrant workers, 83
migration, *p* 10-11, 42-43
Miller, Joaquin, 75
minerals, 59, 60, 97-103; *p* 98-99, 101-103; *m* 96; *chart* 97
    borates, 102
    coal, 99-100; *chart* 97
    copper, 100-101, 102, 116; *p* 101
    energy fuels, 97, 99-100; *p* 98-99; *m* 96; *chart* 97
    gold, 56, 97, 100, 101-102
    iron ore, 102
    lead, 101, 116
    limestone, 102
    manganese, 102
    molybdenum, 102
    natural gas, 99, 118, 126; *chart* 97
    oil, 97, 99, 118, 126; *p* 98-99, 126; *m* 96; *chart* 97
    potash, 102
    salt, 57-58, 102
    sand and gravel, 102, 126; *p* 102-103
    silver, 97, 100, 101-102
    stone, 102
    uranium, 102
    vanadium, 102
    zinc, 100, 101, 116
minority groups, 70
Montana, *p* 16; *m* 8, 61, 115; *chart* 107
    climate, 33; *p* 32-33
    farming, 86-88; *p* 91
    forests, *m* 107
    minerals, 100-101, 102
Monument Valley, *p* 26-27
Moran, Thomas, 74
Mount McKinley, 125; *m* 125
Mount Rainier, *p* 31
Mount Whitney, 21-22; *m* 8
music, *see* arts

Native Americans, *see* people, Indians
natural gas, *see* minerals
natural resources and energy, 92-111; *p* 92-95, 98-99, 101-110; *m* 96, 107; *charts* 97, 107, 108
Nevada, *p* 20-21; *m* 8, 61, 115
    climate, 27
    minerals, 97, 101, 102

New Mexico, p 10-11; m 8, 61, 115
　climate, 37
　energy fuels, 99
　farming, 85
　minerals, 102
　people, 46, 47, 50
North America, 7; m 5, 7
nuclear energy, 97, 102; chart 97

Oakland, California, 54, 119-120; m 61; chart 53
oceans, 5-6; p 6; m 5
oil, see minerals
O'Keeffe, Georgia, 74; p 76
Oregon, p 45; m 8, 61, 115; chart 107
　climate, 30
　farming, 85, 91
　fishing, 109-111; chart 108
　forests, 104; m 107
　people, 44, 46
Oregon Trail, 43

Pacific Mountains and Valleys, see land regions of the West
painters, see arts
people, 40-51, 62, 71, 73, 125, 126, 128; p 40-43, 47-51, 72
　Aleuts, 125
　of Asian descent, 49-50, 56, 70, 128; p 49
　blacks, 48-49, 70; p 48, 65
　of European descent, 46, 128
　Eskimos, 125
　Indians, 50-51, 70, 125; p 50, 51
　Latinos, 70
　Mexican-Americans, 46-48; p 47
　Polynesians, 128
petroleum, see minerals, oil
Phoenix, Arizona, 60-61, 122-123; p 60; m 61
Plateau Country, see land regions of the West
population, 10, 13, 14, 24, 43, 44, 46, 50, 53, 54, 116, 125; m 46; chart 53
Portland, Oregon, 46, 120, 122; p 45; m 61

ports, 53-54, 56, 57, 58-59, 108, 117, 118, 125, 128
Provo, Utah, 123; m 61
Pueblo, Colorado, 123; m 61
Puget (pū′jit) Sound, 23, 58, 112, 120
Puget-Willamette (pū′jit wə lam′-ət) Lowland, 23, 44-46, 91, 120-122; p 45; m 24

recreation, 58, 59
redwood trees, 105
Remington, Frederic, 74; p 74-75
reservations, 50, 51; p 51
reservoirs, 83
responsibilities of citizens, 68
rivers, 19, 20; m 94
Rocky Mountains, see land regions of the West
rules and government, see great ideas
Russell, Charles M., 74

Sacramento River, 22; m 94
Salt Lake City, Utah, 123; m 61
Salt River, 60; m 94
Salt River Valley, 60, 82-83
San Diego, California, 35, 44, 57-58, 118-119; p 4-5, 35, 56-57; m 61; chart 53
San Diego Bay, 57
San Francisco, California, 44, 54-56, 119-120; p 42-43, 47, 54-55; m 61; chart 53
San Francisco Bay, 23, 44, 54-56; p 1, 54-55; m 8
San Francisco Bay Area, 119-120
San Francisco-Oakland Bay Bridge, 56
San Joaquin River, 22-23; m 94
San Jose, California, 119; m 61
Saroyan, William, 76
schools, see education
Seattle, Washington, 44, 46, 58-59, 63, 120; p 58-59, 62-63, 121, 122; m 61; chart 53
sheep, see farm products
Sierra Nevada, (sē er′ ə nə vad′ ə), 21-22, 30-31, 33, 105; p 22-23; m 24

social problems, 68-73
　crime, 69, 70
　discrimination, 70, 71
　education, 71, 73
solar energy, 97
spacecraft, 4-5
Spokane, Washington, 123; m 61
Steinbeck, John, 76; p 76
sugar beets, see farm products

Tacoma, Washington, 120; m 61
temperature, see climate
Terminal Island, California, 108
Tobey, Mark, 74-75
transportation, 46
Tucson, Arizona, 122-123

United States, 7, 10; m 7-10
Utah, m 8, 61

vegetables, see farm products
volcanoes, 21, 127

Washington, 93-95; p 31, 62-63, 92-93, 112-113, 121, 122; m 8, 61, 115; chart 107
　climate, 28, 30
　farming, 85, 88, 91
　fishing, 111; chart 108
　forests, 104; m 107
　people, 44, 46, 50
water, 5-6, 20-21, 93-96
　flood control, 94
　irrigation, 94-96; p 94-95; m 94
　uses of, 93-96; m 94
waterpower, 94, 116; chart 97
Watts section, see Los Angeles, California
Western Hemisphere (hem′ ə sfir), 7; m 5
wheat, see farm products
Willamette River, 23, 120; m 94
wind erosion, 87
World War II, 49
writers, see arts
Wyoming, p 16-17; m 8, 61, 115
　farming, 88, 90

Yosemite National Park, p 22-23

zinc, see minerals

PRONUNCIATION KEY: hat, āge, cāre, fär; let, ēqual, tėrm; it, īce; hot, ōpen, ôrder; oil, out; cup, put, rüle, ūse; child; long; thin; ᴛHen; zh, measure; ə represents a in about, e in taken, i in pencil, o in lemon, u in circus.

The West 131

Acknowledgments

Grateful acknowledgment is made to the following for permission to use the illustrations found in this book:

A. Devaney, Inc.: Page 39
Alaska Pictorial Service: Page 124 by Steve and Delores McCutcheon
Alpha Photo Associates, Inc.: Pages 42-43 by Mac Fadyen
Annan Photo Features: Page 91
Boeing: Pages 118-119 and 122
Buddy Mays: Pages 10-11 and 51
Camera Hawaii: Page 127
Camerique Stock Photos: Page 50
City of Los Angeles, Office of the Mayor: Page 65
City of Phoenix, Office of the Mayor: Page 60
City of San Diego: Pages 4-5
Clyde Sunderland: Page 52
Crown Zellerbach Corporation: Pages 112-113, 113, and 114
De Wys, Inc.: Pages 2-3 and 47
Doug Wilson: Pages 31, 48, and 49
Dudley, Hardin, and Yang, Inc.: Pages 58-59
Freelance Photographers Guild: Pages 16-17, 22-23, 40-41, and 54-55; pages 80-81 and 90 by Willinger; pages 92-93 by Gene Ahrens; pages 106-107 by Spring
Grant Heilman: Pages 14-15, 56-57, 94-95, and 110
H. Armstrong Roberts: Pages 102-103
Jon Brenneis: Page 121
Josef Muench: Pages 26-27 and 36-37
Kaiser Steel Corporation: Pages 116-117

Los Angeles Philharmonic: Page 77
Markow Photography: Pages 18-19
Montana Chamber of Commerce: Page 16 by Browning
NASA: Page 6
NBC Studios, Burbank California: Page 117, singer Mac Davis
Oregon State Highway: Page 45
Photo Researchers, Inc.: Pages 32-33 by Joe Munroe; pages 98-99 by Jack Fields
Ray Atkeson: Page 18
San Diego March of Dimes: Page 67
San Francisco Convention & Visitors Bureau: Page 1
Shostal Associates, Inc.: Pages 23, 25, 28-29, 104-105, 123, and 128; pages 12-13, 78-79, and 84-85 by Manley
Sohio: Page 126
Sterling and Francine Clark Art Institute: Pages 74-75
The Bettmann Archive: Page 76 (right)
Tom Myers: Pages 88-89
Tuna Research Foundation: Pages 108-109
Van Cleve Photography: Pages 20-21 by David Muench
West Stock, Inc.: Pages 62-63 by Steve Meltzer
Western Ways: Page 101 by Charles W. Herbert
Wide World Photos: Pages 69, 72, and 76 (left)

Grateful acknowledgment is made to Scott, Foresman and Company for the pronunciation system used in this book, which is taken from the Thorndike-Barnhart Dictionary Series.

Grateful acknowledgment is made to the following for permission to use cartographic data in this book: Creative Arts: Pages 34 and 35; Base maps courtesy of the Nystrom Raised Relief Map Company, Chicago 60618: Page 24; Panoramic Studios: Page 5; Rand McNally & Company: Pages 8 and 9; United States Department of Commerce, Bureau of the Census: Pages 46, 86, and 87.

States of the West

Arizona	134
California	135
Colorado	137
Idaho	139
Montana	140
Nevada	141
New Mexico	142
Oregon	143
Utah	145
Washington	146
Wyoming	148

**In the Cascade Range of Washington (left)
Death Valley in California (below)**

Arizona

STATE BIRD: Cactus wren
STATE FLOWER: Saguaro cactus
STATE TREE: Paloverde

Although Arizona lies entirely in the Plateau Country, it may be divided into two main sections. Most of northern Arizona is part of the Colorado Plateau, and the rest of the state is in the Basin and Range Country.

The Colorado Plateau. Most of the land in the Colorado Plateau section of Arizona is more than a mile above sea level. Here are the deepest and widest canyons in the state. In this section is the famous Grand Canyon, which is more than a mile deep in some places.

Arizona lies entirely within the Plateau Country of the West. However, this state has mountains and plains as well as plateaus.

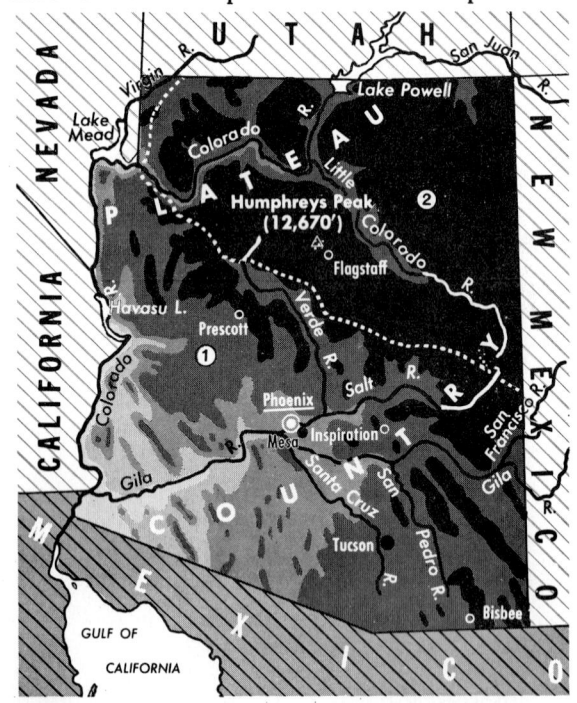

Facts About Arizona	Number or Value	Rank
Area (square miles)	113,909	6
(square kilometers)	295,013	
Population	2,296,000	32
Capital — Phoenix		
Admission Date: February 14, 1912		48
Colleges and Universities	21	31
Farm Products	$1,240,120,000	30
Cattle and calves	408,839,000	13
Cotton	271,369,000	4
Vegetables	123,224,000	11
Fish	$ 4,000	44
Timber Harvested (cubic feet)	94,179,000	28
Minerals	$1,562,234,000	9
Copper	1,327,678,000	1
Molybdenum	57,067,000	2
Sand and gravel	41,906,000	11
Manufactures*	$1,916,900,000	34
Electrical equipment and supplies	335,500,000	21
Primary metals industries	310,300,000	18
Nonelectrical machinery	309,100,000	22

Many of Arizona's highest mountains rise near the southern edge of the Colorado Plateau. (See map at left.) Some of the high peaks in this area are volcanoes that are no longer active. Humphreys Peak, near the city of Flagstaff, is the highest mountain in the state. It is more than two miles high.

The Basin and Range Country. In Arizona, this section is made up mainly of high plains. Scattered through the area, however, are many narrow mountain ranges that rise sharply from the surrounding land. In some places there are also small, flat-topped hills called mesas. The land in southwestern Arizona is generally lower and more level than the land in the southeast. Between the widely separated mountain ranges in this area are broad basins and river valleys.

*See Glossary

134 The West

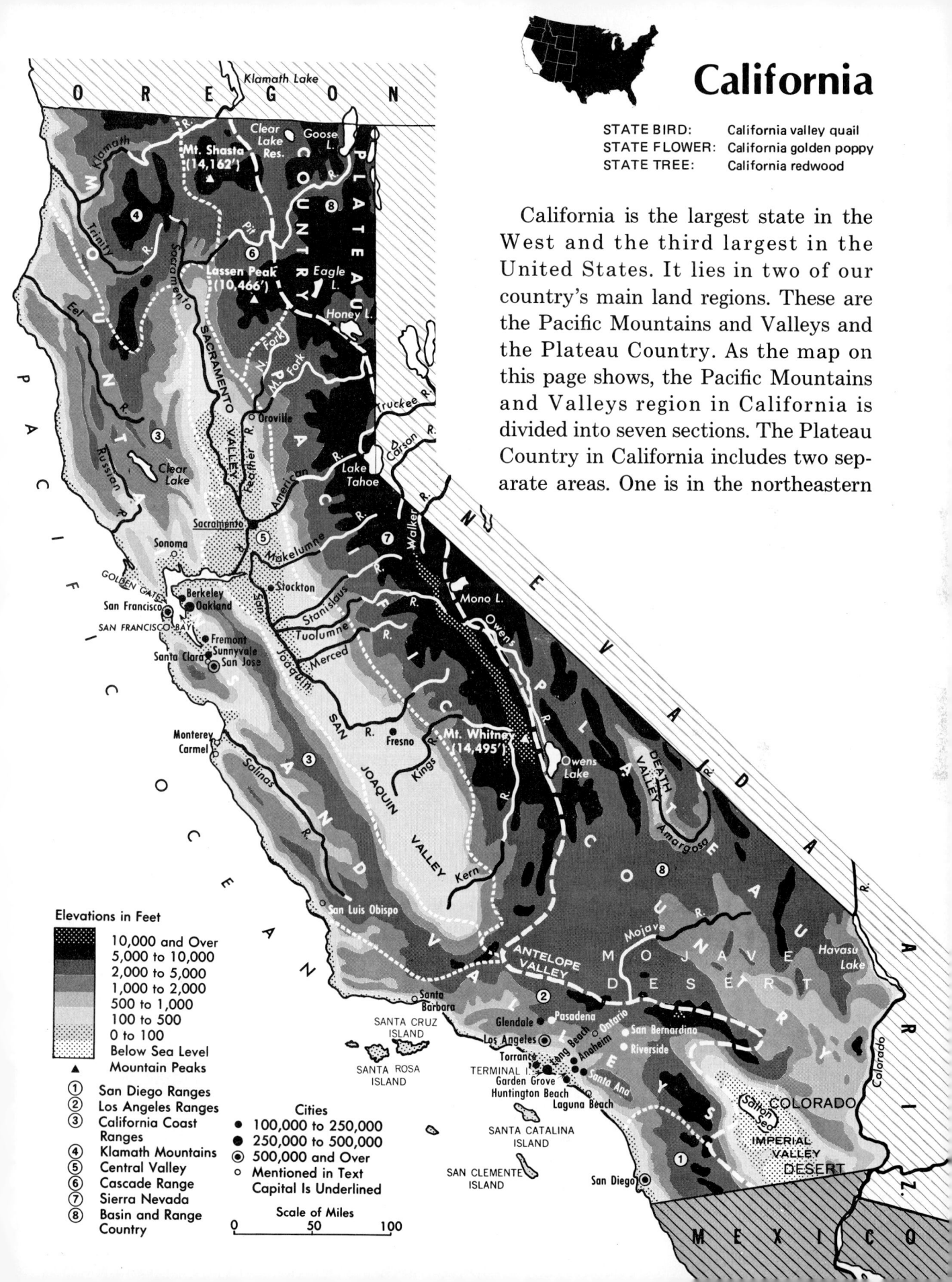

California

STATE BIRD: California valley quail
STATE FLOWER: California golden poppy
STATE TREE: California redwood

California is the largest state in the West and the third largest in the United States. It lies in two of our country's main land regions. These are the Pacific Mountains and Valleys and the Plateau Country. As the map on this page shows, the Pacific Mountains and Valleys region in California is divided into seven sections. The Plateau Country in California includes two separate areas. One is in the northeastern

Elevations in Feet
- 10,000 and Over
- 5,000 to 10,000
- 2,000 to 5,000
- 1,000 to 2,000
- 500 to 1,000
- 100 to 500
- 0 to 100
- Below Sea Level
- ▲ Mountain Peaks

① San Diego Ranges
② Los Angeles Ranges
③ California Coast Ranges
④ Klamath Mountains
⑤ Central Valley
⑥ Cascade Range
⑦ Sierra Nevada
⑧ Basin and Range Country

Cities
- • 100,000 to 250,000
- ● 250,000 to 500,000
- ◉ 500,000 and Over
- ○ Mentioned in Text
- Capital Is Underlined

Scale of Miles
0   50   100

Facts About California		
	Number or Value	Rank
Area (square miles)	158,693	3
(square kilometers)	410,999	
Population	21,896,000	1
Capital — Sacramento		
Admission Date: September 9, 1850		31
Colleges and Universities	221	2
Farm Products	$ 9,101,860,000	1
Fruits and nuts	1,646,380,000	1
Vegetables	1,595,794,000	1
Cattle and calves	1,101,408,000	6
Dairy products	1,088,678,000	2
Fish	$ 140,338,000	2
Timber Harvested (cubic feet)	843,723,000	3
Minerals	$ 2,797,080,000	3
Petroleum	1,710,350,000	3
Cement	210,520,000	2
Sand and gravel	176,213,000	1
Manufactures*	$31,382,700,000	1
Transportation equipment	6,736,000,000	2
Food and kindred products	4,020,400,000	1
Electrical equipment and supplies	3,378,600,000	1

corner of the state and the other is in the southeast. Both of these areas are part of the Basin and Range Country.

The Pacific Mountains and Valleys. A long chain of mountains extends along the Pacific coast of California. It includes several groups of mountains. These are the San Diego Ranges, the Los Angeles Ranges, the California Coast Ranges, and the Klamath Mountains. (See map.) Between the mountain ranges are many small lowland areas. Some of California's largest cities are in these lowlands. Among these cities are Los Angeles, San Diego, San Jose, and Oakland.

A large bay cuts eastward through the mountains along the coast of central California. This is San Francisco Bay, one of the world's finest harbors. The city of San Francisco is located at the entrance to this bay. North of the bay, many of the coastal mountains are covered with dense, green forests. South of the bay, the climate is drier. There the mountains are covered with grass, bushes, and scattered trees.

East of the coastal mountains is a long lowland called the Central Valley. Here the land is almost flat, and the soil is fertile. Nearly all the land in the Central Valley is used for farming. Farmers in the valley grow cotton, fruits, vegetables, and many other kinds of crops.

To the north and east of the Central Valley are two high mountain ranges. These are the Cascade Range and the Sierra Nevada. In the Cascade Range are several high peaks that were formed by volcanoes long ago. The Sierra Nevada is the highest and longest mountain range in California. Many of the mountain slopes here are covered with dense forests of evergreen trees. In the Sierra Nevada are three national parks—Yosemite, Kings Canyon, and Sequoia. They attract thousands of visitors each year.

The Basin and Range Country. Part of the Basin and Range Country lies east of the Cascade Range in northeastern California. The land here is high above sea level and very hilly. Grazing is the main type of farming in this thinly populated area.

Another part of the Basin and Range Country lies in southeastern California. The land here is very dry. There are rugged mountain ranges and low valleys dotted with desert plants. By irrigating their land, farmers are able to grow good crops in some of these desert valleys.

*See Glossary

STATE BIRD: Lark bunting
STATE FLOWER: Rocky Mountain columbine
STATE TREE: Colorado blue spruce

Colorado

Colorado may be divided into three main land areas. The Rocky Mountains extend from north to south through the middle of the state. To the east of the Rockies are the Great Plains. To the west is the Colorado Plateau.

The Rocky Mountains. The highest peaks of the Rocky Mountains are in Colorado. More than fifty of them are over two and one-half miles high. Among the highest are Pikes Peak and Longs Peak. Mount Elbert, which rises 14,431 feet, is the highest of all. The highest mountain peaks in Colorado are covered with snow all year round. Forests of evergreen trees blanket many of the lower slopes. Sparkling streams flow through narrow valleys between the mountains.

Colorado is famous for its beautiful mountain scenery. Millions of people

Elevations in Feet
- 10,000 and Over
- 5,000 to 10,000
- 2,000 to 5,000
- ▲ Mountain Peaks

Cities
- • 100,000 to 250,000
- ⊙ 500,000 and Over
- ○ Mentioned in Text
- Capital Is Underlined

Scale of Miles 0 50 100

Colorado may be divided into three main land areas. The Rocky Mountains extend through the middle of the state. To the east of the Rockies are the Great Plains, and to the west is the Colorado Plateau.

visit the state each year. Many camp in Rocky Mountain National Park.

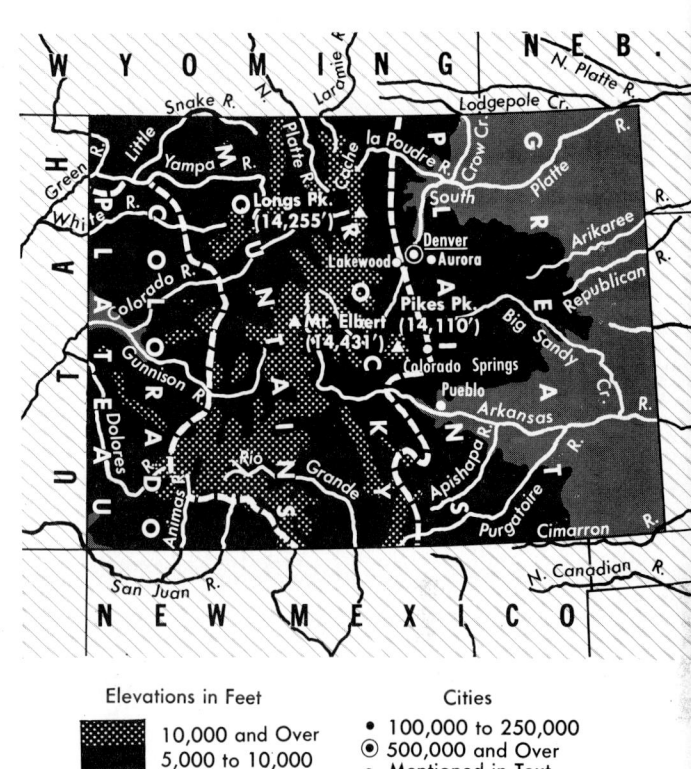

An imaginary line called the Continental Divide runs through the Colorado Rockies. All rivers on one side of this line flow toward the Atlantic Ocean. All rivers on the other side flow toward the Pacific. Four of the largest rivers in the West begin in Colorado. These are the Platte, the Arkansas, the Rio Grande, and the Colorado. (See map above.)

Few people make their homes in the Rocky Mountains of Colorado. The

Facts About Colorado		
	Number or Value	Rank
Area (square miles)	104,247	8
(square kilometers)	269,989	
Population	2,619,000	28
Capital — Denver		
Admission Date: August 1, 1876		38
Colleges and Universities	33	27
Farm Products	$1,976,608,000	16
Cattle and calves	1,163,167,000	5
Wheat	129,956,000	15
Corn	108,388,000	15
Vegetables	96,349,000	13
Timber Harvested (cubic feet)	54,140,000	30
Minerals	$ 750,299,000	20
Petroleum	283,904,000	11
Molybdenum	not available	1
Coal	64,677,000	11
Manufactures*	$2,455,000,000	32
Food and kindred products	513,700,000	25
Nonelectrical machinery	275,700,000	24
Transportation equipment	260,900,000	23

*See Glossary

Denver is the capital and largest city of Colorado. It is located near the western edge of the Great Plains. To the west of Denver rise the snowcapped peaks of the Rocky Mountains.

steep-sided mountains and deep canyons make it hard to build roads and railroads through this area. In most places, the land is too rugged and the climate is too cool for growing crops. But large herds of cattle and sheep graze on mountain pastures. In the mountains there are rich deposits of lead, silver, molybdenum, and other minerals.

The Great Plains. In the Great Plains section of Colorado, most of the land is flat or gently rolling. Large amounts of wheat are grown in some areas. In other places, there are grassy pastures where herds of cattle graze. Crops such as sugar beets and vegetables are grown in irrigated river valleys.

Colorado's largest cities are all located near the western edge of the Great Plains. These include Denver, Colorado Springs, and Pueblo.

The Colorado Plateau. Most of western Colorado lies in the Colorado Plateau. Rivers have cut deep canyons in the surface of the land here. Not many people live in this dry, rugged area. In some places there are deposits of valuable minerals, such as oil, natural gas, and uranium.

STATE BIRD: Mountain bluebird
STATE FLOWER: Syringa
STATE TREE: Western white pine

Idaho

Idaho lies in two main regions of the West. A little more than half of the state is in the Rocky Mountains, and the rest is part of the Plateau Country.

Idaho lies partly in the Rocky Mountains and partly in the Plateau Country of the West. The northernmost part of the state is long and narrow. It is known as the Idaho Panhandle.

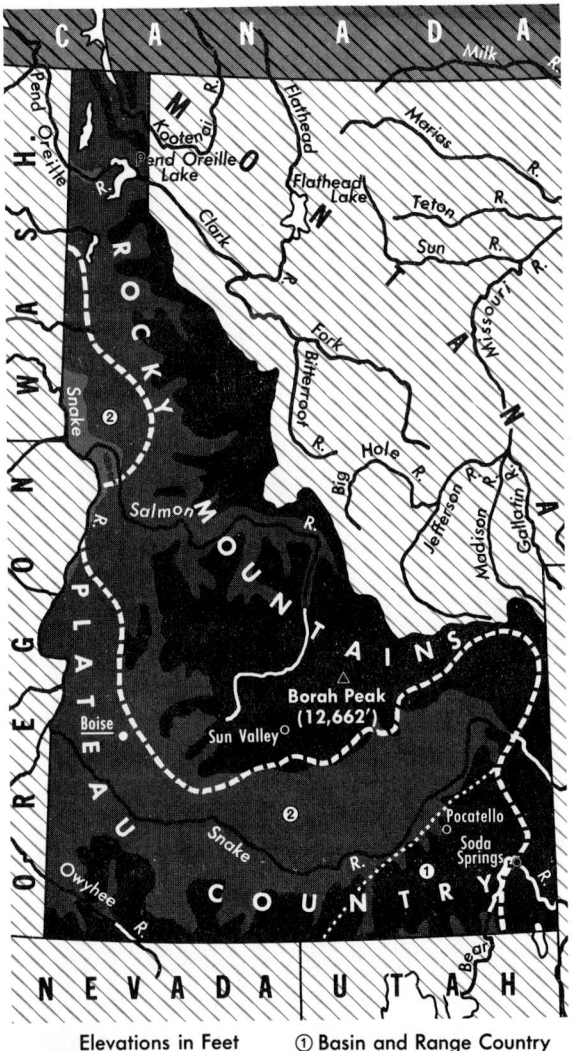

Facts About Idaho	Number or Value	Rank
Area (square miles)	83,557	13
(square kilometers)	216,404	
Population	857,000	41
Capital — Boise		
Admission Date: July 3, 1890		43
Colleges and Universities	9	40
Farm Products	$1,248,420,000	29
Vegetables	362,998,000	3
Cattle and calves	267,812,000	22
Wheat	164,371,000	13
Dairy products	136,492,000	21
Fish	$ 45,000	40
Timber Harvested (cubic feet)	325,951,000	14
Minerals	$ 208,558,000	31
Silver	58,572,000	1
Phosphate rock	not available	
Zinc	28,339,000	5
Manufactures*	$ 749,800,000	41
Lumber and wood products	262,900,000	13
Food and kindred products	258,200,000	31
Chemicals and allied products	58,500,000	35

The Rocky Mountains. Rugged mountains separated by deep valleys cover most of northern and central Idaho. These are part of the Rocky Mountains. The highest peaks rise to more than twelve thousand feet. On the slopes are dense evergreen forests.

The Plateau Country. Much of southern and western Idaho lies in the Plateau Country. Thousands of years ago, molten lava from deep within the earth covered large parts of this area. The top layers of this lava have turned into rich soil.

Idaho's largest cities and most important croplands are in the valley of the Snake River. (See map.) Dams on this river hold back water for use in irrigating potatoes and other vegetable crops. Cattle ranches and wheat farms cover some parts of the Plateau Country.

*See Glossary

The West 139

Montana

STATE BIRD: Western meadowlark
STATE FLOWER: Bitterroot
STATE TREE: Ponderosa pine

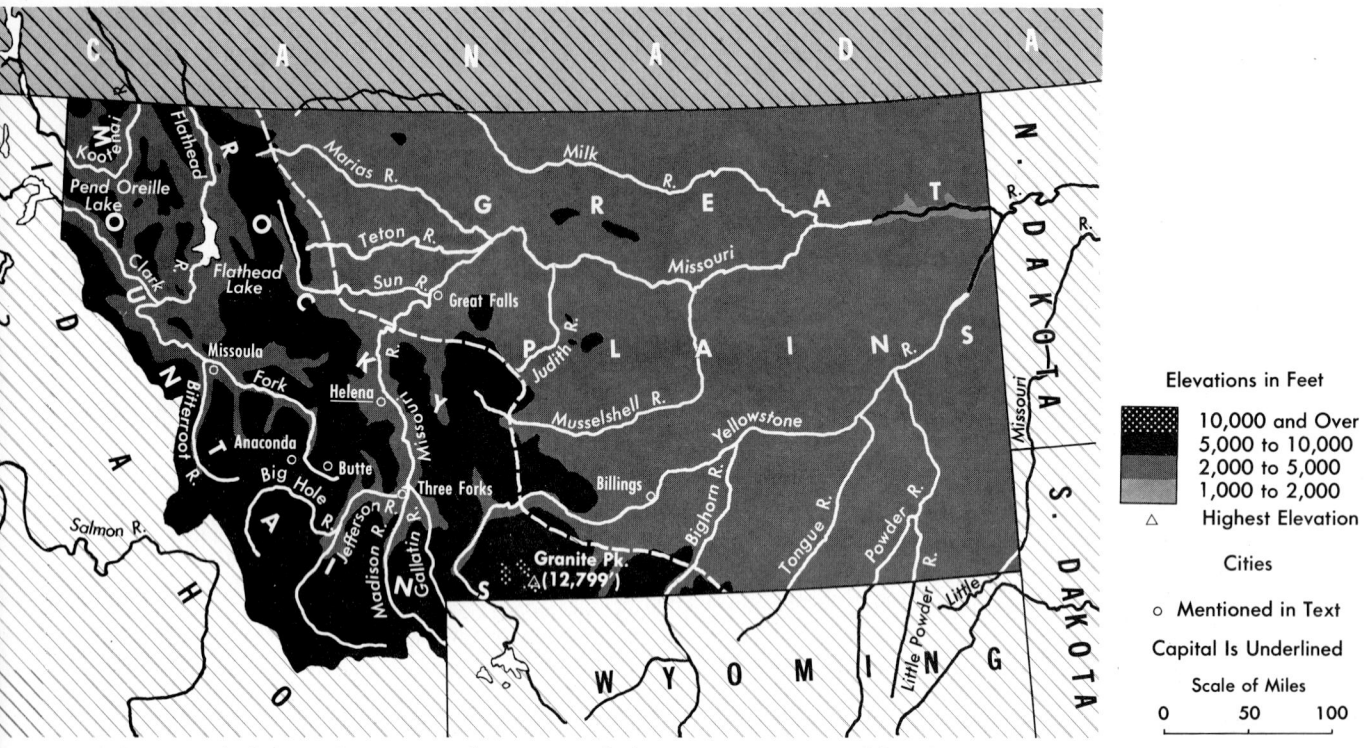

Montana is larger than any other state of the West except California. About three fifths of the state lies in the Great Plains. These plains slope gently upward from east to west. The Missouri River begins in Montana's Rocky Mountains and flows generally eastward across the state.

Facts About Montana	Number or Value	Rank
Area (square miles)	147,138	4
(square kilometers)	381,073	
Population	761,000	43
Capital — Helena		
Admission Date: November 8, 1889		41
Colleges and Universities	12	38
Farm Products	$996,975,000	33
Wheat	394,717,000	4
Cattle and calves	375,331,000	14
Barley	80,376,000	3
Dairy products	24,293,000	44
Fish	$ 91,000	36
Timber Harvested (cubic feet)	279,560,000	16
Minerals	$574,801,000	22
Petroleum	229,802,000	14
Copper	202,728,000	4
Coal	54,961,000	12
Manufactures*	$457,500,000	43
Lumber and wood products	147,700,000	23
Food and kindred products	64,600,000	46
Petroleum and coal products	43,500,000	16

Montana is partly in the Great Plains and partly in the Rocky Mountains. The Great Plains cover about three fifths of the state. The western part of Montana lies in the Rocky Mountains.

The Rocky Mountains. In Montana, the Rockies include several ranges with interesting names, such as Bitterroot, Flathead, and Beartooth. Between the ranges are beautiful forested river valleys. Glacier National Park is located in the Rockies of northwestern Montana.

The Great Plains. The Great Plains in Montana slope gently upward from east to west, reaching an altitude of about four thousand feet at the foot of the Rockies. Dotting the plains are several small mountain ranges.

*See Glossary

STATE BIRD: Mountain bluebird
STATE FLOWER: Sagebrush
STATE TREE: Single-leaf piñon

Nevada

south across the Plateau Country of Nevada. Dry valleys and basins lie between the ranges. Much of the land here is used for grazing cattle. There is too little rain to grow any crops without irrigation. The Humboldt River provides water for many farms in the northern part of the state.

Most parts of Nevada's Plateau Country are very thinly populated. The only cities with more than 50,000 people are Las Vegas and Reno. They are popular vacation places, with many large hotels and nightclubs.

The Sierra Nevada. The peaks in this area overlook beautiful Lake Tahoe, which lies partly in California. Each year, millions of visitors come here to enjoy the lake and the nearby mountains. Some people fish in the lake or in the swift mountain streams. Others hunt wild animals such as deer.

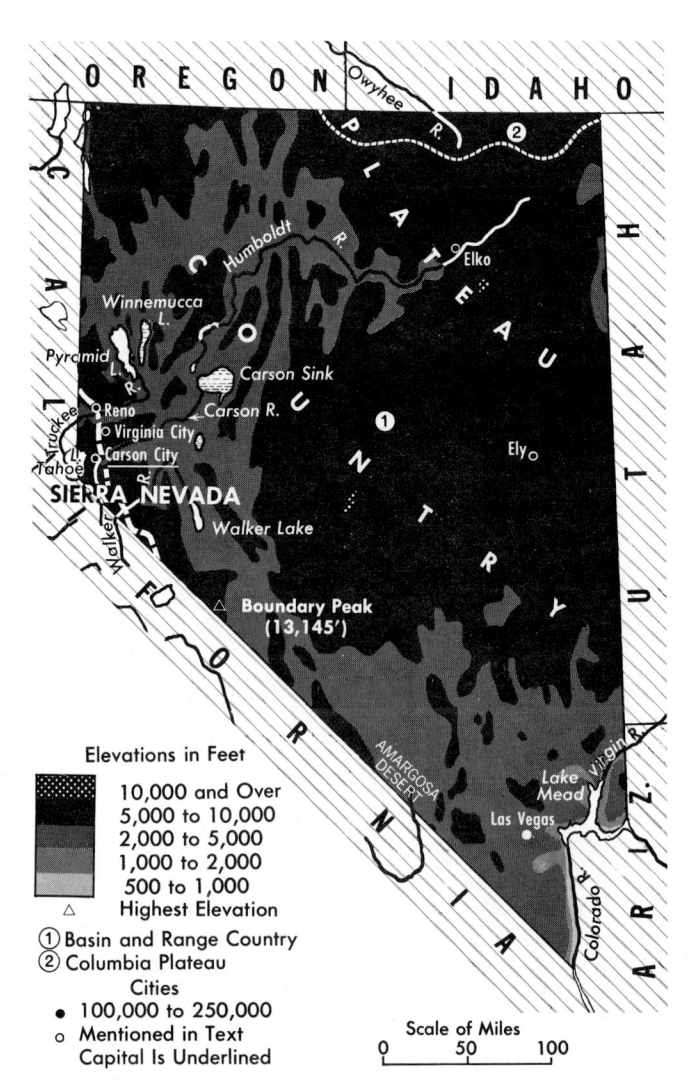

Nevada lies almost entirely in the Plateau Country. The land here is very high. There are many small mountain ranges separated by dry valleys.

Nevada is the driest state in our country. Most parts of this state receive less than ten inches of rainfall a year.

Nearly all of Nevada lies in the Plateau Country. (See map above.) The mountain range called the Sierra Nevada reaches into the far western part of the state.

The Plateau Country. Many small ranges of mountains extend from north to

Map Legend

Elevations in Feet
- 10,000 and Over
- 5,000 to 10,000
- 2,000 to 5,000
- 1,000 to 2,000
- 500 to 1,000
- △ Highest Elevation

① Basin and Range Country
② Columbia Plateau

Cities
- • 100,000 to 250,000
- ○ Mentioned in Text
- Capital Is Underlined

Facts About Nevada	Number or Value	Rank
Area (square miles)	110,540	7
(square kilometers)	286,288	
Population	633,000	46
Capital — Carson City		
Admission Date: October 31, 1864		36
Colleges and Universities	6	43
Farm Products	$149,772,000	46
Cattle and calves	81,022,000	36
Hay	21,299,000	22
Dairy products	16,598,000	46
Vegetables	12,680,000	36
Timber Harvested (cubic feet)	572,000	50
Minerals	$257,876,000	30
Copper	130,021,000	5
Gold	47,723,000	2
Sand and gravel	14,515,000	31
Manufactures*	$215,600,000	47
Stone, glass, and clay products	45,600,000	37
Chemicals and allied products	37,400,000	37
Food and kindred products	28,300,000	49

*See Glossary

The West 141

New Mexico

STATE BIRD: Roadrunner
STATE FLOWER: Yucca
STATE TREE: Piñon

Facts About New Mexico		
	Number or Value	Rank
Area (square miles)	121,666	5
(square kilometers)	315,103	
Population	1,190,000	37
Capital — Santa Fe		
Admission Date: January 6, 1912		47
Colleges and Universities	11	39
Farm Products	$ 712,325,000	35
Cattle and calves	426,162,000	12
Dairy products	44,260,000	41
Vegetables	40,173,000	24
Hay	36,108,000	14
Timber Harvested (cubic feet)	47,592,000	33
Minerals	$1,941,544,000	8
Petroleum	712,578,000	6
Natural gas	390,861,000	4
Copper	303,920,000	3
Manufactures*	$ 366,200,000	45
Food and kindred products	68,300,000	44
Nonelectrical machinery	37,800,000	43
Electrical equipment	34,100,000	41

The map at right shows us that the eastern part of New Mexico is in the Great Plains. A small section of the north central part of the state is in the Rocky Mountains. The rest of the state lies in the Plateau Country.

The Rocky Mountains. The Rockies extend from Colorado into north central New Mexico. They are divided into two parts by the valley of the Rio Grande, New Mexico's largest and most important river. East of the river is Wheeler Peak, the highest point in the state. This peak rises more than thirteen thousand feet above sea level.

The Plateau Country. In the Plateau Country of New Mexico, rugged mountain ranges alternate with dry basins and valleys. In some places, streams have cut deep canyons. Much of the land here is used for grazing. The Rio Grande flows southward through the Plateau Country. Water from this river is used to irrigate crops such as cotton, alfalfa, and wheat.

The Great Plains. The Great Plains cover more than one third of New Mexico. Much of the land is nearly level, but there are deep canyons and river valleys in some places. As in other parts of the Great Plains, farmers here raise wheat and livestock.

Many people go to southeastern New Mexico to visit Carlsbad Caverns National Park. This park contains the largest underground caves in the world.

*See Glossary

New Mexico. Plains and plateaus make up most of the land in this state. A small area lies in the Rocky Mountains.

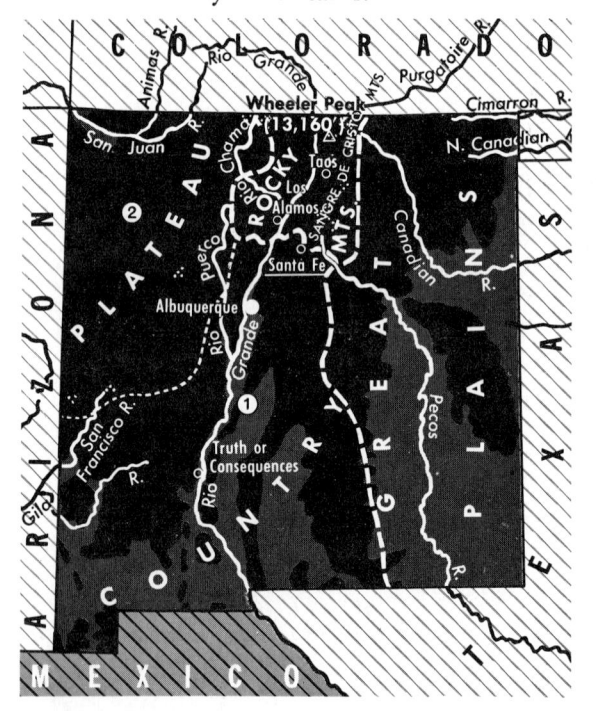

Elevations in Feet
- 10,000 and Over
- 5,000 to 10,000
- 2,000 to 5,000
- △ Highest Elevation

① Basin and Range Country
② Colorado Plateau

Cities
- ● 250,000 to 500,000
- ○ Mentioned in Text
- Capital Is Underlined

Scale of Miles
0 50 100

142 The West

STATE BIRD: Western meadowlark
STATE FLOWER: Oregon grape
STATE TREE: Douglas fir

Oregon

Oregon lies on the Pacific coast. The western third of the state is in the Pacific Mountains and Valleys region. (See map below.) A tiny area along the eastern border of the state is in the Rocky Mountains. The rest of Oregon is in the Plateau Country.

The Pacific Mountains and Valleys. Two mountain chains extend from north to south through western Oregon. These are the Cascade Range and the mountains along the coast.

The Cascade Range is rugged and thickly forested. Mount Hood, in the

Oregon. The western third of Oregon is in the Pacific Mountains and Valleys region. The rest of the state is mainly in the Plateau Country. The Pacific Ocean borders Oregon on the west.

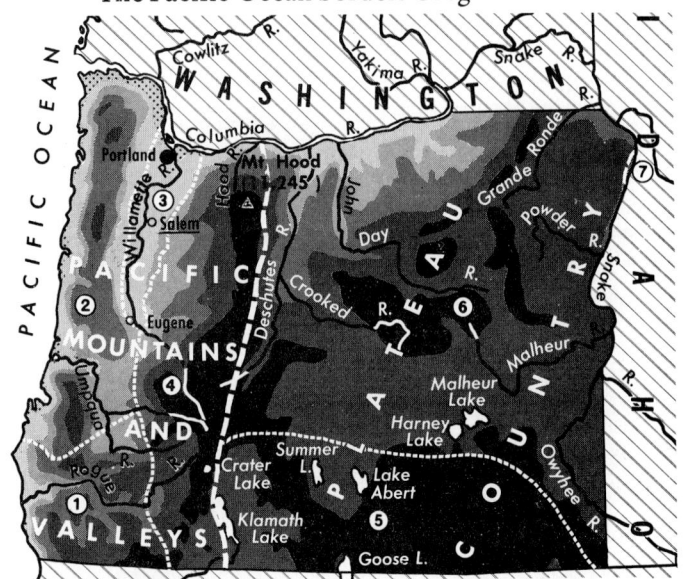

Facts About Oregon	Number or Value	Rank
Area (square miles)	96,981	10
(square kilometers)	251,171	
Population	2,376,000	30
Capital — Salem		
Admission Date: February 14, 1859		33
Colleges and Universities	40	25
Farm Products	$1,022,476,000	32
Wheat	167,060,000	12
Cattle and calves	165,433,000	30
Vegetables	164,803,000	9
Dairy products	101,495,000	28
Fish	$ 37,207,000	9
Timber Harvested (cubic feet)	1,529,041,000	1
Minerals	$ 103,920,000	40
Stone	43,406,000	20
Sand and gravel	30,948,000	17
Cement	not available	
Manufactures*	$3,471,200,000	27
Lumber and wood products	1,487,200,000	1
Food and kindred products	399,800,000	27
Paper and allied products	301,200,000	21

Cascade Range, is the highest peak in the state. It rises more than two miles above sea level. In the Cascade Range in southern Oregon is Crater Lake National Park. Here, brilliant blue water fills the crater of a volcano* that is no longer active.

The mountains along the coast are not as high as those in the Cascade Range. In southern Oregon they are called the Klamath Mountains. The dense forests that cover the mountain slopes here make this an important lumbering area. North of the Klamath Mountains is the Oregon Coast Range.

In northwestern Oregon, a broad valley lies between the Coast Range and the Cascade Range. This is the valley of the Willamette River. It is part of the Puget-Willamette Lowland.* Much of the land in the Willamette Valley is nearly level. Farmers here grow many

*See Glossary

The West 143

kinds of crops, including vegetables, fruit, wheat, and alfalfa. There are also many dairy and poultry farms in this valley.

More people live in the Willamette Valley than in any other part of Oregon. Portland, the state's largest city, is located at the place where the Willamette River flows into the Columbia River.

The Plateau Country. Two sections of the Plateau Country extend through eastern Oregon. These are the Columbia Plateau and the Basin and Range Country. (See map.)

Thousands of years ago, the area that is now the Columbia Plateau was covered with melted lava from volcanoes. The top layers of lava have turned into rich soil that is good for growing wheat. Rivers have cut deep canyons in the land. In northeastern Oregon, mountain peaks rise from the plateau. These peaks were too high to be covered by the lava that formed the plateau.

The southeastern part of Oregon lies in the Basin and Range Country. Here there are dry basins separated by ranges of low mountains. Much of the land is used for grazing livestock.

The Hood River valley is surrounded by the snowy peaks of the Cascade Range in north central Oregon. (See map.) Apples, pears, and other fruit are raised on large orchards in this fertile valley.

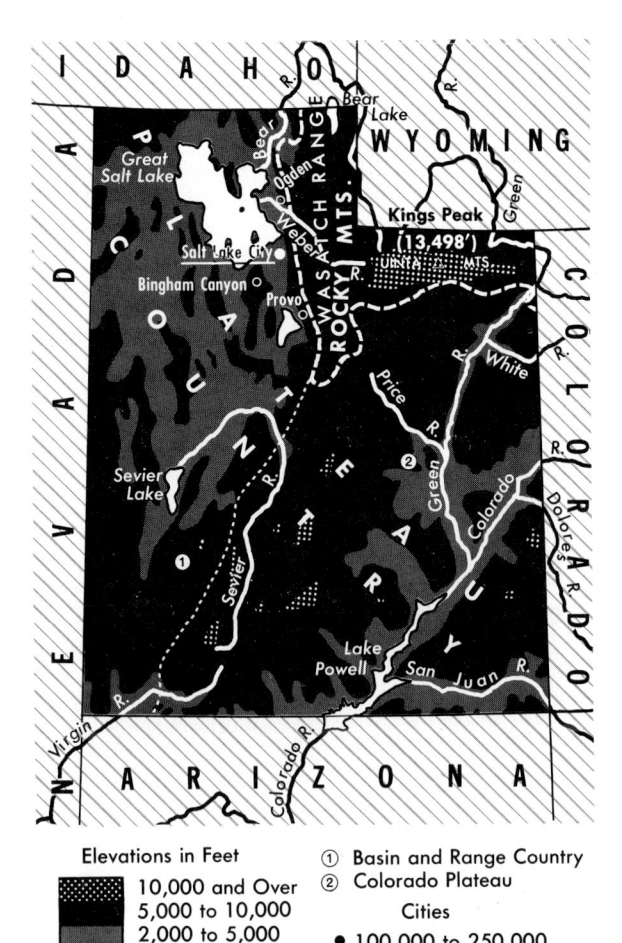

STATE BIRD: Seagull
STATE FLOWER: Sego lily
STATE TREE: Blue spruce

Utah

Utah lies mainly in the Plateau Country of the West. Two ranges of the Rocky Mountains extend into the northeastern part of the state.

Most of Utah is in the Plateau Country. A small area in the northeastern part of the state is in the Rocky Mountains. (See map above.)

The Plateau Country. The eastern part of Utah's Plateau Country lies in the Colorado Plateau. The Colorado River and its branches have cut deep canyons in this high, dry tableland. Few people live in this part of Utah. However, there are several national parks here. Among these are Bryce Canyon, Zion, and Canyonlands.

To the west of the Colorado Plateau is the Basin and Range Country. (See map.) Here there are many small mountain ranges separated by dry basins. Great Salt Lake is located in the northern part of Utah's Basin and Range Country. West of the lake is Great Salt Lake Desert.

Most of Utah's people live along the eastern edge of the Basin and Range Country near Great Salt Lake. Here, streams flowing down from the Wasatch Mountains provide water for farms and factories. Utah's largest cities are located here. They are Salt Lake City, Ogden, and Provo.

The Rocky Mountains. Two ranges of the Rockies extend into northeastern Utah. These are the Wasatch Range and the Uinta Mountains. People come here for skiing, fishing, and other sports.

Facts About Utah		
	Number or Value	Rank
Area (square miles)	84,916	11
(square kilometers)	219,924	
Population	1,268,000	36
Capital — Salt Lake City		
Admission Date: January 4, 1896		45
Colleges and Universities	13	37
Farm Products	$ 359,307,000	39
Cattle and calves	97,177,000	35
Dairy products	87,756,000	30
Poultry	38,169,000	31
Hay	29,883,000	17
Timber Harvested (cubic feet)	12,441,000	42
Minerals	$ 952,045,000	17
Copper	356,497,000	2
Petroleum	279,858,000	12
Coal	71,699,000	7
Manufactures*	$1,005,900,000	40
Food and kindred products	141,500,000	39
Nonelectrical machinery	96,800,000	37
Transportation equipment	81,700,000	30

*See Glossary

The West 145

Washington

STATE BIRD: Willow goldfinch
STATE FLOWER: Coast rhododendron
STATE TREE: Western hemlock

Washington is divided into three main regions. (See map below.) The western part of the state is in the Pacific Mountains and Valleys. Most of eastern Washington is in the Plateau Country. The far northeastern part of the state is in the Rocky Mountains.

The Pacific Mountains and Valleys. A chain of rugged mountains extends along the coast of Washington. The northern part of this chain is called the Olympic Mountains. It is one of the rainiest parts of the United States. Dense forests cover much of the land here. South of the Olympic Mountains is the Oregon Coast Range.

To the east of the coastal mountains is a broad valley. It is part of the Puget-Willamette Lowland. In southern Washington, the valley is a rich farming area. In the northern part of the valley is a long, crooked arm of the ocean called Puget Sound.

The rugged, forested mountains of the Cascade Range rise to the east of the Puget-Willamette Lowland. In the

Facts About Washington	Number or Value	Rank
Area (square miles)	68,192	20
(square kilometers)	176,610	
Population	3,658,000	22
Capital — Olympia		
Admission Date: November 11, 1889		42
Colleges and Universities	43	23
Farm Products	$1,754,267,000	20
Wheat	466,311,000	3
Vegetables	242,624,000	4
Dairy products	240,182,000	12
Cattle and calves	188,530,000	27
Fish	$ 58,336,000	7
Timber Harvested (cubic feet)	1,397,901,000	2
Minerals	$ 143,916,000	36
Cement	36,540,000	13
Sand and gravel	35,030,000	14
Stone	24,483,000	26
Manufactures*	$4,570,500,000	25
Transportation equipment	1,125,100,000	11
Lumber and wood products	934,900,000	3
Food and kindred products	540,600,000	24

*See Glossary

Washington lies on the Pacific coast of the United States. Canada borders Washington on the north.

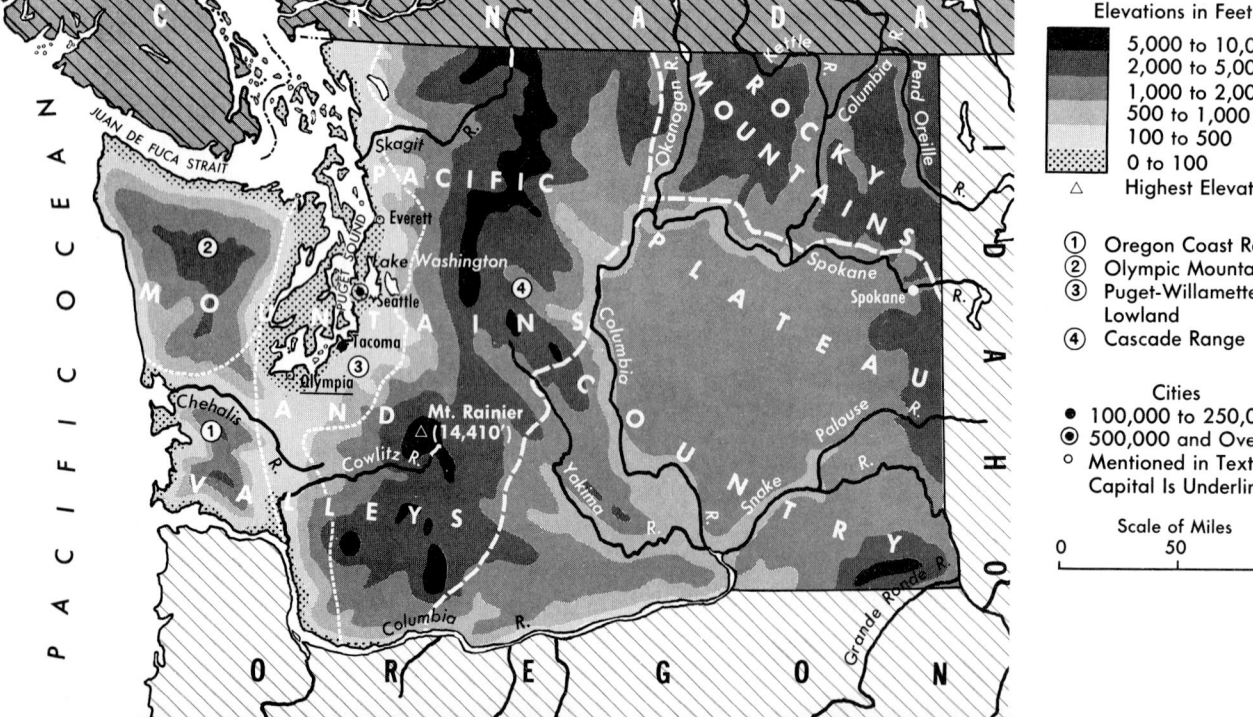

Elevations in Feet
- 5,000 to 10,000
- 2,000 to 5,000
- 1,000 to 2,000
- 500 to 1,000
- 100 to 500
- 0 to 100
- △ Highest Elevation

① Oregon Coast Range
② Olympic Mountains
③ Puget-Willamette Lowland
④ Cascade Range

Cities
● 100,000 to 250,000
◉ 500,000 and Over
○ Mentioned in Text
Capital Is Underlined

Reflection Lake and Mount Rainier are in the Cascade Range of Washington. Mount Rainier is the state's highest peak. Glistening snow and ice cover the top of this mountain all year round.

Cascade Range is Mount Rainier, the state's highest peak. Like several other peaks in the Cascade Range, it was formed by volcanoes long ago.

The Plateau Country. The Plateau Country of eastern Washington is part of the Columbia Plateau. Washington's two largest rivers flow through this region. These are the Columbia and the Snake. In the Plateau Country, there are rolling hills with soil that is very fertile. Some parts of this region are covered with vast wheat fields. In other places, there are dry pasturelands where herds of cattle graze. Apples, peaches, cherries, and other fruits are grown in irrigated valleys near the western edge of the Plateau Country.

The Rocky Mountains. Two ranges of the Rockies extend into northeastern Washington. Herds of cattle and sheep graze on mountain pastures here. In some places, the mountain slopes are covered with pine forests.

Wyoming

STATE BIRD: Western meadowlark
STATE FLOWER: Indian paintbrush
STATE TREE: Plains cottonwood

Wyoming is the highest state in our country except for Colorado. About two thirds of the state lies in the Rocky Mountains region. The rest is in the Great Plains.

The Rocky Mountains. In northwestern Wyoming, the Rockies are high and rugged. Some of the high mountains in this area lie along an imaginary line called the Continental Divide. All rivers east of the divide, such as the North Platte, flow toward the Atlantic Ocean. Rivers west of the divide, such as the Snake, flow toward the Pacific.

Between the mountain ranges in the Rockies are several large, flat basins. Herds of cattle and sheep graze in these dry, treeless areas.

Yellowstone and Grand Teton national parks are located in northwestern Wyoming. Many thousands of tourists visit these parks each year. Yellowstone is our country's oldest national park. Here you can see rushing waterfalls, rugged canyons, and geysers. A geyser is a hot spring that throws water and steam high into the air.

The Great Plains. This part of Wyoming is mostly flat or gently rolling grassland. Much of the land here is used for grazing cattle and sheep. The Black Hills extend into northeastern Wyoming. These rugged, forested hills lie mainly in South Dakota.

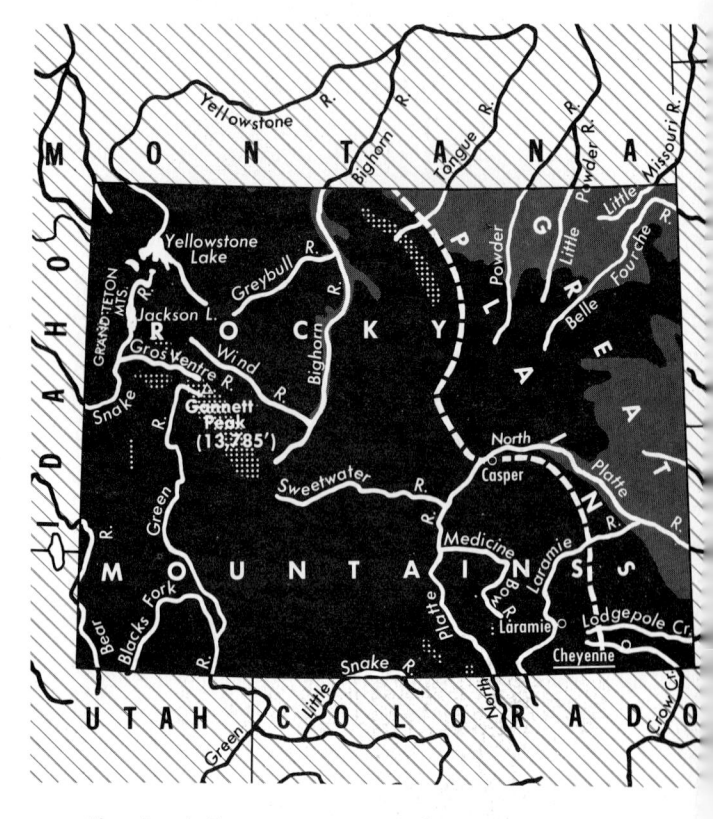

Wyoming lies partly in the Rocky Mountains region and partly in the Great Plains. Most of this state is more than one mile above sea level.

Facts About Wyoming

	Number or Value	Rank
Area (square miles)	97,914	9
(square kilometers)	253,587	
Population	406,000	50
Capital — Cheyenne		
Admission Date: July 10, 1890		44
Colleges and Universities	8	41
Farm Products	$ 386,101,000	38
Cattle and calves	255,336,000	23
Sugar beets	23,310,000	9
Sheep and lambs	20,688,000	6
Wheat	18,198,000	25
Timber Harvested (cubic feet)	33,685,000	37
Minerals	$1,437,200,000	10
Petroleum	914,360,000	4
Sodium compounds	not available	
Coal	103,915,000	10
Manufactures*	$ 148,400,000	50
Petroleum and coal products	53,100,000	14
Stone, glass, and clay products	19,900,000	46
Food and kindred products	19,400,000	50

*See Glossary

PICTORIAL STORY OF OUR COUNTRY

Mount Rushmore, in South Dakota, honors four of our presidents.

Our Country

Our country, the United States of America, was established just over two hundred years ago. At that time, the United States was small and weak. It was the home of less than three million people. Most of these people lived on farms or in small villages near the Atlantic coast of North America.

Today the United States is one of the largest and richest countries on earth. It stretches almost three thousand miles, from the Atlantic Ocean to the Pacific. (See the map on pages 60-61.) It also includes the far northern state of Alaska and the island state of Hawaii. Within this huge country are many large, modern cities.

Nearly 220 million people live in the United States today. Each year they produce billions of dollars' worth of goods and services. As a result, Americans live more comfortably than people in most parts of the world. Also, they enjoy a great deal of freedom to live as they please and to take part in their own government.

In the following pages, you will discover how the United States grew from a small, weak country into the powerful nation that it is today. As you read, look for certain ideas or ways of living that have helped to build our nation.

In 1976, the United States was two hundred years old. The picture at the right shows people marching in a parade to celebrate our nation's birthday. Their clothes are like the ones that people wore at the time our country was started. Two hundred years ago, the United States was small and weak. Today it is one of the largest and richest countries in the world. Are there certain ideas that helped the United States to grow? If so, what are they? This book will help you answer these questions.

History 3

Using Natural Resources

See Great Ideas

An Iroquois* Indian village in what is now the state of New York. Many different groups of Indians lived in North America long ago. They used a number of things they found in the world around them to help them meet their needs. These gifts of nature are called "natural resources." What natural resources are being used by the people in the picture? Look in this book and other books to discover facts that will help you answer this question.

1 People Build Communities in America

■ Who were the first Americans?

People have been living in what is now the United States for many thousands of years. The first Americans were people with brown skin, dark eyes, and straight, black hair. They were divided into many different groups, or tribes. Most tribes called themselves by names that meant simply "the men" or "the people." Today these early people

*See Glossary

4 History

of America are usually known as Indians, or as Native Americans.

The Indians may have come to North America from Asia. No one knows for certain how the Indians first came to North America. But many scientists believe that these people came from the continent* of Asia. There are two main reasons why they think this. First, many Indians look somewhat like the people of Asia. Second, Asia and North America are very close together in the far north. They are separated only by a narrow strip of water called the Bering Strait. (Compare map at right with map of Alaska on page 60.) Long ago, the oceans of the world were not as deep as they are today. A bridge of land may have connected Asia and North America. It would have been possible to travel from one continent to another across this land bridge.

Scientists believe that people began coming to North America at least 25,000 years ago, and possibly more than 100,000 years ago. These people may have been hunting wild animals for food. Or they may have been trying to get away from enemies. As time passed, the Indians settled in many parts of North and South America. (See map at right.)

The Indian tribes of North America were not all alike. They spoke hundreds of different languages, and they had very different ways of life. For example, some tribes got most of their food by hunting animals such as deer and buffalo. Other tribes grew crops such as corn and squash for food. Still others lived mostly on fruit, seeds, and roots they gathered from wild plants.

The Indians are believed to have come from Asia across the Bering Strait. They settled in many parts of North and South America.

ROUTES OF INDIAN SETTLERS

History 5

A European trading ship in the 1500's. People in Europe were eager to trade with countries in eastern Asia. Why? How did the desire for trade cause Europeans to find out about America?

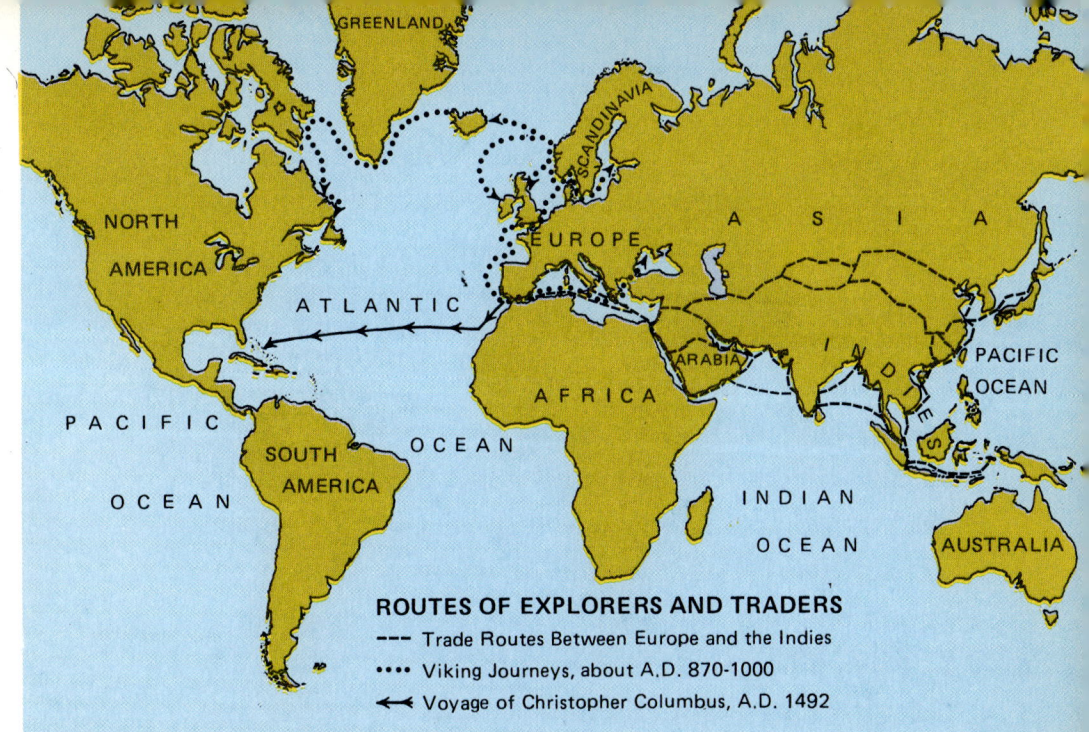

ROUTES OF EXPLORERS AND TRADERS
- - - Trade Routes Between Europe and the Indies
•••• Viking Journeys, about A.D. 870-1000
◄— Voyage of Christopher Columbus, A.D. 1492

■ **How did Europeans learn about America?**

Sailors from Europe began making journeys to faraway lands. Far to the east of America, across the broad Atlantic Ocean, lay the continent of Europe. For thousands of years, people had lived in Europe without knowing anything about the lands on the other side of the ocean. Sailing ships in those days were small and not very safe. Also, sailors did not have any way to find out where they were if they sailed out of sight of land. Many people believed that the ocean was the home of terrible monsters. It is not surprising that only the most daring sailors were willing to sail very far out into the ocean.

Now and then, a ship from Europe may have reached America. For example, it seems certain that bold Viking* sailors landed on the Atlantic coast of North America about one thousand years ago. (See map above.) But news spread slowly in those days, and most Europeans never learned about such journeys.

During the early 1400's, people in Europe began to take more interest in visiting other parts of the world. Better ships and new kinds of tools to help sailors find their way had been developed. As a result, people were able to make longer ocean journeys.

At that time, people in Europe were eager to carry on trade with the lands in eastern Asia known as the Indies. In these lands, it was possible to get spices, silk, and other valuable goods. For years, Asian traders had been bringing these goods by land to ports on the eastern shore of the Mediterranean Sea.* Here, traders from Italy loaded the goods on their ships and carried them to cities in Europe. The prices that Europeans had to pay for these goods were much higher than the prices that the Asian traders had paid for them. Many Europeans wanted to find an ocean route to the Indies so they could buy goods directly from traders there. Then they would no longer have to pay high prices to Italian traders.

Columbus sailed westward and reached America. Some people hoped to find an ocean route to the Indies by sailing east from the southern tip of Africa. But one man had a different plan. He was an Italian sailor named Christopher Columbus. At that time, many Europeans were already saying that the earth was round. Columbus agreed with them. He was sure he could reach Asia by sailing westward across the Atlantic Ocean.

Queen Isabella of Spain agreed to give Columbus the money and ships that he needed for his journey. In August of 1492, Columbus and his crew left Spain in three tiny ships. They sailed for many weeks until they reached a small island off the coast of North America. Columbus thought he had reached the Indies, so he called the people he found there "Indians." After visiting other islands, he returned to Spain with the news of his exciting discovery.

Before long, other explorers from European countries were sailing westward to see the lands Columbus had found. They soon realized that Columbus had not reached Asia after all. Instead, he had reached a completely new part of the world.

Many people came from Europe to America. In the years that followed the voyage of Columbus, people from several European countries came to America. Some of them were searching for a water route through America to Asia. Others were hoping to find gold and silver or other kinds of treasure. Still others wanted to bring their religion, Christianity, to the Indians.

A Spanish explorer named Francisco Coronado was one of the first Europeans to visit the southwestern part of the United States. He led an army through this area in 1540. Why did Coronado come? What were some of the other reasons why people from Europe came to America?

■ What part did the Spanish play in settling America?

The Spanish built missions and forts in what is now the United States. The first Europeans to settle in America at this time came from Spain. Spanish explorers found rich Indian cities in Mexico and South America. They fought the Indians and took over their lands. In this way, they won a great fortune in gold and silver for Spain.

Hoping to find more riches, other Spaniards journeyed far into North America. They found little gold and silver there. But their journeys made it possible for Spain to claim a large area in what is now the United States.

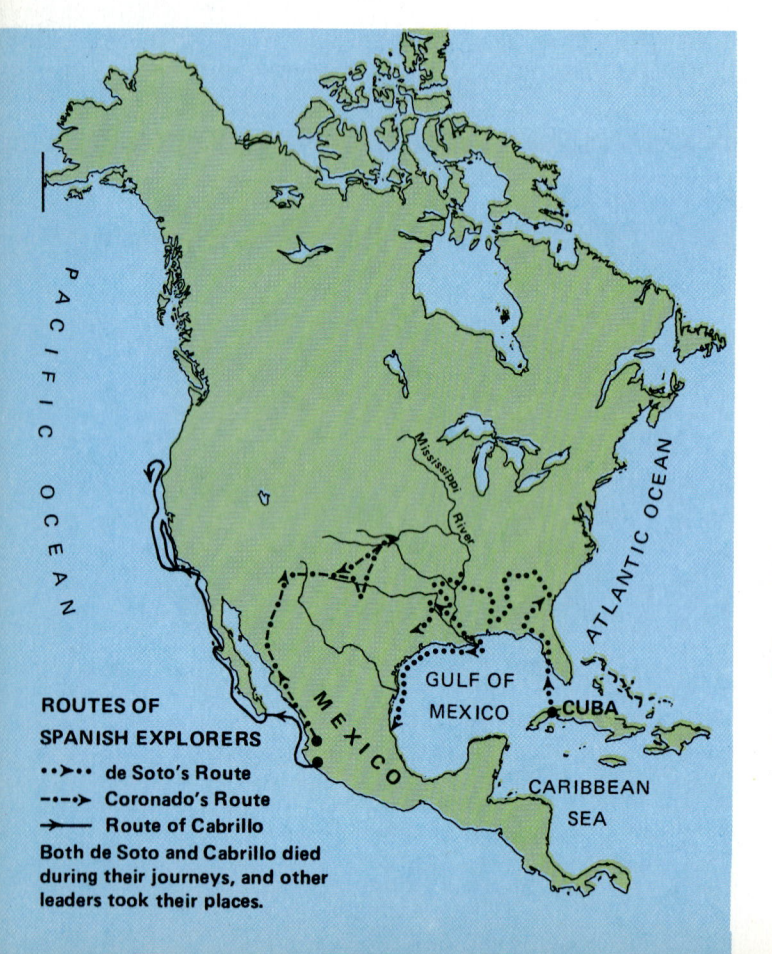

ROUTES OF SPANISH EXPLORERS
··▸·· de Soto's Route
—·—▸ Coronado's Route
——▸ Route of Cabrillo

Both de Soto and Cabrillo died during their journeys, and other leaders took their places.

The map at the left shows the routes of three Spaniards who visited different parts of North America in the 1500's. In 1539, Hernando de Soto started on a journey through what is now the southeastern part of our country. He was the first European to see the Mississippi River. In 1540, Francisco Coronado started out from Mexico to look for rich cities that were said to lie farther north. He journeyed for hundreds of miles over deserts and mountains, but he never found the cities he was seeking. Juan Cabrillo was the first European to visit California. He sailed along the Pacific coast in 1542.

The mission of San Xavier is near Tucson, Arizona. (See map on pages 60-61.) It was built by Spanish missionaries in the 1700's. What is a missionary? If you do not know, look in the Glossary at the back of this book. The missionaries spent much time learning to speak the languages spoken by the Indians. Why was it important for them to do this? If people do not speak the same language, how can they tell their ideas to one another?

Language

See Great Ideas

As time passed, Spanish settlers began coming here to live. They built missions where the Indians could come to learn about Christianity. (See the picture above.) They also built forts to protect their settlements from being attacked by enemy Indians or by soldiers from other European countries. The first Spanish settlements were established in Florida during the 1500's. Later, other Spanish settlements were started in Texas, New Mexico, Arizona, and California.

History 11

Father Jacques Marquette was a French missionary. He and a fur trader named Louis Joliet went much of the way down the Mississippi River in 1673. They were searching for a water route that would lead to Asia. Do you think they found it? Give reasons for your answer.

■ Which lands were settled by the French, Dutch, and Swedish?

France claimed a huge amount of land in North America. People from France also visited North America during the 1500's and 1600's. Some sailed along the Atlantic coast. Others traveled up the St. Lawrence River in what is now Canada. (See the map on pages 60-61.) Later, other French explorers made journeys through the Great Lakes* and along the Mississippi River. They claimed a huge amount of land for France. The left-hand map on page 21 shows the French territory in North America.

During the 1600's and 1700's, people from France came to North America to live. Some were traders who bought valuable furs from the Indians in exchange for goods such as cloth, knives, and beads. These furs were sent to Europe, where they could be sold for high prices. Other French people who came to America were soldiers, missionaries, fishers, or farmers.

New Amsterdam was a Dutch settlement along the Hudson River. It later became New York City. What does the picture tell you about New Amsterdam?

The Dutch and Swedish settled near the Atlantic coast. Other European countries also started settlements in North America during the 1600's. Two of these countries were Holland and Sweden. There were Dutch* settlements along the Hudson River in what is now New York State. (See map at right.) The Swedish settled along the Delaware River. But these settlements were small and weak. By 1700, all of them had been taken over by the country of England.

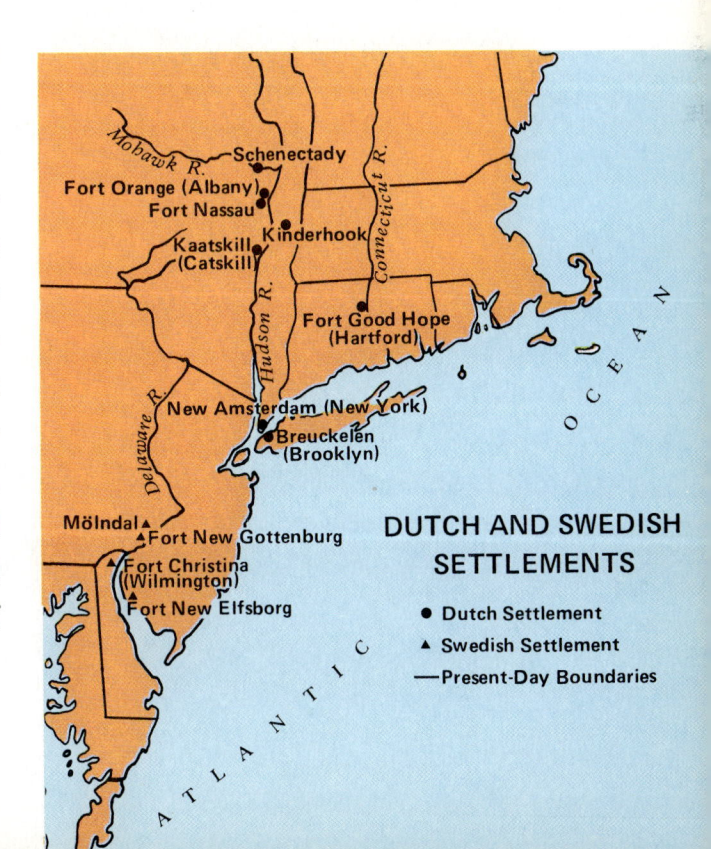

DUTCH AND SWEDISH SETTLEMENTS

- Dutch Settlement
▲ Swedish Settlement
— Present-Day Boundaries

■ Why did the English decide to start settlements in America?

The English were slow to settle the lands they claimed. The first explorer from England to visit America was John Cabot. In 1497 he and his men sailed westward across the Atlantic Ocean in search of a water route to the Indies. When they reached the coast of Canada, they claimed the land for the English king.

For many years, the English did not try to settle the lands that Cabot had visited. But as time went on, English leaders became more interested in starting colonies* in America.

From these colonies, the English could buy goods that they could not produce in large enough amounts in England. Among these goods were logs and animal furs. In return, traders in England could sell large amounts of cloth, hardware, and other English goods to the American settlers. At that time, England, France, Holland, and Spain were all rivals of one another. The English decided that if they started colonies along the Atlantic coast, the other European countries would be less likely to claim this land for themselves.

An English settlement was started in Virginia. In 1607, a group of English traders sent about one hundred people to what is now Virginia. There the colonists started a settlement called Jamestown. This was the first successful English settlement in America. At first, life was very hard for the settlers. Many of them died of hunger or sickness. Others were killed by the Indians, who were angry because the settlers often treated them badly. In spite of these troubles, Jamestown kept going. During the years that followed, people from England started many other settlements along the Atlantic coast of North America.

People came to America in search of freedom and a better way of life. Why were so many English people willing to leave their homes and make the long,

Loyalty

See Great Ideas

John Cabot landed on the Atlantic coast of Canada in 1497. Do you think sailors like Cabot could have made successful journeys without the help of loyal followers? Explain your answer. What might have happened if these followers had not been loyal?

dangerous journey to America? For one thing, people who lived in England at that time did not have very much freedom. All English men and women were expected to belong to the Church of England, which was headed by the king. People who belonged to other churches could be put into prison. This was why the Pilgrims* and certain other groups of people decided to move to America. In that faraway land, they would be free to worship as they pleased.

During the 1600's, it was hard to make a good living in England. Most of the farmland was owned by a small number of wealthy families. In earlier times, many English people had been farmers who rented land from these rich landowners. But as time passed, the landowners found they could make more money by

Using Tools

See Great Ideas

Jamestown, Virginia, was the first long-lasting English settlement in America. The picture below shows the settlers building a fort along the banks of the James River. What tools are the people in this picture using? Can you think of some other tools that the settlers might have needed in order to build their fort? Would it have been possible for the European settlers to make homes in the wilderness without using tools? Explain your answer.

raising sheep for wool. They began using their fields as pastures for sheep. Many farmers could not find any land to rent, and it was not easy to get other jobs.

In America, there were large areas of fertile land that had not yet been settled. Farmers could get all the land they wanted free, or at a very low cost. All kinds of workers were needed in America, so anyone who was willing to work hard could be fairly sure of getting a good job. The hope of a better life brought many settlers to America.

■ What was life in the British colonies like?

The colonies grew in population. As the years passed, more and more people made their homes in England's colonies. Settlers came not only from England but also from Ireland, Germany, France, and other European countries. In the meantime, England had joined with the neighboring country of Scotland to form the kingdom of Great Britain.

By 1750 there were thirteen British colonies in North America. (See the map above.) Together these colonies had a population of more than one million. Most of the colonists lived on the Atlantic coast or along

Thirteen British colonies grew up along the Atlantic coast of North America. Which four colonies made up the area known as New England? What were the four Middle Colonies? What were the five Southern Colonies?

rivers that flowed into the ocean. The rest of what is now the United States was mostly a wilderness.

How people in the British colonies made their living. About nine out of every ten colonists in America earned their living by farming. However, there were fewer farmers in New England than in the other colonies. Much of the land in New England was hilly, and the soil was thin and stony. But there were valuable forests in New England, and the

History 17

Exchange

See Great Ideas

A street in Philadelphia, the largest city in the British colonies. Philadelphia grew up along the Delaware River. Ships could sail up the river from the Atlantic Ocean to load and unload their goods. As time passed, Philadelphia became an important center for trade. Another word for trade is "exchange." How do you think exchange helped the thirteen colonies to grow?

Atlantic Ocean was rich in fish. Along the coast were many bays where ships could be safe from storms. Boston and other busy cities grew up here. Many people in New England earned their living from the sea. Some of them built ships. Others were sailors, fishers, or traders.

In the Middle Colonies, there were larger areas of level land with rich soil. Farmers here produced large amounts of wheat, beef, and other goods. They sold these goods to people in all of the colonies and also Great Britain. The Middle Colonies were rich in iron ore,* wood, and other resources. Cities like New York and Philadelphia grew up along the Atlantic coast, where there were good harbors for ships.

In the Southern Colonies, the land and climate* were good for farming. Summers were long and hot. There was plenty of rainfall, and the soil in many places was rich. Some of the colonists started large farms called plantations. There they grew crops such as tobacco and indigo.* These crops could be shipped to Europe and sold there for high prices. Much of the work on the plantations was done by black people who had been brought from Africa as slaves.

In colonial days, slavery was carried on in many parts of the world. To get slaves, traders from England and other European countries sailed along the coast of Africa. They gave cloth and other valuable goods to African rulers in exchange for prisoners who had been captured in war. The prisoners were loaded into ships and taken to America. Many died of hunger or sickness along the way. Those who lived were sold to the American settlers. By the late 1700's, about one fifth of all the people in the British colonies were black men and women from Africa.

Discover Our Country's Story

1. Why did the first people who lived in America become known as Indians?
2. Why did people in Europe want to find an all-water route to Asia?
3. How did Christopher Columbus hope to reach Asia? Was he successful? Explain your answer.
4. What parts of the United States were settled by people from Spain?
5. What happened to the Dutch and Swedish settlements in America?
6. Why was Jamestown important in American history?
7. Why did the Pilgrims decide to come to America?
8. Why were there fewer farmers in New England than in the other colonies?
9. Why were the Southern Colonies so well suited to farming?
10. In colonial days, most people did not think it was wrong to own slaves. Why do you suppose they felt this way?

2 The American Communities Form a Nation

■ How did Britain win control of France's lands in North America?

France and Great Britain went to war. At the same time the British colonies were growing larger, France and Great Britain began to quarrel. Both countries claimed an area that lay mostly between the Appalachian Mountains and the Mississippi River. (Compare the left-hand map on page 21 with the map on pages 60-61.) This helped to bring about the French and Indian War,* which began in 1754.

At first, the French seemed to be winning the war. They had good army leaders, and they were helped by several Indian tribes. But there were about twenty times as many people in the British colonies as in the French colonies. Also, Britain had a stronger navy than France. As a result, the British could send more troops and supplies to America.

After years of fighting, the British defeated the French. A treaty* of peace was signed in 1763. Under this treaty, France lost its huge empire in North America. (See right-hand map on page 21.) Britain now ruled over nearly all the land in the eastern part of the continent.

■ Why were the American colonists unhappy under British rule?

A quarrel arose between Great Britain and the colonies. After the French and Indian War, the American colonists began to grow more and more unhappy under British rule. One reason for this was that the colonists were not free to carry on business as they pleased. For example, Britain would not allow the colonists to sell goods directly to foreign countries such as France and Holland. These goods had to be sent to England first. Also, goods that were shipped into and out of the colonies had to be carried in British ships. Some kinds of goods that were made in America could not be sold anywhere except in the colony where they were made. The purpose of all these laws was to help traders and shipowners in Great Britain.

Most people in the colonies strongly disliked the British trade laws. They believed these laws hurt their business and caused them to pay higher prices for goods they bought

*See Glossary

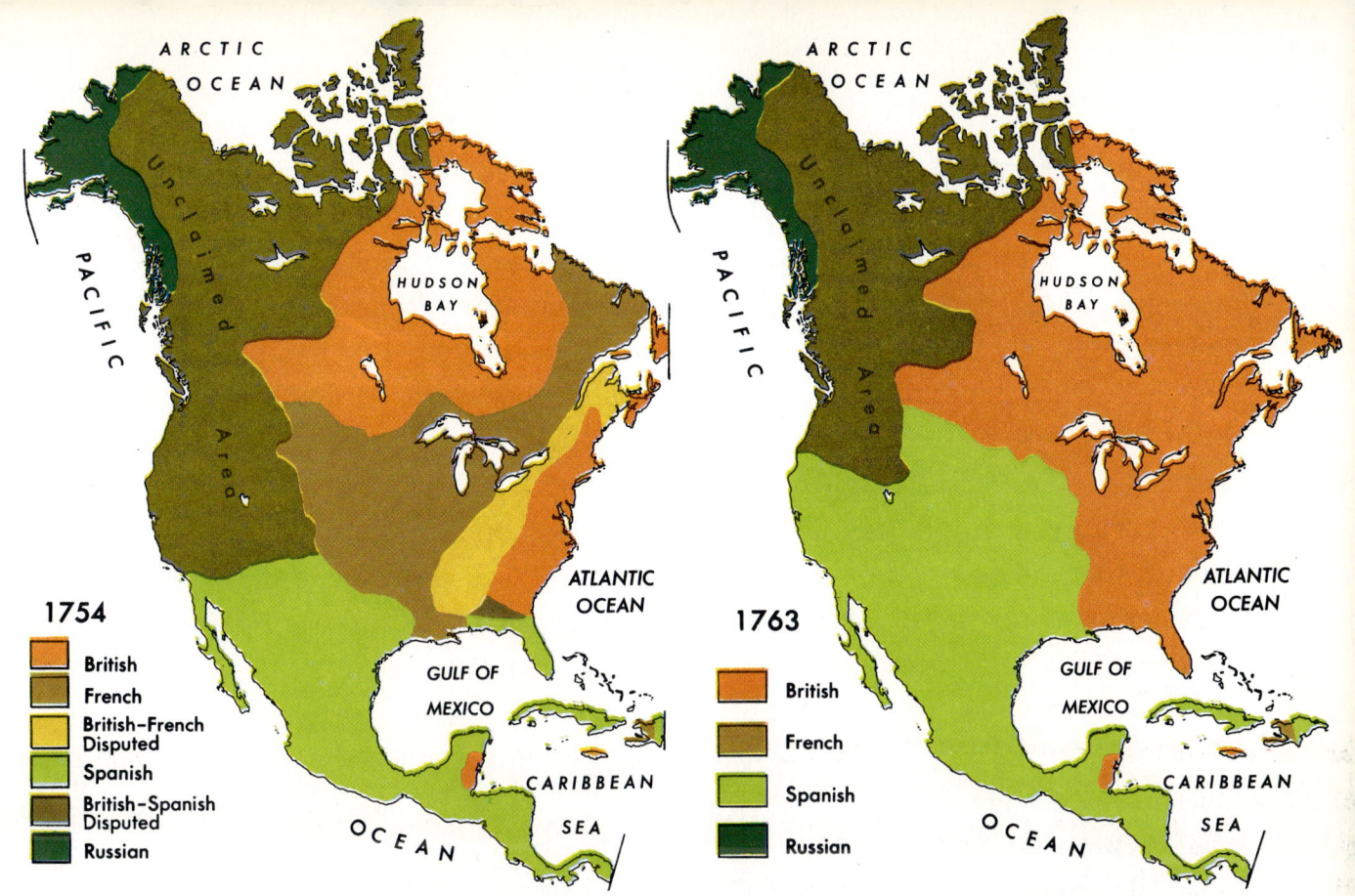

Before and after the French and Indian War. These maps show the lands in North America that belonged to different countries of Europe. The French and Indian War started in 1754. At that time, Great Britain and France both claimed huge amounts of land in North America. At the end of the war, in 1763, France had to give up nearly all of its great empire.

from Britain and other lands. Many colonists broke the laws by trading secretly with foreign countries.

In order to make sure that the trade laws were obeyed, British officers were sent to the colonies to hunt for people who were breaking these laws. The officers were given papers called writs of assistance, which allowed them to search any home or business place in the colonies. The colonists felt that the writs of assistance took away some of their rights as British citizens.

Many colonists had expected that they would be allowed to settle west of the Appalachian Mountains after the French were defeated. But the British were afraid that this would cause trouble with the Indians who lived there. In 1763 the British government sent out an order telling the settlers not to move into the lands west of the Appalachian Mountains.

The colonists became even more unhappy when the British Parliament* passed laws that made them pay certain taxes to Britain. The

History 21

colonists were not allowed to choose any people to represent them in Parliament, so they felt Parliament had no right to tax them. In the past, the lawmaking body of each colony had decided what taxes people would have to pay. It seemed to the colonists that the British leaders were trying to take away their right to govern themselves.

Americans protested against the British laws. The colonists showed their anger toward Britain in several ways. In some communities, British officers were attacked by groups of citizens. Sometimes British goods were destroyed. For example, colonists who were dressed as Indians dumped a load of tea into the harbor of Boston. This was known as the Boston Tea Party. Many colonists refused to buy any more goods from Great Britain until the laws were changed.

■ How did the colonists gain their independence?

The Revolutionary War began. As time went on, it became clear that the British government was not going to change its ways. Many Americans began to think that stronger measures were needed. In 1774, a number of colonial leaders met in Philadelphia to talk about their troubles with Britain. This meeting was known as the First Continental Congress.* In each colony, groups of citizens began to gather weapons and meet for army drill. In Massachusetts these people were called minutemen, because they could be ready for battle only a few minutes after receiving a warning.

In April of 1775, the British general in Massachusetts sent a group of soldiers from Boston to the nearby villages of Lexington and Concord. The soldiers were ordered to get the weapons and gunpowder that had been stored there by the colonists. Fighting broke out between the British soldiers and a group of minutemen. This was the start of the Revolutionary War.

News of the fighting soon spread from Massachusetts to the other colonies. A short time later, the Second Continental Congress met in Philadelphia. For several years, this Congress led the thirteen colonies in their fight against Britain.

Freedom

See Great Ideas

The picture at the left shows an American lawyer named James Otis speaking in a courtroom against the writs of assistance. (See page 21.) Do you think that the American colonists were used to having very much freedom? Explain. What part do you think the idea of freedom played in the colonists' fight against British rule?

The picture above shows the Second Continental Congress meeting in Philadelphia on July 4, 1776. The Declaration of Independence is being presented to the Congress for its approval.

Colonial leaders signed the Declaration of Independence. When the war began, most of the American colonists still felt a strong loyalty toward Great Britain. But as the fighting went on, many people came to feel that the colonies should break away from Britain and form an independent nation. If the colonies were no longer under British rule, they could govern themselves as they pleased. They could build up new industries and trade freely with all countries. People could settle anywhere without having to ask the British government.

By the summer of 1776, most members of the Second Continental

Why did most people in the Congress believe that the American colonies should break away from Britain? Why did they feel it was important to have a written Declaration of Independence?

Congress were in favor of independence. Thomas Jefferson and several others were asked to prepare a statement that would explain why the colonists wanted to be free of British rule. This statement became known as the Declaration of Independence. It was approved by the Second Continental Congress on July 4, 1776. Today, we think of July 4 as the "birthday" of our country.

Americans finally won their fight for freedom. Even after the Declaration of Independence was signed, the colonists were not yet free of British rule. The Revolutionary War went on for seven more years. At times, it seemed certain that the

History 25

Americans would be defeated. They were fighting a rich and powerful nation. The American soldiers did not have much training. Also, they lacked proper food, clothing, and weapons. Many people in America were not in favor of independence. These people helped the British in a number of ways.

In spite of these troubles, the colonists refused to give up. The American soldiers were fighting to win freedom and to protect their homes, so they showed great loyalty and bravery. The American general, George Washington, was a wise and strong leader. Also, the colonists received much valuable aid from Britain's enemy, France. The French government gave money, weapons, and soldiers to help the Americans.

At Yorktown, Virginia, in 1781, a British army gave itself up to American and French troops led by George Washington. What problems did the American colonists face during the Revolutionary War? Why were they able to overcome these problems and win their freedom from British rule?

In 1781, a British army gave itself up to General Washington at the village of Yorktown, Virginia. Now the British government knew that it had lost the war. A treaty of peace was signed in 1783. In this treaty, Britain agreed that the United States was a fully independent country. The new nation stretched from the Atlantic Ocean to the Mississippi River, and from Canada to Florida. (See the map on page 34.)

■ What kind of government was established in the new nation?

The United States did not have a strong national government. When the war ended, the American people faced an important problem. The thirteen states that had won their independence were not really united. Most people had a greater feeling of loyalty to the state in which they lived than they did to the nation.

The national government of the United States was very weak. It could pass laws, but it had no way of making sure that these laws were carried out. Also, it did not have the power to raise the money it needed to carry on its work. Many people were afraid that there would soon be thirteen small, weak countries instead of one large, strong nation.

A new plan of government was written. In 1787, leaders from the different states held a meeting in Philadelphia. They wanted to talk about ways of making the national government stronger. These people decided to write a new plan of government, or constitution,* for the United States.

For almost four months, the American leaders argued about the kind of government that the United States should have. There were many different ideas. Sometimes it seemed that the meeting would never reach

Cooperation

See Great Ideas

The picture at the right shows a crowd of people watching George Washington become the first president of the United States. This happened in New York City in 1789. Do you think cooperation was needed in order to set up a new government for the United States? Could this government have been successful if people had not been willing to work together? Explain.

its goal. But the people at the meeting knew that if they did not cooperate, the United States might fall apart. They agreed to settle their differences.

At last, the leaders in Philadelphia were done with their work. On September 17, 1787, most of them signed their names to the new Constitution of the United States.

The Constitution set up a federal* form of government. Under this plan, the national government would be much stronger than it had been before. For example, it would be able to carry out national laws and settle arguments between states. It would also be able to collect taxes to carry on its work. But the states would still have power to deal with many other kinds of matters.

The national government would be divided into three branches. One branch, Congress, would make the laws. Another branch—headed by the president—would see that the laws were carried out. The third branch would be made up of the Supreme Court* and other national courts.

The Constitution was approved. Before the new plan of government could become law, it had to be accepted by at least nine states. Many people did not want the Constitution. They thought it gave too much power to the national government. Others were in favor of the Constitution, because they thought a strong national government would be able to take care of some of the country's problems.

By the summer of 1788, nine states had approved the Constitution. Now the new government could begin work.

Elections were held to choose a president, a vice-president, and members of Congress. George Washington was elected president. He chose a group of people to help him run the government. This group became known as the Cabinet. Plans were made to build a capital city called Washington in an area along the Potomac River known as the District of Columbia. (Find Washington, D.C., on the map on pages 60-61.)

Discover Our Country's Story
1. Why were the British able to win the French and Indian War?
2. Why did the colonists feel that the British Parliament had no right to tax them?
3. How did the Revolutionary War begin?
4. What caused the British government to decide that it had lost the war in America?
5. Why was a constitution needed for the United States? Is the United States Constitution still being used today? How can you find out?
6. Why were some people against the new Constitution? Why were other people in favor of it? Which side won?

History 29

3 The Nation Grows

■ Why did many Americans move west of the Appalachian Mountains?

Pioneers built homes in the wilderness. After the United States became a nation, thousands of settlers moved from the Atlantic coast to the lands west of the Appalachian Mountains. (See map on pages 60-61.) Here they could buy good farmland at a very low cost. Some of the settlers followed trails that led through passes in the mountains. Others went by boat down the Ohio River.

The settlers who built new homes west of the mountains faced many hardships and dangers. Often, thick forests had to be cleared away be-

Rules and Government

See Great Ideas

This picture shows Daniel Boone leading settlers through a pass in the Appalachian Mountains. During the late 1700's, many American families moved west of the mountains to make new homes. Do you think these settlers needed to follow certain rules in order to get along with one another? Do you think they needed some form of government? Explain your answer.

fore the land could be used for farming. The pioneer families had to raise their own food and build their own cabins. They also had to make most of their own furniture and clothing. Sometimes they were attacked by Indians who did not want strangers moving into their hunting grounds. Many settlers died of diseases such as smallpox* and cholera.*

In spite of these troubles, more and more people came to the lands west of the Appalachian Mountains. Towns and cities began to grow up here. As the territories between the Appalachians and the Mississippi River grew in population, they were allowed to enter the Union* as states.

■ How did life in America change during the early 1800's?

Factories were built to make goods needed by Americans. At the time the United States became a nation, most of the goods people used in their homes were made by hand. But a great change was taking place in England. Machines were being made that could do spinning, weaving, and other jobs that people had always done by hand. These machines were too large to be put in people's homes. Instead, large buildings called factories were built. Then workers were hired to come to the factories and run the machines.

Near the end of the 1700's, people in America learned how to make some of the new machines. They built a number of textile* mills, where cotton was spun into thread. These were the first real factories in the United States.

New England was very well suited to manufacturing. In this part of the country, there were wealthy business people

*See Glossary

who had money to spend for building factories. Since there was little good farmland in New England, many people were looking for other ways to earn a living. They could be hired to work in factories. Also, New England had a number of rivers and streams that could supply waterpower to run the new machinery.

By the early 1800's, there were many factories in New England. They made clothing, guns, tools, and many other things needed by America's growing population.

Better means of transportation were developed. When the United States was started, it was hard to go from one part of the country to another. Nearly all the roads were narrow, bumpy, and often muddy. People journeyed over these roads on horseback, or in wagons or stagecoaches. Often it was easier to go by boat, but water transportation was very slow. Because it cost so much to ship goods from place to place, there was little trade between different parts of the country.

A railroad train in New Jersey during the 1830's. How is this train different from the ones that are used today? What other kinds of transportation do you see in this picture?

During the early 1800's, great improvements were made in transportation. New roads with hard surfaces were built in many places. Canals were dug to connect waterways such as rivers and lakes. The most important was the Erie Canal in New York State. By using the Erie Canal, people could go by water from the Atlantic coast to the Great Lakes. Large amounts of goods were also carried over this route.

At the same time, people were starting to use a new form of power to run machinery. This was steam power. The first successful steam* engine had been made in the 1760's. Before long, steam engines were being used to run boats and trains. By the middle 1800's, there were hundreds of steamboats on our country's rivers and on the Great Lakes. Railroad lines were being built to connect all the important cities in the United States.

Our country grew rapidly in population. In the early 1800's, the number of people who lived in the United

In the 1800's, trains and steamboats became important means of transportation in the United States. How do you suppose this affected trade between different parts of our country?

—Present-Day Boundaries of States

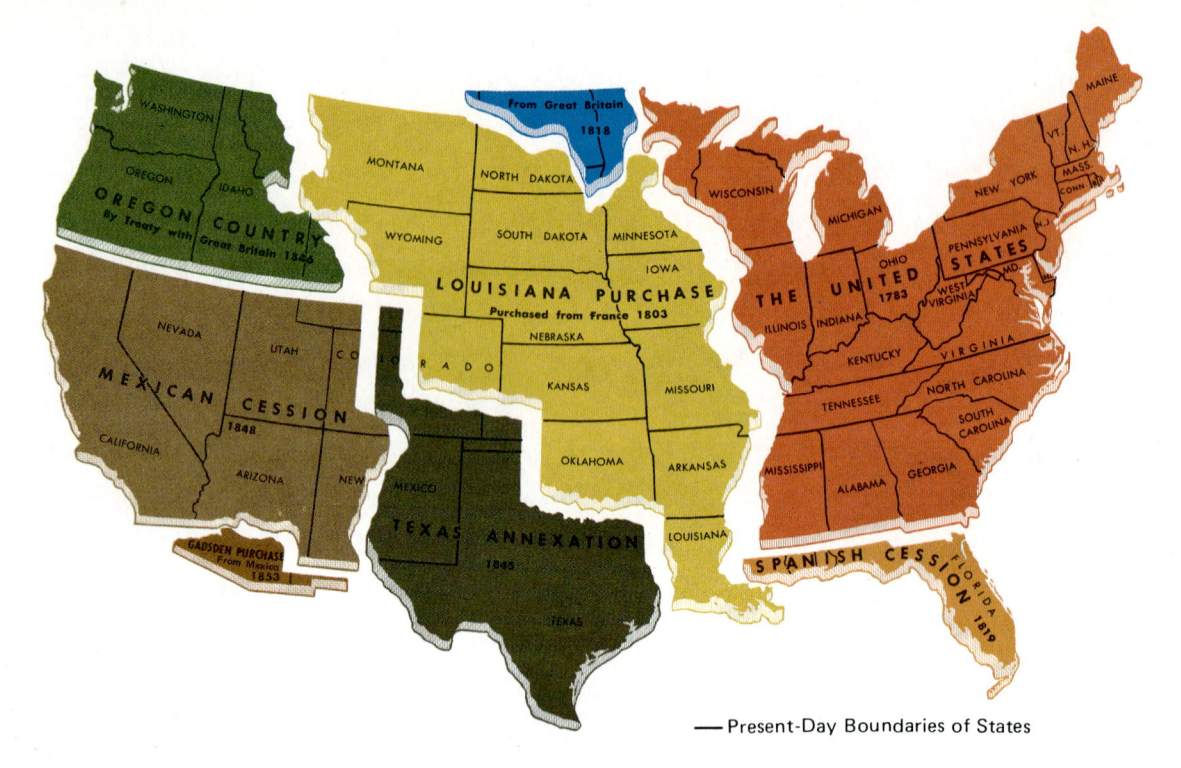

How our country grew. The red area on this map shows the size of the United States at the time that our country won its freedom from Great Britain. Later, other pieces of land were added to our country. For example, the United States gained Florida from Spain in 1819.

States grew larger than ever before. More than two million people came here from Ireland, Germany, and other places in Europe. Most of these people were seeking greater freedom or a better way of life. Many of them settled in cities along the Atlantic coast. Others went westward to build new homes on the frontier.

■ How did the United States gain land west of the Mississippi?

The United States bought Louisiana. To the west of the Mississippi River lay a huge piece of land called Louisiana. In 1803, the United States bought this land from France. (See map above.) President Thomas Jefferson sent a group of explorers led by Meriwether Lewis and William Clark to learn more about this new part of our country. Lewis and Clark journeyed all the way across the Louisiana Territory. (See map on page 36.) Then they went westward through the mountains to the Pacific Ocean. They brought back many useful facts about the places they had visited. During the years that followed, thousands of settlers moved

34 History

into the Louisiana Territory to make their homes.

Texas became part of the Union. In 1821, the people of Mexico won their freedom from Spain. At that time, Mexico took over all the Spanish lands in the western part of North America. (Compare the map below with the maps on page 21.) There were Mexican settlements in Texas, California, and other places. However, these settlements were mostly small and far apart.

During the 1820's, settlers from the United States began moving into Texas. The government of Mexico had told them they could settle there. But as time passed, a quarrel arose between the American settlers and the Mexican government. Even though the settlers had promised to be loyal to Mexico, they still thought of themselves as Americans. In 1835, the settlers revolted. About a year later, they were able to break away from Mexican rule.

The settlers had won their independence from Mexico, but they did not want Texas to remain a separate country. They hoped it would become part of the United States. In 1845, our government annexed* Texas. This made people in Mexico angry. They believed the United States had been trying all along to take over this area.

The United States gained California and other lands from Mexico. About the same time, American settlers were also moving into California. Like the Texans, these people did not wish to live under Mexican rule. They wanted the United States to take over California too.

In 1846, a war broke out between Mexico and the United States. After about a year of fighting, the United States won this war. Mexico then had to sell California and other lands

THE UNITED STATES AND MEXICO IN 1821

----- Present-Day Boundary Between the United States and Mexico

History 35

in the Southwest to the United States. (See map on page 34.)

Britain and the United States divided the Oregon Country. Along the Pacific coast was a large piece of land known as the Oregon Country. Both the United States and Great Britain wanted to own it. For a time, it seemed likely that the two countries would go to war over the Oregon Country. But in 1846 they settled their differences by signing a treaty. Under this agreement, the United States got nearly all of the Oregon Country south of a line that stretched from the Rocky Mountains to the Pacific Ocean. Britain took the land north of this line.

■ Why did many people come to the western part of our country?

Pioneers in covered wagons traveled across the West. Years before the United States gained part of the Oregon Country, Americans were coming to this area. In the Oregon Country, there were pleasant valleys where the soil and climate were very good for farming. Many Americans wanted to move to the Oregon Country because they thought they could make a better living there.

Most of the settlers went westward over a route known as the Oregon Trail. (See map on this page.) They carried their belongings in covered wagons that were pulled by oxen or horses. The journey along the two-thousand-mile trail took about six months. It was very hard and dangerous. The settlers had to cross high mountains, wide rivers, and empty deserts. Many people died of sickness or were killed in fights with Indians. But settlers kept on coming.

The search for gold and silver brought many settlers. In 1848, a discovery was made that brought thousands of people to California. An American settler found tiny bits

ROUTES TO THE WEST

----- Westbound Route of Lewis and Clark, 1804-1805
—— Oregon Trail
······ First Railroad Across the West
—— Present-Day Boundaries of States

36 History

Pioneers going to the Oregon Country. These people have removed the wheels from their covered wagon and put it on a raft to float down a river. During the 1800's, many people moved to the West to make use of the natural resources there. What were some of these resources?

of gold in a mountain stream near Sacramento. (See map at left.) News of this exciting discovery soon spread to the eastern part of the United States. Before long, thousands of settlers were going to California by ship or by covered wagon in order to hunt for gold. This was known as the "gold rush." The number of people in California grew rapidly. Only two years later, California became a state in the Union.

In the years that followed, large deposits of gold and silver were found in Nevada, Colorado, and other parts of the West. Each discovery brought many miners. Large towns grew up quickly wherever gold and silver were found. Most of these "boomtowns" lasted only a few years, until the gold and silver ran out. But a few mining towns—such as Denver, Colorado—grew into important cities.

Railroads brought many people to the West. For years, people had dreamed of a railroad that would connect the eastern part of the United States with the Pacific coast. In the 1860's, two companies began this difficult task. Workers for one company began laying track westward from Omaha, Nebraska. (See map on page 36.) The other company's workers started east from Sacramento, California. The two railroad lines finally met near Great Salt Lake in Utah in 1869.

As time passed, other railroads were built across the West. Now settlers could travel westward by train instead of making the long, dangerous journey by covered wagon. Soon, people were moving west in growing numbers.

An Indian camp on the Great Plains. Why were the Indians unhappy to see white settlers coming to the West? What changes took place in the Indians' way of life after the settlers came?

The Indians lost their land and their way of life. Many different tribes of Indians lived in the West at the time that white people began coming here. The Indians did not like to have white people settle on their land. Often they had good reasons for being unhappy. For example, in the early 1800's huge herds of buffalo roamed the Great Plains.* The Indians of the plains hunted buffalo to get meat, hides, and other things they needed. But as the years passed, most of the buffalo were killed by white hunters. Then the Indians could no longer find enough buffalo to meet their needs.

In the last half of the 1800's, a number of battles took place between the Indians and United States soldiers. The Indians fought bravely. But they were much fewer in number than the white people, and some of the tribes were not willing to cooperate with each other. Also, the whites had better weapons. At last, the Indians gave up. They had to sell most of their land to the whites and move to places called reservations.*

Farmers came to the Great Plains to make their homes. After railroads were built across the Great Plains, many farmers began to settle in this part of the country. They came because they could get good farmland free or at a very low price. In return for building railroad lines, some companies had been given large amounts of land by the government. They were willing to sell this land cheaply to settlers. Also, the government gave land to people who were willing to farm it for five years.

Life was not easy for the families who settled on the Great Plains. Summers were hot and winters were freezing cold. In most places, the land was covered with thick grass that made it hard to plow the soil. Strong winds or hail sometimes destroyed whole fields of crops. Weeks or months might pass without any rain. Often farmers had to dig deep wells in order to get water. They had to put fences of barbed wire around their fields to keep wandering herds of cattle from eating their crops.

Pioneer farmers on the Great Plains. These people are plowing land so they can plant crops. Why was life very hard for many of the families who settled on the Great Plains?

Some settlers became so unhappy with their hard life that they moved back east. But others refused to give up. Through hard work and courage, they changed the Great Plains into an important farming area.

Discover Our Country's Story
1. What were some problems faced by the settlers who moved west of the Appalachian Mountains?
2. Why was New England a good place for building factories?
3. Why was there little trade at first between different parts of our country?
4. Why was Lewis and Clark's journey important to the United States?
5. Why were the people of Mexico angry when Texas became part of the United States?
6. Why did large numbers of people begin coming to California in 1848?
7. What were "boomtowns"? What happened to most of these towns?
8. How was the building of railroads important to the history of the West?
9. Why did the Indians lose most of the battles they fought against United States soldiers?
10. Why did many farmers come to the Great Plains during the last half of the 1800's?

4 The Union Is Saved

■ How did the United States become a divided country?

The North and the South had different ways of life. In the early 1800's, there were important differences between the northern and southern parts of our country. Hundreds of factories had been built in the North. Many people there lived in cities or large towns. In the South, there were few cities and only a small number of factories. Most people made their living by farming. In some places, there were plantations. On these large farms, cotton was usually the main crop. The owners sold large amounts of cotton to factories in the North and in Europe.

Loyalty

See Great Ideas

Abraham Lincoln was president of the United States at the time that a war broke out between the northern and southern parts of our country. This great struggle became known as the Civil War. Why is Abraham Lincoln remembered today as one of our greatest presidents? How did Lincoln show his loyalty to his country? How did he show his loyalty to certain ideas, such as the idea of freedom for all people? You will need to read more about Lincoln in other books to find the answers to these questions.

Large numbers of slaves worked on plantations in the South. Much of the work on southern farms was done by black people. On page 18, you read how blacks were brought from Africa in colonial days as slaves. These people did not have the freedom to live where they wished or to work at jobs of their own choosing. They had to work all their lives for the white plantation owners.

In colonial days, slavery had been allowed in the North also. But it had never been very profitable there, because farms were much smaller. Also, many people in the North believed that slavery was wrong. By 1800, most states in the North had passed laws saying that people could not own slaves.

Americans disagreed about slavery and other matters. Some people in the North believed that slavery should be ended everywhere in the United States. These people made speeches and wrote books attacking

A **slave market in Virginia** before the Civil War. White people in the South often said that black people did not mind being slaves. Do you think they were right? Why? Why not? Do you think that human beings everywhere have a deep desire for freedom? Explain.

A Divided Country

The map at the right shows the United States at the time of the Civil War. Slavery was allowed in all the Confederate states. It was not allowed in most states of the Union. These were known as free states. A few states, such as Missouri and Kentucky, allowed slavery but remained loyal to the Union. The western part of Virginia stayed with the Union when the rest of the state joined the Confederacy. It later became the state of West Virginia.

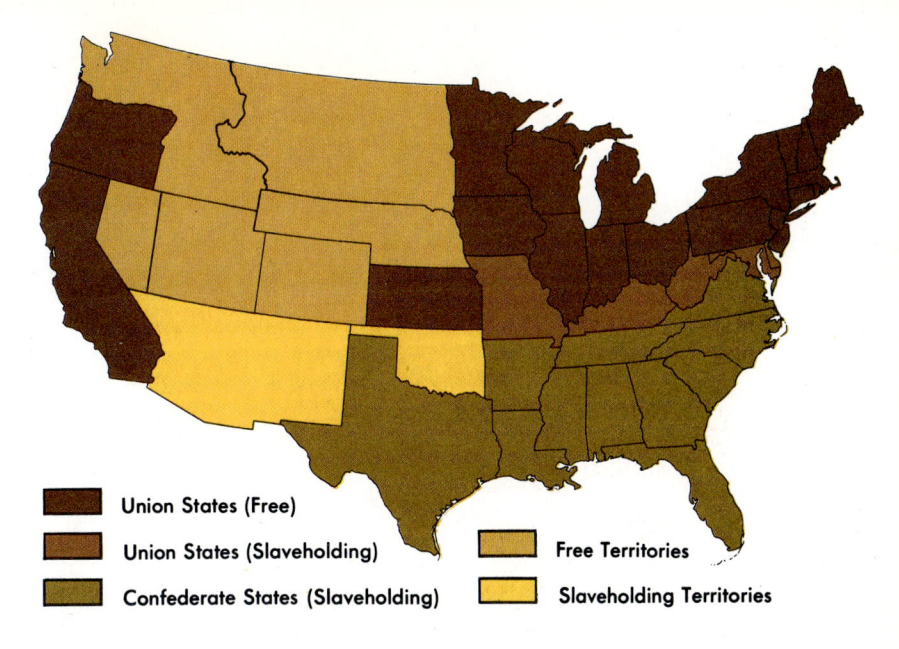

- Union States (Free)
- Union States (Slaveholding)
- Confederate States (Slaveholding)
- Free Territories
- Slaveholding Territories

slavery. Sometimes they helped black people in the South to escape from their masters. As time passed, more people in the North began to agree with their views.

This movement to do away with slavery made most white people in the South very angry. They were afraid they would not be able to keep up their way of life if they did not have slaves to work for them.

People in the North and the South also disagreed about other matters. One of these was the question of states' rights. Most leaders in the North believed that laws made by the federal government should always be obeyed by the states. On the other hand, many southern leaders believed that states did not have to obey federal laws if they thought these laws were unfair. Some even said that states had the right to leave the Union.

■ How did the Civil War affect our country?

The quarrel between the North and the South led to war. In 1860, Abraham Lincoln became president of the United States. This alarmed many white people in the South, because they thought Lincoln would try to end slavery. Before long, eleven states in the South broke away

History 43

The Battle of Mobile Bay was an important navy battle in the Civil War. It took place in 1864 near Mobile, Alabama. (See map on pages 60-61.) Who won the Battle of Mobile Bay? Why was this battle so important? Look in other books to find answers to these questions.

44 History

from the Union. They formed a new nation known as the Confederate States of America, or the Confederacy.

In April, 1861, a war broke out between the North and the South. This became known as the Civil War.* It lasted four years and took the lives of more than half a million Americans.

The war ended in victory for the North. For a time, the South appeared to be winning the war. But the North was stronger in several ways. It had more than twice as many people as the South, and much more wealth. There were more factories in the North to make weapons and other things the soldiers needed. In addition, the North had better railroads. The North was aided by thousands of black soldiers who fought for the Union. Also, President Lincoln was a very wise and strong leader.

These advantages helped the North to win the war. In the spring of 1865, the Confederate armies surrendered to the armies of the Union.

Two important results of the Civil War. The victory of the North caused two important things to happen. First, the eleven Confederate states were brought back into the Union. Second, slavery was ended in all parts of the United States.

*See Glossary

Discover Our Country's Story
1. What were some important differences between the North and the South during the early 1800's?
2. Why did slavery come to an end in the North?
3. How did people in the North and the South disagree on the question of states' rights?
4. Why were many white people in the South alarmed when Abraham Lincoln became president?
5. Why was the North able to win the Civil War?

History 45

5 Our Country Becomes a World Leader

■ How did the United States become a great manufacturing nation?

The Civil War helped industry to grow. During the Civil War, industry grew rapidly in the United States. The American soldiers needed large amounts of such things as clothing, food, and weapons. To help meet these needs, new factories were started. And many older factories made more goods than ever before.

After the war, industry grew even faster. There were now more people in the United States, so there were more customers for the goods that factories made. Also, the new railroads made it possible to ship goods quickly and cheaply from one place to another. Because of this, factories could sell their goods to people in all parts of the country.

Inventors discovered new ways of making goods. Another reason why industry grew so rapidly was that people found new ways to make use of our country's rich natural resources. For example, there were large deposits of coal and iron ore in the United States. Coal and iron ore could be used in making steel. Although steel was a very useful metal, it had always been slow and costly to produce. But in the 1850's,

Using Natural Resources
See Great Ideas

The picture at right shows a group of ironworkers in New York State. During the last half of the 1800's, Americans discovered new ways of using certain natural resources to meet their needs. What were some of these resources? How did the new discoveries affect the growth of industry in the United States?

people found a way to make large amounts of steel rapidly and cheaply. Soon many steel plants were built in the United States. The steel was used by other factories in making many different kinds of goods.

People were also discovering new ways of using natural resources to produce heat, light, and power. One of these resources was a dark, oily liquid that came out of the ground in certain places. This was called petroleum. For a long time, people thought petroleum was worthless. But then they found that it could be made into kerosene* and other valuable products. Kerosene became widely used as a fuel in lamps and stoves.

People in America were also learning about a new form of power called electricity. In 1879, Thomas Edison made the first successful electric light. Edison and other inventors also developed machines that could make large amounts of electricity.

*See Glossary

Photograph courtesy of the Ford Archives

Using Tools

See Great Ideas

The picture above shows Henry Ford and his wife, Clara Bryant Ford, in a workshop behind their home in Detroit, Michigan. The year was 1896, and Henry Ford was just finishing work on his first automobile. Ford was not the first person ever to build an automobile, but he was the first to make cars that were cheap enough for most people to buy. Can you explain how he did this?

Soon electricity was being used to run many kinds of machinery.

About the same time, people were discovering new ways of sending messages from place to place. Alexander Graham Bell invented the first telephone in 1876. Radio was another new form of communication.* It was developed in the early 1900's.

Because of new inventions, transportation was also improved. The first automobiles were built in the late 1800's by people in Europe and the United States. In 1903, two brothers from Ohio named Wilbur and Orville Wright built the first successful airplane.

Factory owners discovered better ways of making goods. As the years passed, factory owners in the United States found new and better ways of making goods. One of the most important of these was the assembly-line method. It was developed mostly by an auto maker named Henry Ford. The frame of an automobile was put on a large belt that moved slowly past a line of workers. Each worker added a different part to the frame until the car was finished.

The assembly-line method made it possible to build large numbers of cars at a price most people could pay. It worked so well that factories began to use it in making many different kinds of goods.

All of these new discoveries helped industry to grow rapidly in the United States. By the early 1900's, our country was producing more factory goods than any other country.

■ How did great cities grow up in the United States?

People moved from farms to cities. Before the Civil War, only one out of every five Americans lived in a city or large town. But in the years that followed, great changes took place in people's way of living. Farmers began to use new machines and better ways of farming. These made it possible for one farmer to raise enough food for many people. At the same time, more workers than ever before were needed in factories, stores, and offices. Thousands of people moved from farms to cities to get jobs. As more and more newcomers arrived, the cities grew rapidly. For example, Chicago was more than twenty times as large in 1910 as it was in 1860. By 1910 nearly half of all Americans lived in cities or large towns.

Immigrants* came from many lands. Many of the people who settled in the growing cities were immigrants from other lands. Between 1865 and 1915, more than twenty-six million people came to the United States to live. Most of them were from European countries such as Germany, Italy, Sweden, and Poland. Some also came from Mexico, Canada, and other countries in North and South America. A much smaller

*See Glossary

Division of Labor

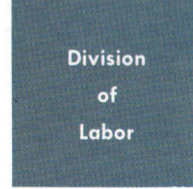

See Great Ideas

The picture above shows a famous street called the Bowery in New York City during the 1890's. In the years that followed the Civil War, American cities grew rapidly. What were some of the reasons for this? Was there *more* division of labor in the cities than in the country? Or was there *less*? How do you think this affected the number of people who wanted to move from the farms to the cities? Look for "Great Ideas" on the Contents page to find information that will help answer these questions.

number of people came from China, Japan, and other countries in Asia.

Most of these people came to America because they had heard it was a "land of opportunity." In the lands where they were born, they had found it hard to earn a good living. They hoped it would be easier to find good jobs in America. Some people came to America because they wanted more freedom than they could have in their own countries.

Life was not easy for most of the immigrants at first. These people were often very poor. Because most of them did not have any special training, they could not get good jobs. Many could not speak English when they arrived. Often they found it hard to give up their old ways of

50 History

doing things and learn a new way of life. Some of them were treated unkindly by other people in America. This was partly because they seemed strange and "different." Also, many Americans were afraid the newcomers would take their jobs away from them by working for less money.

As time passed, life became easier for most of the immigrants. The children and many of the older people went to school. There they learned the English language and American ways. As they gained more education, they were able to get better jobs. Many of our country's leaders during the last one hundred years have been immigrants or sons and daughters of immigrants.

■ How did the United States become involved in world problems?

Americans began to take more interest in other countries. During the 1700's and 1800's, most Americans paid little attention to what was happening in other parts of the world. Wide oceans separated America from Europe, Asia, and Africa. Transportation and communication were still quite slow. Americans were interested mostly in developing the resources of their own huge country.

As time passed, an important change began to take place. The United States was now becoming one of the richest and strongest countries in the world. It was carrying on more and more trade with other nations. Many Americans felt the United States should play a more important part in the world.

A chance to do this came in 1898, when the United States went to war against Spain. At that time, Spain ruled the island of Cuba in the West Indies. American soldiers were sent to Cuba to help the people of that island win their independence from Spain. After a few months of fighting, the Americans defeated the Spanish. Spain had to give Cuba its freedom. The United States became owner of two Spanish possessions. These were the island of Puerto Rico, in the West Indies, and the Philippine Islands, off the coast of Asia. About the same time, the United States took over the Hawaiian Islands.

The United States entered a war in Europe. In 1914, a terrible war broke out between two groups of countries in Europe. On one side were the Central Powers, which included Germany and Austria-Hungary. On the other side were Britain, France, Russia, and several other countries. They were called the Allies. The great struggle between the Allies and the Central Powers became known as World War I.

At first, the United States tried to stay out of the war in Europe. But German submarines began to attack Allied ships in the Atlantic Ocean. A number of Americans on these ships were killed. The Germans also did other things that made the American people angry. In 1917 the United States joined the war on the side of the Allies. American soldiers were sent to Europe to fight. In the fall of 1918, the Central Powers finally gave up.

Another war took the lives of many Americans. For a few years, there was peace in most parts of the world. But in 1933 a group of people called the Nazis* took over the government in Germany. Their leader, Adolf Hitler, wanted to conquer other countries and make Germany the most powerful nation in Europe. The leaders of Italy and Japan also decided to go to war to gain more lands. Together, these three countries became known as the Axis. They were opposed by Britain, France, the Soviet Union, and other countries. In 1939, Germany attacked the neighboring country of Poland. This was the start of World War II.

Again, people in the United States hoped to stay out of war. But in 1941, Japanese airplanes made a surprise attack on a large group of American warships docked at Pearl Harbor in the Hawaiian Islands. This attack brought our country into the war against the Axis. Millions of Americans were sent to fight in many parts of the world.

By working together, the United States and its allies were able to defeat the Axis. First Italy and then Germany surrendered to the Allied armies. In the meantime, scientists who were working for the United States government built a powerful new weapon called the atomic bomb. In August, 1945, atomic bombs destroyed two Japanese cities. Partly because of this, Japan gave up the war a short time later.

The United Nations was formed to work for world peace. By the end of World War II, many people had come to believe that there must never again be a world war. Atomic bombs and other weapons had become too powerful. If these new weapons were ever used in another war, they might destroy all life on earth.

An American battleship on fire after the Japanese attack at Pearl Harbor in 1941. Where is Pearl Harbor? Why was the attack at Pearl Harbor so important in American history?

Cooperation

See Great Ideas

The picture above shows people from different countries at a meeting of the United Nations in New York City. What is the United Nations? Why was the United Nations formed? Do you think it is important for countries to cooperate with one another in order to solve their problems? Give facts to explain your answer. What sometimes happens when countries do not cooperate?

In 1945, most countries of the world joined together in forming a new organization to work for world peace. This was the United Nations. Today about 150 countries are members of the United Nations, which meets in New York City. The United Nations tries to settle disagreements that might lead to war. It also tries to help the poorer countries of the world provide a better way of life for their people.

Communism spread to many parts of the world. After World War II ended, the United States was faced with a new problem. For almost thirty years, the Soviet Union had been ruled by a group of people who were known as Communists.* The Communists believed that industry, trade, and most other activities in a country should be run by the government. They wanted people all over the world to follow the Communist way of life.

For a time, it seemed to many Americans that the Communists might reach their goal. Communist governments came to power in several countries of eastern Europe, such as Poland and Hungary. In 1949 the huge country of China also fell under Communist rule.

Most people in the United States were strongly against communism. They were afraid it could take away their freedom. The United States made agreements with a number of friendly countries in Europe and Asia. These countries promised to help each other in case of a Communist attack.

The struggle between the Communist countries and the non-Communist countries became known as the Cold War. Both sides made their armies larger. They also developed new weapons and war equipment, such as hydrogen* bombs and guided* missiles. Sometimes real fighting broke out between the two sides. For example, there was a war between Communist and non-Communist forces in the small Asian country of Korea. This war lasted from 1950 to 1953. Another war took place in the Asian country of Vietnam from 1957 to 1975. About half a million American soldiers were killed or wounded in these two wars.

In the last few years, the Communist and non-Communist countries have grown a little more friendly toward one another. Some people believe that the Cold War is mostly over. Other people think that the Cold War will last as long as the Communist and non-Communist countries have such different ways of life.

Discover Our Country's Story
1. How did the Civil War help American industry to grow? Why did industry keep on growing after the war was over?
2. What important changes took place in transportation and communication during the late 1800's and early 1900's?
3. Why did many people from Europe come to America after 1865?
4. Why did many immigrants have a hard time when they first came to America?
5. Why did most Americans take little interest in other countries during the 1700's and 1800's?
6. What were some things that happened because of the Spanish-American War?
7. Why did the United States take part in World War I? Why did it take part in World War II?
8. What was the Cold War, and how did it come about?

History 55

6 Years of Amazing Change

■ How have science and industry changed American life?

In the last thirty years, great changes have taken place in our country. Today our way of life is very different from what it was in the past.

Changes brought about by science. Some of these changes have been brought about by science. For example, scientists have learned how to use the energy* stored in atoms.* This energy can be used to make powerful weapons. It can be used to produce electricity. Also, rockets have been built to carry people far from the earth. American astronauts* have already landed on the moon. Someday they may be able to make even longer trips in space.

Changes caused by industry. Important changes have also been taking place in industry. Many new machines have been invented. Some of these machines do not need people to guide them. They can run by themselves. The use of

*See Glossary

A giant rocket takes off from the earth for a flight into space. Do you think space flights will be important to Americans in years to come? Explain.

machines like these is called automation. Other new machines can do the hardest math problems in a few seconds. These machines are called computers.

The new machines have helped industry to grow. By using them, workers can produce more goods than ever before. (See the charts below.) This is why most Americans have a comfortable way of life. They can afford to buy many kinds of goods. For example, most American families own cars and television sets. This is not true in many other countries. There, only a few rich families can buy such things.

Pollution is a serious problem. The growth of our industry has brought many good things to people in the United States. But it has also led to some major problems. One of these is pollution.*

Air pollution is caused in several ways. People burn fuels such as coal and oil to heat their buildings. They also burn these fuels to produce electricity. Sometimes rubbish is burned to get rid of it. The smoke from all these fires goes into the air. There

Great changes have taken place in our country in the last thirty years. Some of these changes are shown on the charts below. The chart at left shows the number of people in the United States. Our population has grown from about 152 million in 1950 to almost 220 million today. The middle chart shows the value of all goods and services produced in our country. As you can see, production has grown very rapidly since 1950. The chart at right shows the average family income in the United States. The average family income grew from about $3,300 in 1950 to about $13,700 in 1975. It is still growing rapidly today.

Our Changing Nation

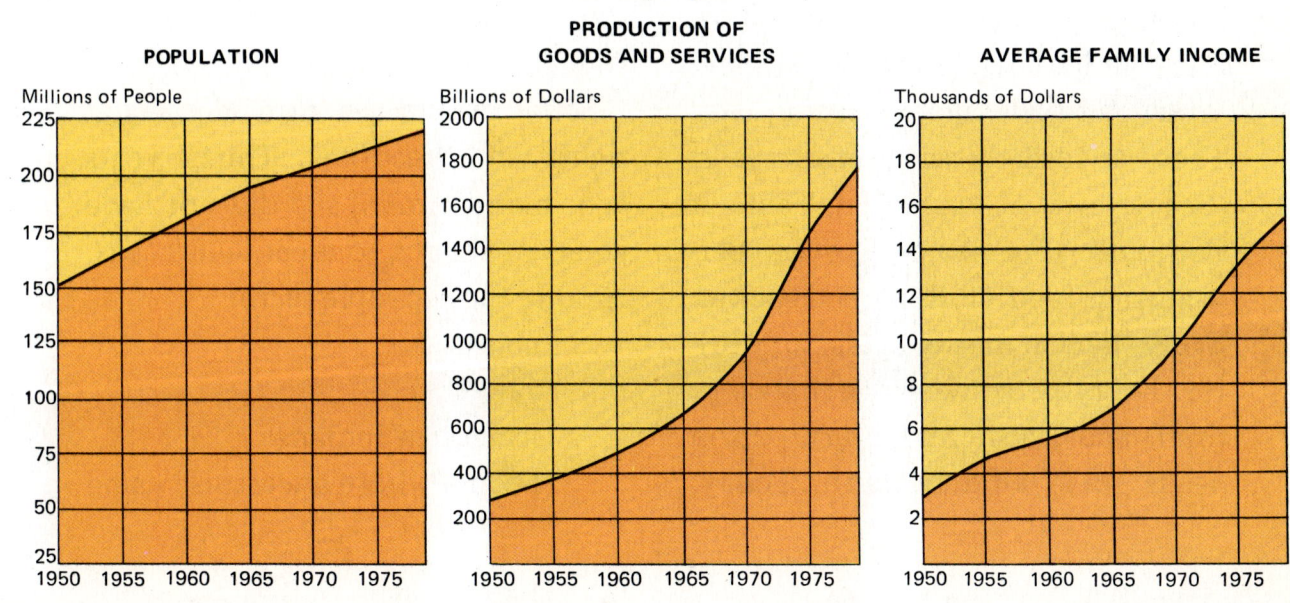

POPULATION

PRODUCTION OF GOODS AND SERVICES

AVERAGE FAMILY INCOME

it mixes with fumes from cars, trucks, buses, and airplanes.

Water can become polluted also. This happens when cities and factories dump their waste materials into rivers and lakes.

Today many Americans are worried about pollution. Scientists have found that people can become very sick from breathing polluted air. Polluted water is not safe for drinking, bathing, and other uses. Our country's leaders are seeking ways to stop pollution. They want to make our air and water clean again.

The need to use resources carefully. The growth of industry has led to another problem. Each year, American factories use huge amounts of natural resources. Today some of these resources are starting to run out. For example, we no longer produce enough oil, or petroleum,* to meet our needs. So we must buy large amounts of oil from other countries. If these countries ever stopped selling us oil, we would be in serious trouble.

In the future, we will have to use our resources more carefully to keep from running out. We must also find new ways of getting the things we need. For instance, sunlight is a source of energy that will never be used up. Some people are now using sunlight to heat their houses. Someday it may also be possible to use sunlight in producing electric power.

■ How has the concern for human needs changed American life?

Basic needs of people. All people on earth are alike in certain ways. They all have needs they must meet in order to live happy, useful lives. These are called basic human needs. (See "Needs of People" in Table of Contents.) For example, every person needs food, clothing, and shelter. Every person needs goals to work for. Every person needs a chance to think and learn. And every person needs some kind of faith. Today, Americans are trying to make sure that all our citizens have a chance to meet their basic human needs.

Some people did not have equal rights and freedoms. Thirty years ago, many Americans did not have an equal chance to meet their needs. Among these people were:

... blacks
... Jews*
... American Indians
... people whose ancestors* came

from certain countries, such as Mexico, Puerto Rico, China, and Japan.

These people lacked a number of the rights and freedoms that other Americans enjoyed. For example, in some places black children could not go to the same schools as white children. Some hotels and resorts would not admit Jews as guests. Mexican-Americans were sometimes

Freedom

See Great Ideas

The picture above shows a civil rights march in Boston, Massachusetts, during the 1960's. What do we mean by "civil rights"? Why did some Americans feel they needed to hold marches for civil rights? Did the civil rights movement succeed in reaching its goals? Give facts to back up your answer. Are there still any people in our country today who do not enjoy the same rights and freedoms as other Americans? If so, who are they?

History 59

130°
125°
120°
115°
110°
105°
100°
C A N
Vancouver
Calgary
Regina
Seattle
Olympia
Tacoma
WASHINGTON
Spokane
River
CASCADE RANGE
ROCKY MOUNTAINS
IDAHO
Great Falls
MONTANA
Missouri
Helena
Butte
Yellowstone River
Billings
NORTH DAKOTA
Bismarck
River
45°
Portland
Columbia
Salem
Eugene
OREGON
COAST RANGES
Boise
Snake
Idaho Falls
River
WYOMING
SOUTH DAKOTA
Pierre
Missouri
40°
Great Salt Lake
Ogden
Salt Lake City
Provo
WASATCH RANGE
Casper
Cheyenne
NEBRASKA
North Platte River
Greeley
South
Denver
COLORADO
Pueblo
KANSAS
Arkansas
NEVADA
UTAH
Carson City
Sacramento
San Francisco
San Francisco Bay
Berkeley
Oakland
CALIFORNIA
SIERRA NEVADA
Mt. Whitney
35°
Las Vegas
Hoover Dam
GRAND CANYON
River
Colorado
Los Angeles
Long Beach
San Diego
ARIZONA
Phoenix
Tucson
Santa Fe
Albuquerque
NEW MEXICO
Amarillo
Oklahoma City
OKLA
Lubbock
Fort Worth
El Paso
TEXAS
Rio Grande
Austin
San Antonio
MEX.
Brownsville
30°
PACIFIC OCEAN
120°
115°
110°
105°
100°
25°
SOVIET UNION
180°
160°
ARCTIC OCEAN
Point Barrow
70°
60°
BERING STRAIT
ARCTIC CIRCLE
Yukon River
Nome
Mt. McKinley 20,320 Ft.
Fairbanks
BERING SEA
CANADA
Anchorage
Palmer
Seward
GULF OF ALASKA
Juneau
Sitka
Ketchikan
Kodiak
ALASKA
0 100 200 300 Miles
0 100 200 300 Kilometers
ALEUTIAN ISLANDS
180°
160°
140°
KAUAI
OAHU
Honolulu
MAUI
Mauna Kea
Hilo
HAWAII
20°
0 50 100 150 200 Miles
0 50 100 150 200 Kilometers
MIDWAY IS.
170°
160°
PACIFIC OCEAN
HAWAII
0 100 200 300 Miles
0 100 200 300 Kilometers
25°
HAWAIIAN ISLANDS
TROPIC OF CANCER
KAUAI
Honolulu
OAHU
HAWAII
20°

UNITED STATES
0 100 200 300 Miles
0 100 200 300 Kilometers
National Capitals
State Capitals
Other Cities
Shading from green through yellow, brown, and red indicates increase in altitude. Figures show approximate altitude for corresponding color.
5,000 ft. (1,524 m.)
2,000 ft. (610 m.)
1,000 ft. (305 m.)
500 ft. (152 m.)
COPYRIGHT BY RAND MCNALLY & CO. MADE IN U.S.A.
C A N A D A
MINNESOTA
WISCONSIN
MICHIGAN
IOWA
ILLINOIS
INDIANA
OHIO
PENNSYLVANIA
NEW YORK
VT.
N.H.
MAINE
MASS.
CONN.
R.I.
N.J.
MD.
DEL.
D.C.
WEST VIRGINIA
VIRGINIA
KENTUCKY
TENNESSEE
NORTH CAROLINA
SOUTH CAROLINA
GEORGIA
ALABAMA
MISSISSIPPI
LOUISIANA
ARKANSAS
MISSOURI
FLORIDA
OZARK PLATEAU
APPALACHIAN MOUNTAINS
ATLANTIC OCEAN
STRAITS OF FLORIDA
TROPIC OF CANCER
NORTH LATITUDE
WEST LONGITUDE
Lake Superior
Lake Michigan
Lake Huron
Lake Erie
Lake Ontario
St. Lawrence River
Red River of the North
Mississippi River
Ohio River
Winnipeg
Fargo
Duluth
St. Paul
Minneapolis
Sioux Falls
Sioux City
Omaha
Lincoln
Topeka
Kansas City
Wichita
Tulsa
Ft. Smith
Little Rock
Dallas
Shreveport
Houston
Galveston
Beaumont
Baton Rouge
New Orleans
Jackson
Mobile
Pensacola
Tallahassee
Jacksonville
Tampa
St. Petersburg
Miami
Havana
Montgomery
Birmingham
Atlanta
Macon
Savannah
Charleston
Columbia
Charlotte
Raleigh
Norfolk
Richmond
Washington
Annapolis
Baltimore
Dover
Philadelphia
Trenton
New York
Hartford
Providence
Boston
Albany
Concord
Montpelier
Portland
Lewiston
Augusta
Quebec
Montreal
Ottawa
Toronto
Rochester
Buffalo
Harrisburg
Pittsburgh
Cleveland
Akron
Toledo
Detroit
Columbus
Cincinnati
Charleston
Frankfort
Lexington
Louisville
Nashville
Memphis
Indianapolis
Gary
Chicago
Milwaukee
Madison
Davenport
Des Moines
Peoria
Springfield
St. Louis
Jefferson City
Lansing
Grand Rapids
Flint
Saginaw
Sault Ste. Marie
95°
90°
85°
80°
75°
70°
65°
45°
40°
35°
30°
25°

refused jobs that other Americans could get easily. Some people would not sell houses or rent apartments to Indian families.

Women, too, were often treated unfairly in our country. For example, some companies would not hire women for certain jobs. If they did hire women, they would often pay them less money than men. This was true even if the women did exactly the same kind of work.

People work for equal rights and freedoms. During the 1950's, an important change took place. Some of the people who had been treated unfairly began to demand equal rights. They held marches and public meetings to call attention to what they wanted. Soon they were joined by other Americans who supported their fight for freedom. This became known as the civil* rights movement.

As time passed, the civil rights movement began to reach its goals. Our federal and state governments passed laws to protect the rights of minority* groups. Today it is against the law to treat a person unfairly just because that person belongs to a certain group. Women and minority groups now enjoy more rights than ever before in our history.

Today some people cannot meet their needs. Even today, however, many Americans find it hard to meet their needs. For example, millions of people cannot find steady jobs. Sometimes this is because they are too old, or their health is poor. They may not have the education or the skills needed to get a well-paying job. Sometimes there are simply not enough jobs for all the people who need them.

Usually, people who lack steady jobs do not have much money. They cannot afford to buy the proper kinds of food, clothing, and shelter. Many of them live in run-down areas called slums. When they become ill, they cannot afford medical care. Sometimes their illnesses keep them from holding full-time jobs.

Business and government are helping. Many things are being done to help Americans who have trouble meeting their needs. For instance, our government runs training programs for workers without jobs. Here, people learn skills they can use in industry. Business companies also carry on programs of this kind. Many cities have built apartment buildings where people can live without paying very much money. Our government provides money for people who are too old or too ill to hold steady jobs.

Government programs have helped many Americans to meet their needs. But these programs often cost a lot of money. Also, many people are needed to carry them out. Today, more than sixteen million Americans work for the government. Our national government spends more than thirteen times as much money each year as it did in 1948. Most of this money comes from taxes that our citizens must pay to the government.

Doing our part as citizens. In the years to come, many more exciting

Rules and Government

See Great Ideas

The picture below shows a woman scientist at work. In the past, women could work only at certain kinds of jobs. Today, all kinds of jobs are open to women. How did laws help to bring about this change? Sometimes people think that laws take away part of their freedom. But can laws also protect a person's freedom? If so, how?

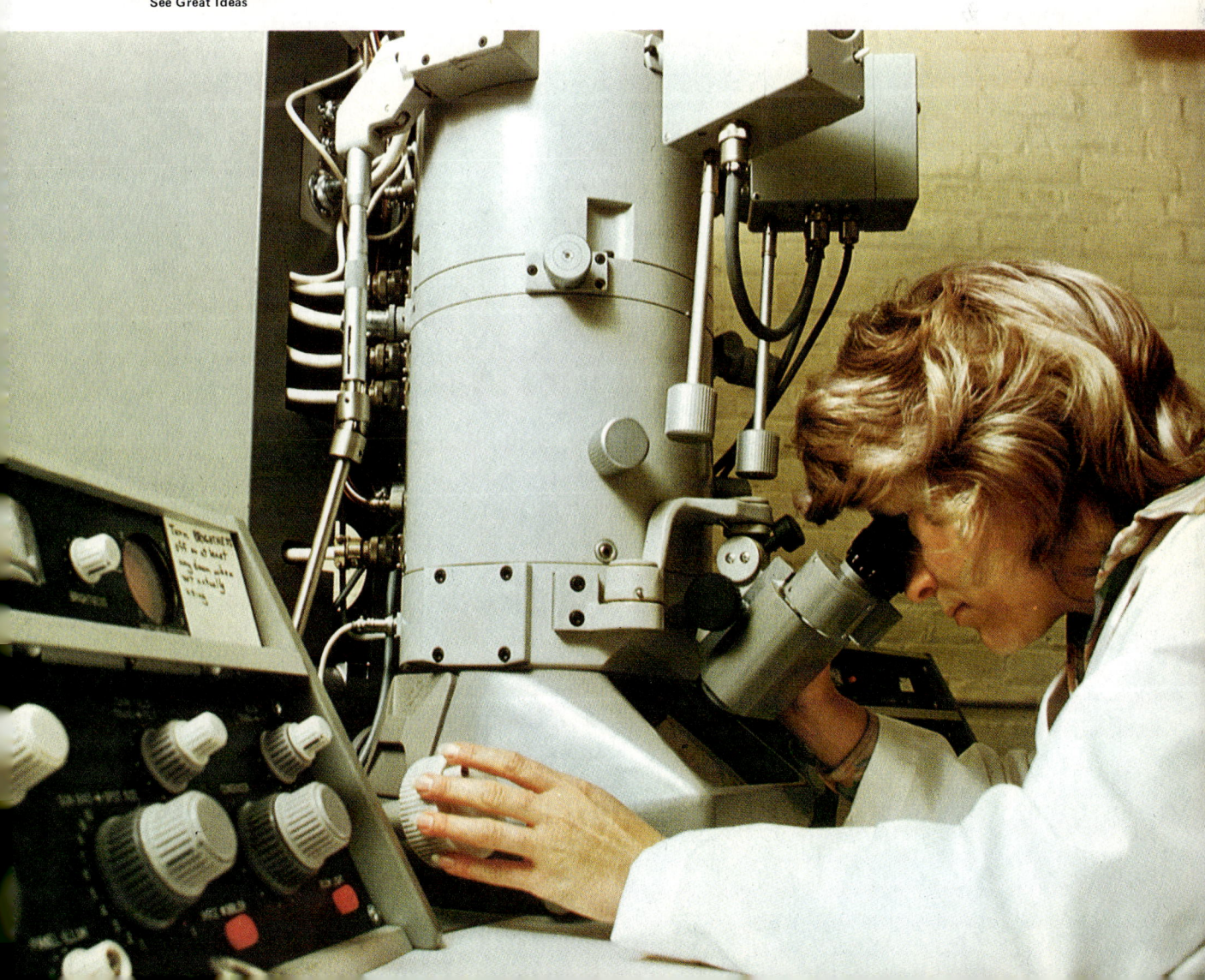

Education

See Great Ideas

Working on a classroom project. In our country today, most young people have a chance to get a good education. Nearly all children attend grade school and high school. Many students also go on to college. Do you think education is one of the great ideas that have built our nation? What would happen if most of our citizens did not have a good education? Would our government be able to do its job well? Give reasons for your answers.

changes will take place in our country. Will these changes be good or bad? The answer is largely up to us. We must all do our part as citizens. We must continue to live by the great ideas that built our nation—ideas such as freedom, loyalty, and cooperation. In this way, we can make our country even better and stronger than it is today.

Discover Our Country's Story

1. What important changes have taken place in the United States during the last thirty years? How have these changes affected your family?
2. Why is pollution a serious problem today? What are some examples of pollution in your own community?
3. What is being done today to help people who have trouble meeting their needs?
4. In what ways do you think the United States will change in the years ahead?

Index

Explanation of abbreviations used in this Index: *p* — picture   *m* — map

Allies, 52
animals, 5, 17, 39
Asia, 5, 8, 9
assembly-line method, 49
astronauts, 56
atomic bomb, 53
automation, 57
automobiles, 49; *p* 48

Battle of Mobile Bay, *p* 44-45
Bell, Alexander Graham, 48
Bering Strait, 5; *m* 5
birthday of our country, 25; *p* 2-3
blacks, *see* people
Boone, Daniel, *p* 30-31
Boston, Massachusetts, 18; *p* 59
Boston Tea Party, 22
Britain, *see* Great Britain

Cabinet, 29
Cabot, John, 14; *p* 14-15
Cabrillo (kä brēl' yō), **Juan**, *m* 10
California, 11, 35
Chicago, Illinois, 49
China, 55
cities, 49. See also names of cities
civil rights, 62; *p* 59
Civil War, 43-45, 46; *p* 44-45; *m* 43
coal, *see* minerals
Cold War, 55
colonies,
　British, 17-18, 20; *m* 17
　English, 14-15, 17
　French, 20
　Middle Colonies, 18; *m* 17
　New England, 17-18; *m* 17
　Southern Colonies, 18; *m* 17
Columbus, Christopher, 8-9; *m* 7
communism, 54-55
communities, early, 4-18
computers, 57
Confederate States of America, 45; *m* 43
Congress, 28, 29
Constitution, (kon' stə tü' shən) of the United States, 27-28
Continental Congress, First, 23
Continental Congress, Second, 23, 24-25; *p* 24-25
Coronado, Francisco, *p* 8-9; *m* 10
covered wagon, *p* 37
Cuba, 51-52

de Soto, Hernando, *m* 10
Declaration of Independence, 24, 25; *p* 24-25
divided country, 41; *m* 43

earning a living, 17, 41, 50, 51
Edison, Thomas, 47
electricity, 47-48, 56, 58
energy, 56, 58
Erie Canal, 33
Europeans, *see* people
explorers, 8-10, 12, 14; *p* 8-9, 12-13; *m* 7, 10

factories, 31, 32, 41, 45
farmers, 16, 17, 18, 39; *p* 40
farm products, 5, 18, 41
Ford, Henry, 49; *p* 48
forts, 10, 11
France, 26, 52
freedom, *see* great ideas
French and Indian War, 20; *m* 21

Germany, 52
gold, *see* minerals
goods and services, *chart* 57
government,
　British, 23
　national, 27-28
　spending, 62, 63
Great Britain, 17, 18, 24
great ideas,
　cooperation, *p* 28-29, 54
　division of labor, *p* 50-51
　education, *p* 64
　exchange, *p* 18-19
　freedom, 2, 16, 55, 58, 59; *p* 22-23, 59
　language, *p* 10-11
　loyalty, *p* 14-15, 41
　rules and government, 43; *p* 30-31, 63
　using natural resources, 4, 46, 58; *p* 4, 37, 46-47
　using tools, 8; *p* 16, 48
Great Lakes, 12, 33
Great Plains, 39-40; *p* 40
guided missiles, 55

Hawaiian Islands, 52, 53
Hitler, Adolf, 52
hydrogen bombs, 55

immigrants, 49-51
income, family, *chart* 57
Indians, *see* people
Indies, 8, 14; *m* 7
industry, 46-47, 56, 57, 58; *p* 46-47; *chart* 57
inventions, 48-49, 56
iron ore, *see* minerals

Jamestown, Virginia, 15; *p* 16
Japan, 52, 53
Jefferson, Thomas, 25, 34
Joliet, Louis, *p* 12-13

Korean War, 55

laws, 22, 62
Lewis and Clark, 34; *m* 36
Lincoln, Abraham, 43, 45; *p* 41
Louisiana Purchase, 34-35; *m* 34

machines, 31, 56-57
manufacturing, 31-32
Marquette, Father Jacques, *p* 12-13
Mexico, 35
minerals,
　coal, 46
　gold, 9, 10, 37-38
　iron ore, 18, 46
　petroleum, 47, 58
　silver, 9, 10, 36-37
minority groups, 62
minutemen, 23
missionaries, 12; *p* 12-13
missions, 10, 11; *p* 10-11
Mississippi River, 12, 20; *p* 12-13; *m* 10
Mount Rushmore, *p* 1

Native Americans, *see* people, Indians
New Amsterdam, *p* 13
New England, 17-18
New York City, 18; *p* 13, 28-29, 50-51

oil, *see* minerals, petroleum
Oregon Country, 36; *m* 34
Oregon Trail, 36; *m* 36

Parliament, 21-22
Pearl Harbor, 52-53; *p* 52-53
people,
　basic needs, 58
　blacks, 18, 42, 43, 58, 59; *p* 42-43
　Europeans, 7-17; *p* 6-9, 12-16
　first Americans, 4-5
　French, 12
　Indians, 4-5, 9, 10, 11, 12, 20, 21, 31, 39, 58, 62; *p* 4, 38-39; *m* 5
　Jews, 58, 59
　Mexican-Americans, 59
　Spanish, 10-11; *p* 8-9; *m* 10

Pronunciation Key: hat, āge, cãre, fär; let, ēqual, tėrm; it, īce; hot, ōpen, ôrder; oil, out; cup, pút, rüle, ūse; child; long; thin; ᴛHen; zh, measure; ə represents **a** in about, **e** in taken, **i** in pencil, **o** in lemon, **u** in circus.

History 65

petroleum, *see* minerals
Philadelphia, Pennsylvania, 18, 23, 27, 28; *p* 18-19
Pilgrims, 16
pioneers, *see* settlers
plantations, 18
pollution, 57-58
population, 2, 17, 33-34; *chart* 57

radio, 48
railroads, *see* transportation
Revolutionary War, 23-27; *p* 26-27
rockets, 56; *p* 56
Russia, *see* Soviet Union

schools, *p* 64
science, 56; *p* 63
settlements, 11, 13, 15, 35; *p* 13, 16, 18-19; *m* 13
settlers, 5, 11, 17, 21, 30-40; *p* 30-31, 37; *m* 5

silver, *see* minerals
slavery, 18, 42-43; *m* 43
slaves, *p* 42-43
slums, 62
Soviet Union, 52, 54
space flight, 56; *p* 56
Spanish-American War, 51
states' rights, 43
steam engine, 33
steam power, 33
steel, 46-47
Supreme Court, 28

taxes, 21, 63
telephone, 48
Texas, 11, 35; *m* 34
textile mills, 31
trade, 20-21, 32, 51; *p* 6-7
traders, 8, 12, 15, 18; *m* 7
transportation, 32-33; *p* 32-33
treaties, 20, 27

unemployment, 62
Union, the, 45; *m* 43
United Nations, 53-54; *p* 54
United States, *m* 60-61
  growth of, *m* 34
  possessions, 52
using natural resources, *see* great ideas

Vietnam War, 55
Vikings, 7; *m* 7

Washington, D.C., 29
Washington, George, 26, 27, 29; *p* 26-27, 28-29
West Indies, 51, 52
women, 62; *p* 63
World War I, 52
World War II, 52-53; *p* 52-53
Wright brothers, 49

Yorktown, Virginia, 27; *p* 26-27

Acknowledgments

Grateful acknowledgment is made to the following for permission to use the illustrations found in this book:

American Heritage: Pages 8-9, painting by Frederic Remington
Anheuser-Busch, Inc.: Pages 12-13, courtesy of August A. Busch, Jr.
Cincinnati Art Museum: Pages 38-39, bequest of Mrs. W. D. Julian
Confederation Life Collection: Pages 14-15
Ford Archives: Page 48, painting by Norman Rockwell
Francis G. Mayer, Art Color Slides, New York City: Pages 42-43, painting by Eyre Crowe
Grant Heilman: Pages 10-11 by Alan Pitcairn
H. Armstrong Roberts: Pages 1, 2-3, 52-53, and 63
Herb Orth, LIFE Magazine, © Time Inc.: Pages 22-23
Ken Heyman: Page 64
Kennedy Galleries, New York: Pages 32-33
Metropolitan Museum of Art: Pages 46-47, painting by John Ferguson Weir, gift of Lyman G. Bloomingdale, 1901
Museum of the City of New York: Pages 50-51
NASA: Page 56
New York Public Library: Page 13; pages 18-19, engraving by William Birch and Son
Phillip Gendreau: Page 41
The Fideler Company: Pages 4, 6-7, 28-29, 30-31, and 40
Thomas Williams: Page 16
United Nations: Page 54
United States Department of Commerce, Bureau of Public Roads: Page 37
Van Cleve Photography: Page 59 by David Kelley
Wadsworth Atheneum, Hartford, Conn.: Pages 44-45
Yale University Art Gallery: Pages 24-25 and 26-27, paintings by John Trumbull

Grateful acknowledgment is made to Scott, Foresman and Company for the pronunciation system used in this book, which is taken from the Thorndike-Barnhart Dictionary Series. Grateful acknowledgment is made to Rand McNally & Company for cartographic data on pages 60-61 and for permission to use the globes in this book.

SKILLS MANUAL

CONTENTS

Thinking 1
Solving Problems 2
Learning Social Studies Skills 3
   How To Find Information
      You Need 4
   Evaluating Information 5
   Making Reports 7
   Holding a Group Discussion 9
   Working With Others 9
   Building Your Vocabulary 10
Learning Map Skills 10

Thinking

One of the main reasons you are attending school is to learn how to think clearly. Your social studies class is one of the best places in which to grow in the use of your thinking skills. Here you will learn more about using the thinking skills that will help you understand yourself, your country, and your world.

There are seven different kinds of thinking skills. As you use all seven, you will become more successful in school and in life. You will be able to understand yourself and your world much better. You will be a happier and more useful citizen as well.

Seven kinds of thinking

1. **Remembering** is the simplest kind of thinking. Everything you can remember is called your store of knowledge.

   Example: Remembering facts, such as the names of state capitals.

2. **Translation** is changing information from one form into another.

   Example: Reading a map and putting into words the information you find there.

3. **Interpretation** is discovering how things relate to each other, or how things are connected.

   Example: Comparing two pictures to decide in what ways they are alike or in what ways they are different.

4. **Application** is using your knowledge and skills to solve a new problem.

   Example: Using social studies skills to prepare a written report.

5. **Analysis** is the kind of thinking you use when you try to find out how something is organized, or put together. When you

use this kind of thinking, you separate complicated information into its basic parts. Then you can see how they were put together and how they are related to each other.

Example: Separating main ideas from supporting facts.

6. **Synthesis** is putting ideas together in a form that not only has meaning but is also new and original.

Examples: Painting a picture; or writing something original, which might be a paragraph or an entire poem, story, or play.

7. **Evaluation** is the highest level of thinking. It is judging whether or not something meets a given standard.

Example: Deciding which of several different sources of information is the most reliable; or judging the success of a class discussion.

Solving Problems

The social studies will be more worthwhile to you if you learn to think and work as a scientist does. Scientists use a special way of studying called the problem-solving method. During the 1900's, the use of this method has helped people gain much scientific knowledge. In fact, we have gained more scientific knowledge during the 1900's than people had discovered earlier throughout the history of human beings on this planet.

The problem-solving method is more interesting than simply reading a textbook and memorizing answers for a test. By using this method, you can make your own discoveries. Using the problem-solving method will also help you learn how to think clearly. It will involve you in using all of the seven different kinds of thinking skills. To use this method in learning about our country, you will need to follow these steps.

1. **Choose an important, interesting problem** that you would like to solve. (A sample problem to solve is given on the opposite page.) Write the problem down so that you will have clearly in mind what it is you want to find out. If there are small problems that need to be solved in order to solve your big problem, list them, too.

2. **Think about all possible solutions** to your problem. List the ones that seem most likely to be true. These possible solutions are called "educated guesses," or hypotheses. You will try to solve your problem by finding facts to support or to disprove your hypotheses.

Sometimes you may wish to do some general background reading before you make your hypotheses. For example, if you were going to solve the sample problem on the opposite page, you might want first to read about the land features of the Northeast. Then, make your hypotheses based on what you have discovered.

3. **Test your hypotheses** by doing research. This book provides you with four major sources of information. These are the pictures, the text, the maps, and the Glossary. To find the information you need, you may use the Table of Contents and the Index. The suggestions on pages 4-7 will help you find and evaluate other sources of information.

As you do research, make notes of all the information that will either support your hypotheses or disprove them. You may discover that information from one source does not agree with information from another. If this should happen, check still further. Try to decide which facts are correct.

4. Summarize what you have learned. Your summary should be a short statement of the main points you have discovered. Have you been able to support one or more of your hypotheses with facts? Have you been able to prove that one or more of your hypotheses is not correct? What new facts have you learned? Do you need to do more research?

You may want to write a report about the problem. To help other people share the ideas you have come to understand, you may decide to include maps, pictures, or your own drawings with your report. You will find helpful suggestions for writing a good report on pages 7 and 8.

A sample problem to solve

As you study our country, you may wish to try to solve problems about our country as a whole. Or, you may wish to study one major region. The following sample problem to solve is about the Northeast as a region.

Mountains and rolling hills make up much of the Northeast. Very little of this part of our country is low and level. How do the land features of the Northeast affect the lives of the people? In forming hypotheses to solve this problem, you will need to think about how the land features of the Northeast affect the following:

a. where the cities grew up
b. industry
c. farming

The suggestions on the next two pages will help you find the information you need for solving this problem.

Learning Social Studies Skills

What is a skill?

A skill is something that you have learned to do well. To learn some skills, such as swimming or playing baseball, you must train the muscles of your arms and legs. To learn others, such as typing, you must train your fingers. Still other skills call for you to train your mind. For instance, reading with understanding is a skill that calls for much mental training. The skills that you use in the social studies are largely mental skills.

Why are skills important?

Mastering different skills will help you to have a happier and more satisfying life. You will be healthier and enjoy your free time more if you develop skills needed to take part in different sports. By developing art and music skills, you will be able to share your feelings more fully. It is even more important for you to develop your mental skills. These skills are the tools that you will use in getting and using the knowledge you need to live successfully in today's world.

Developing a skill

If you were to ask fine athletes or musicians how they gained their skills, they would probably say, "Through practice."

To develop mental skills, you must practice also. Remember, however, that a person cannot become a good ballplayer if he or she keeps throwing the ball in the wrong way. A person cannot become a fine musician by practicing the wrong notes. The same thing is true of mental skills. To master them, you must practice them correctly.

The following pages have suggestions about how to perform correctly several important skills needed in the social studies. For example, to succeed in the social studies you must know how to find the information you need. You need to know how to prepare reports and how to work with others on group projects. Study these skills carefully, and use them.

How To Find Information You Need

Each day of your life you seek information. Sometimes you want to know certain facts just because you are curious. Most of the time, however, you want information for some certain reason. If you enjoy baseball, for instance, you may want to know how to figure batting averages. If you collect stamps, you need to know how to find out what countries they come from. As a student in today's world, you need information for many reasons. As an adult, you will need even more knowledge in order to live successfully in tomorrow's world.

You may wonder how you can possibly learn all the facts you are going to need during your lifetime. The answer is that you can't. Therefore, knowing how to find information when you need it is very important to you. Following are suggestions for finding good sources of information and for using these sources to find the facts that you need.

Written Sources of Information

Books

You may be able to find the information you need in books that you have at home or in your classroom. To see if a textbook or other nonfiction* book has the information you need, look at the table of contents and the index.

Sometimes, you will need to go to your school or neighborhood library to find books that have the information you want. To make the best use of a library, you should learn to use the card catalog. This is a file that contains information about the books in the library. Each nonfiction book has at least three cards, filed in alphabetical order. One is for the title, one is for the author, and one is for the subject of the book. Each card gives the book's special number. This number will help you to find the book. All the nonfiction books in the library are arranged on the shelves in numerical order. If you cannot find a book that you want, the librarian will help you.

Reference volumes

You will find much useful information in certain books known as reference volumes. Among these are dictionaries, encyclopedias, atlases, and other special books. Some companies publish a book each year with facts and figures and general information about the events of the year before. Such books are generally called yearbooks, annuals, or almanacs.

Newspapers and magazines

These are important sources of up-to-date information. Sometimes you will want to look for information in papers or magazines that you do not have at home. You can almost always find the ones you want at the library.

The *Readers' Guide to Periodical Literature* is kept for use in most libraries. It will direct you to magazine articles about the subject you are interested in. This is a series of volumes that list articles by title, author, and subject. In the front of each volume is an explanation of the abbreviations used to indicate the different magazines and their dates.

Booklets, pamphlets, and bulletins

You can get many materials of this kind from local and state governments, as well as from our federal government. Chambers of commerce, travel bureaus, trade organizations, private companies, and embassies of other countries publish materials that have a wealth of information.

Many booklets and bulletins give correct information. Remember, however, that some of them were written to promote certain goods or ideas. Information from such sources should be checked carefully.

*See Glossary

Reading for Information

The following suggestions will help you to save time and work when you are looking for information in books and other written materials.

The table of contents and the index

The table of contents appears at the beginning of the book and generally is a list of the chapters in the book. By looking at this list, you can almost always tell if the book has the kind of information you need.

The index is a more detailed list of the things that are talked about in the book. It will help you find the pages on which specific facts are talked about. In most books, the index is at the back. Encyclopedias often place the index in a separate volume.

At the beginning of an index, you will generally find an explanation that makes it easier to use. For instance, the beginning of the Index for this book tells you that *p* means picture and *m* means map.

The topics, or entries, in the index are arranged in alphabetical order. To find all the information you need, you may have to look under more than one entry. For example, to find out what pages of a social studies book have information about cities, you would look up the entry for cities. You could also see if cities are listed by their own names.

Skim the written material

Before you begin reading a chapter or a page, skim it to see if it has the information you need. In this way you will not waste time reading something that is of little or no value to you. When you skim, you look mainly for topic headings, topic sentences, and key words. Imagine you are looking for the answer to the question: "What are the people in the West doing to conserve their forest resources?" In a book about the West or about the United States, you might look for a topic heading that mentions forest resources. When you find this heading, you might look for the key words, "conserving forests."

Read carefully

When you think you have found the page that has the information you are looking for, read it carefully. Does this page tell you exactly what you want to know? If not, you will need to look further.

Other Ways of Getting Information

Direct experience

What you see or live through for yourself may be a good source of information if you have watched carefully and remembered accurately. Firsthand information can often be obtained by visiting places in your community or nearby, such as museums, factories, or government offices.

Radio and television

Use the listings in your local newspaper to find programs about the subjects in which you are interested.

Movies, filmstrips, recordings, and slides

Materials on many different subjects are available. You can get them from schools, libraries, museums, and private companies.

Resource people

Sometimes, you will be able to get information by talking with a person who has special knowledge. Once in a while, you may wish to invite someone to speak to your class and answer questions.

Evaluating Information

During your lifetime, you will constantly need to evaluate what you see, hear, and read. Information is not true or worthwhile simply because it is presented on television or is written in a book, magazine, or newspaper. The following suggestions will help you in evaluating information.

Primary and secondary sources of information

A primary source of information is a firsthand record. For instance, a photograph taken of something while it is happening is a primary source. So is the report you write about a field trip you take. Original documents, such as the Constitution of the United States, are primary sources also.

A secondary source is a secondhand report. If you write a report about what someone else told you he or she saw, your report will be a secondary source of information. Another example of a secondary source is a history book.

Advanced scholars like to use primary sources whenever possible. However, these sources are often difficult to obtain. Most students in elementary and high school use secondary sources. You should always be aware that you are using secondhand information when you use a secondary source.

Who said it and when was it said?

The next step in evaluating information is to ask, "Who said it?" Was she a person with special training in the subject about which she wrote? Was he a newsman who is known for careful reporting of the facts?

Another question you should ask is "When was it said?" Changes take place rapidly in our world, and the information you are using may be out of date. For instance, suppose you are looking for information about a country. If you use an encyclopedia that is five years old, much of the information you find will not be correct.

Is it mostly fact or opinion?

The next step in evaluating information is to decide if it is based on facts or if it consists mostly of unsupported opinions. You can do this best if you know about these three kinds of statements:

1. <u>Statements of fact that can be checked.</u> For example, "Voters in the United States choose their representatives by secret ballot" is a statement of fact that can be checked by finding out how voting is carried on in different parts of our country.
2. <u>Inferences, or conclusions that are based on facts.</u> The statement "The people of the United States live in a democracy" is an inference. This inference is based on the fact that the citizens choose their representatives by secret ballot, and on other facts that can be proved. It is important to remember that inferences can be false or only partly true, even though they are based on facts.
3. <u>Value judgments, or opinions.</u> The statement "It is always wrong for a country to go to war" is a value judgment. Since a value judgment is an opinion, you need to look at it very carefully. On what facts and inferences is it based? What facts and conclusions do you think form the basis of the opinion, "It is always wrong for a country to go to war"? Do you agree or disagree with these conclusions? Trustworthy writers or reporters are careful to let their readers know which statements are their own opinions. They also try to base their opinions as much as possible on facts that can be proved.

Why was it said?

The next step in evaluating information is to find out the purpose for which it was prepared. Many books and articles are prepared in an honest effort to give you accurate information. Scientists writing about new scientific discoveries will generally try to report their findings as accurately as possible. They will be careful to distinguish between things they have actually seen and conclusions they have drawn from their observations.

Some information, however, is prepared mostly to persuade people to believe or act a certain way. Information of this kind is called propaganda.

Some propaganda is used to promote causes that are generally thought to be good. A picture that shows Smokey the Bear and the words "Only you can prevent forest fires" is an example of this kind of propaganda.

Propaganda is also used to make people support causes they would not agree with if they knew more about them. This kind of propaganda may be made up of information that is true, partly true, or false. Even when it is true, however, the information may be presented in such a way as to mislead you.

Propaganda generally appeals to people's feelings rather than to their thinking ability. For this reason, you should learn to recognize information that is propaganda. Then you can think about it calmly and clearly, and evaluate it intelligently.

Making Reports

There are many times when you need to share information or ideas with others. Sometimes you will need to do this in writing. Other times you will need to do it by speaking. One of the best ways to develop your writing and speaking skills is by making written and oral reports. The success of your report will depend on how well you have organized your material. It will also depend on your skill in presenting it. Here are some guidelines that will help you in preparing a good report.

Decide upon a goal

Have your goal clearly in mind. Are you mostly interested in sharing information? Do you want to give your own ideas on a subject? Or are you trying to persuade other people to agree with you?

Find the information you need

Be sure to use more than one source. If you are not sure how to find information about your subject, read the suggestions on pages 4 and 5.

Take good notes

To remember what you have read, you must take notes. Before you begin taking notes, however, you will need to make a list of the questions you want your report to answer. As you do research, write down the facts that answer these questions. You may find some interesting and important facts that do not answer any of your questions. If you feel that they might be useful in your report, write them down, too. Your notes should be short and in your own words except when you want to use quotations. When you use an exact quotation, be sure to put quotation marks around it.

You will be able to make the best use of your notes if you write them on file cards. Use a separate card for each statement or group of statements that answers one of your questions. To remember where your information came from, write on each card the title, author, and date of the source. When you have finished taking notes, group the cards according to the questions they answer.

Make an outline

After you have reviewed your notes, make an outline. This is a general plan that shows the order and the relationship of the ideas you want to include in your report. The first step in making an outline is to pick out the main ideas. These will be the main headings in your outline. (See sample outline below.) Next, list under each of these headings the ideas and facts that support or explain it. These related ideas are called subheadings. As you arrange your information, ask yourself the following questions.

a. Is there one main idea I must put first because everything else depends on this idea?
b. Have I arranged my facts in such a way as to show relationships among them?

c. Are there some ideas that will be clearer if they come after other ideas have been explained?
d. Have I included enough facts so that I can end my outline with a summary statement or a logical conclusion?

When you have finished your first outline, you may find that some parts of it are too short. If so, you may wish to do more research. When you feel that you have enough information, make your final outline. Remember that this outline will serve as a guide for your finished report.

Example of an outline

The author of this Skills Manual prepared the following outline before writing "Making Reports."

   I. Introduction
  II. Deciding upon a goal
 III. Finding information
 IV. Taking notes
    A. List main ideas to be researched
    B. Write on file cards facts that support or explain these ideas
    C. Group cards according to main ideas
  V. Making an outline
    A. Purpose of an outline
    B. Guidelines for arranging information
    C. Sample outline of this section
 VI. Preparing a written report
VII. Presenting an oral report

Special guidelines for a written report

Using your outline as a guide, write your report. The following suggestions will help you to make your report interesting and clear.

Create word pictures that your readers can see in their minds. Before you begin, imagine that you are going to make a movie of the subject you plan to write about. What scenes would you like to show? Next, think of the words that will bring these same pictures into your readers' minds.

Group your sentences into good paragraphs. It is generally best to begin a paragraph with a topic sentence that says to the reader, "This is what you will learn about in this paragraph." The other sentences in the paragraph should help to support or explain the topic sentence.

A sample paragraph. Below is a sample paragraph from a textbook about the northeastern part of our country. The topic sentence has been underlined. Notice how clear it is and how well the other sentences support it. Also notice how many pictures the paragraph puts in your mind.

> One of the most interesting sights in the Erie-Ontario Lowland is beautiful Niagara Falls. These falls are located on the Niagara River, which forms part of the border between the United States and Canada. The Niagara River flows northward from Lake Erie to Lake Ontario. About halfway between these two lakes, the river plunges over a steep cliff, forming Niagara Falls. Each year, thousands of tourists come to see these famous falls. Waterpower from the falls is used to produce electricity for factories and homes in both the United States and Canada.

Other guidelines. There are two other things to remember in writing a good report. First, use the dictionary to find the spelling of words you are not sure about. Second, make a list of the sources of information you used. Put this list at the beginning or end of your report. This list is called a bibliography.

Special guidelines for an oral report

When you are going to give a report orally, you will also want to arrange your information in a logical order by making an outline. Prepare notes to guide you during your talk. These notes should be complete enough to help you remember all the points you want to make. You may even write out certain parts of your report that you would rather read.

When you present your report, speak directly to your audience. Pronounce your words correctly and clearly. Remember to speak slowly enough for your listeners to follow what you are saying. Use a tone of voice that will hold their interest. Stand up straight, but try not to be too stiff. Remember, the only way to improve your speaking skills is to practice them correctly.

Holding a Group Discussion

One of the important ways in which you learn is by exchanging ideas with other people. You do this often in everyday conversation. You are likely to learn more, however, when you take part in the special kind of group conversation that we call a discussion. A discussion is more orderly than a conversation. It generally has a definite, serious purpose. This purpose may be the sharing of information or the solving of a problem. In order to reach its goal, the discussion group must arrive at a conclusion or make a decision of some kind.

The guidelines below will help you to have a successful discussion.

Be prepared

Think about the subject to be discussed ahead of time. Prepare for the discussion by reading and taking notes. You may also want to make an outline of the ideas you want to share with the group.

Take part

Take part in the discussion. Express your ideas clearly and in as few words as possible. Be sure that the statements you make and the questions you ask deal with the subject being talked about.

Listen and think

Listen thoughtfully to others. Encourage all of the members of the discussion group to express their ideas. Do not make up your mind about a question or a problem until all of the facts have been given.

Be courteous

When you speak, address the whole group. Ask and answer questions politely. When you do not agree with someone, give your reasons in a friendly way.

Working With Others

In school and throughout life, you will find that there are many things that can be done better by a group than by one person working alone. Some of these projects would take too long to finish if they were done by one person. Others have different parts that can be done best by people with different talents.

Before your group begins a project, you should decide several matters. First, decide exactly what goal you are trying to reach. Second, decide what part of the project each person should do. Third, decide when the project is to be finished.

Do your part

Remember that the success of your project depends on every member of the group. Be willing to do your share of the work and to accept your share of the responsibility.

Follow the rules

Help the group decide on reasonable rules. Then follow them. When a difference of opinion cannot be settled by discussion, make a decision by majority* vote.

Share your ideas

Be willing to share your ideas with the group. When you present an idea for discussion, be prepared to see it criticized or even rejected. At the same time, have the courage to stand up for an idea or a belief that is really important to you.

Be friendly, thoughtful, helpful, cheerful

Try to express your opinions seriously and sincerely without hurting others or losing their respect. Listen politely to the ideas of others.

Learn from your mistakes

Look for ways in which you can be a better group member the next time you work with others on a project.

Building Your Vocabulary

When you do research in many different kinds of reading materials, you are likely to find several words you have never seen before. If you skip over these words, you may not fully understand what you are reading. The following suggestions will help you to discover the meanings of new words and build your vocabulary.

1. **See how the word is used in the sentence.** When you come to a new word, don't stop reading. Read on beyond the new word to see if you can discover any hints as to what its meaning might be. Trying to figure out the meaning of a word from the way it is used may not give you the exact definition. However, it will give you a general idea of what the word means.

2. **Sound out the word.** Break the word up into syllables, and try to pronounce it. When you say the word aloud, you may find that you know it after all but have simply never seen it in print.

3. **Look in the dictionary.** When you think you have figured out what a word means and how it is pronounced, look it up in the dictionary. First, check the pronunciation. Have you pronounced it correctly? Then, check the meaning of the word. Remember, most words have more than one meaning. Did you decide on the right definition?

4. **Make a list of the new words you learn.** In your own words, write a definition of each word you place on your list. Review this list from time to time.

Learning Map Skills

The earth is a sphere

Our earth is round like a ball. We call anything with this shape a sphere. The earth is, of course, a very large sphere. Its diameter* is about 8,000 miles (12,874 kilometers*). Its circumference* is about 25,000 miles (40,233 kilometers). The earth is not quite a perfect sphere. It is somewhat flat at the North and South poles.

Globes and maps

The globe in your classroom is also a sphere. It is a small-size copy of the earth. The surface of the globe shows the shapes of the areas of land on the earth. It also shows the shapes of the different bodies of water. By looking at the globe, you can see exactly where the continents,* islands, and oceans are. Globes are made with the North Pole at the top. But they are often tipped to show the way the earth is tipped. Maps are flat drawings. They may show part or all of the earth's surface.

Scale

Globes and maps give information about distance. When you use them, you need to know what distance on the earth is represented by a given distance on the globe or map. This relationship is called the scale. The scale of a globe or map may be shown in several different ways.

On most maps, the scale is shown by a small drawing. For example:

```
           0        200        400  Miles
Scale      |---------|----------|
           0        322        644  Kilometers
```

Sometimes, the scale is shown in this way: 1 inch = 400 miles (644 kilometers).

THE GREAT LAKES

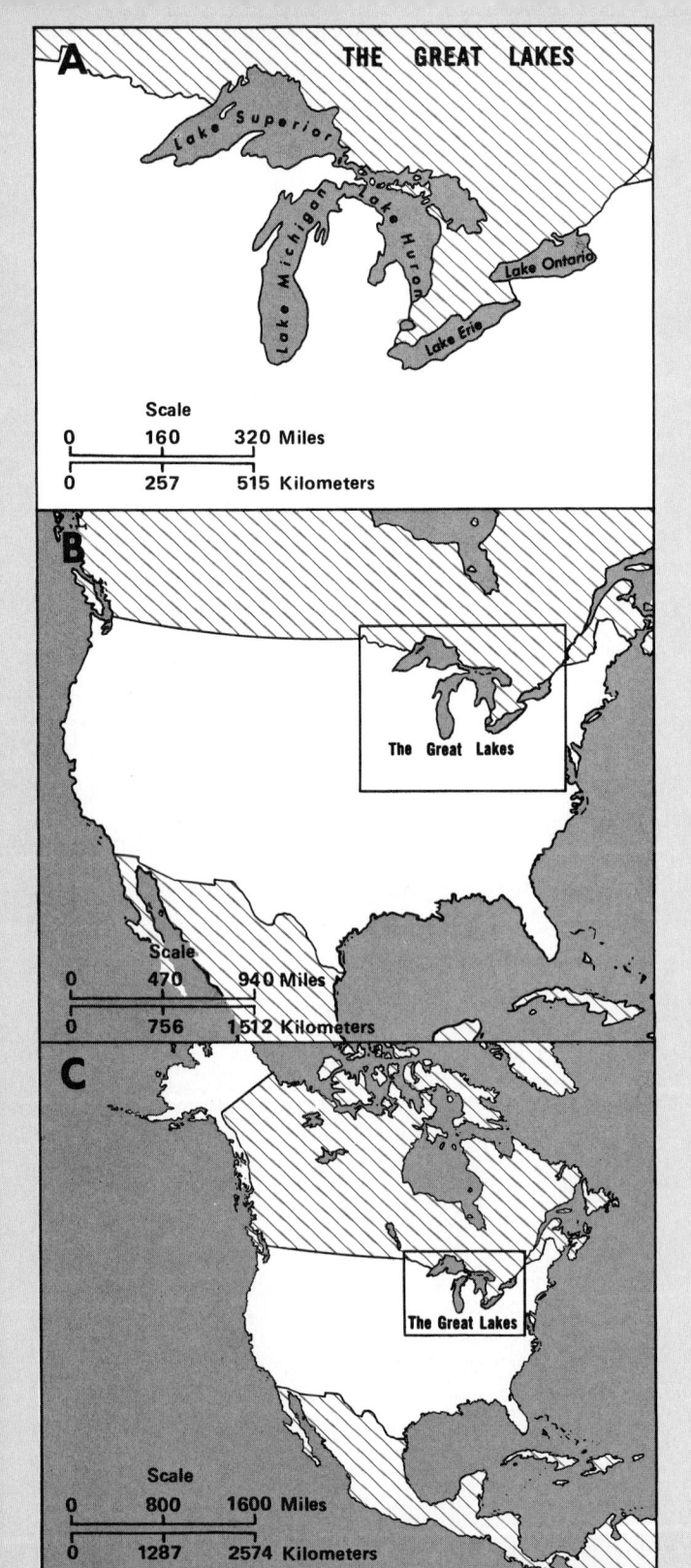

Scale
0 — 160 — 320 Miles
0 — 257 — 515 Kilometers

Scale
0 — 470 — 940 Miles
0 — 756 — 1512 Kilometers

Scale
0 — 800 — 1600 Miles
0 — 1287 — 2574 Kilometers

The Great Lakes area is a different size on each of the three maps above. This is because one inch on each of these maps represents a different distance on the earth.

Finding places on the earth

Map makers, travelers, and other interested people have always wanted to know just where certain places are. Over the years, a very accurate way of giving such information has been worked out. This system is used all over the world.

In order to work out a means of finding anything, you need starting points and a measuring unit. The North and South poles and the equator are the starting points for the system we use to find places on the earth. The measuring unit for our system is called the degree (°).

Parallels show latitude

When we want to find a place on the earth, we first find out how far it is north or south of the equator. This distance measured in degrees is called north or south latitude. The equator stands for zero latitude. The North Pole is located at 90 degrees north latitude. The South Pole is at 90 degrees south latitude.

All points on the earth that have the same latitude are the same distance from the equator. A line connecting such points is called a parallel. This is because it is parallel to the equator. (See globe D on the next page.)

Meridians show longitude

After we know the latitude of a place, we need to know its location in an east-west direction. This is called its longitude. The lines that show longitude are called meridians. They are drawn so as to connect the North and South poles (See globe E on the next page.) Longitude is measured from the meridian that passes through Greenwich, England. This line of zero longitude is called the prime meridian. Distance east or west of this meridian measured in degrees is called east or west longitude. The meridian of 180 degrees west longitude is the same as the one of 180 degrees east longitude. This is because 180 degrees is exactly halfway around the world.

D Parallels Show Latitude

E Meridians Show Longitude

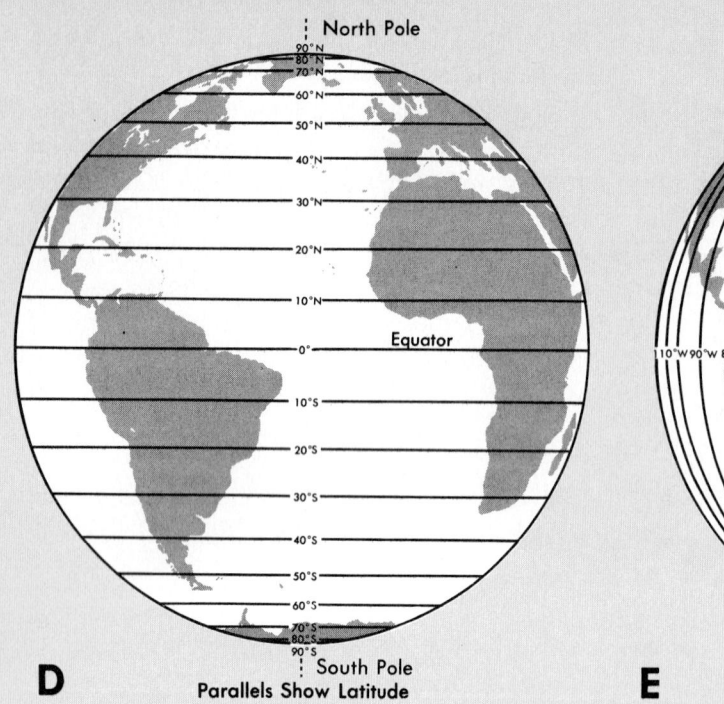

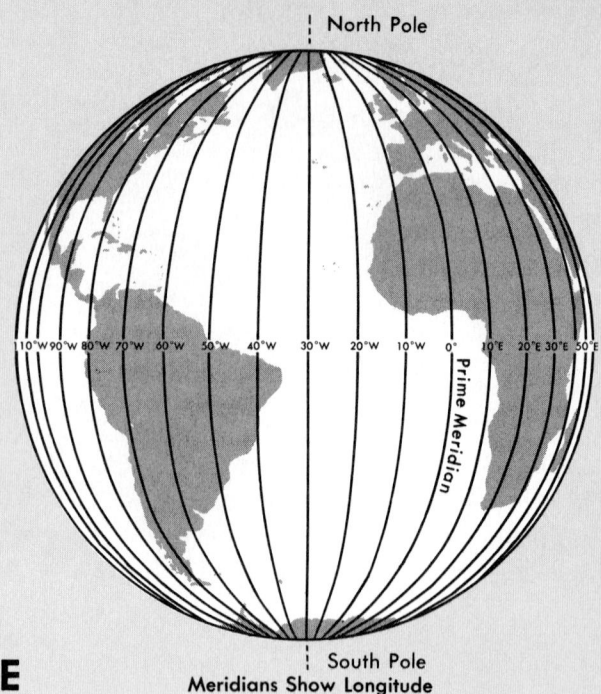

Finding places on a globe

The location of a certain place might be given to you like this: 30° N 90° W. This means that this place is located 30 degrees north of the equator, and 90 degrees west of the prime meridian. See if you can find this place on the globe in your classroom. It is helpful to remember that parallels and meridians are drawn every ten or fifteen degrees on most globes.

The round earth on a flat map

An important fact about a sphere is that you cannot flatten out its surface perfectly. To prove this, you might do the following. Cut an orange in half. Scrape away the fruit. You will not be able to press either piece of orange peel flat without crushing it. If you cut one piece in half, however, you can press these smaller pieces nearly flat. Next, cut one of these pieces of peel into three smaller pieces, shaped like those in drawing F on the opposite page. You will be able to press these pieces quite flat.

A map like the one shown in drawing F can be made by cutting the surface of a globe into twelve pieces shaped like the smallest pieces of your orange peel. Such a map would be accurate. However, an "orange-peel" map is not easy to use, because the continents and oceans are cut apart.

A flat map can never show the earth's surface as truthfully as a globe can. On globes, shape, size, distance, and direction are all accurate. A single flat map of the world cannot be drawn to show all four of these things correctly. But flat maps can be made that show some of these things accurately. The different ways of drawing maps of the world to show different things correctly are called map projections.

The Mercator projection

Drawing G, on the opposite page, shows a world map called a Mercator projection. When you compare this map with a globe, you can see that continents, islands, and oceans have almost the right shape. On this kind of map, however, North America seems larger than Africa. This is not true. On Mercator maps, lands far from the equator appear larger than they are.

Because they show true directions, Mercator maps are very useful to sailors and fliers. For instance, the city of Lisbon, Portugal, lies almost exactly east of Baltimore, Maryland. A Mercator map shows that a ship could reach Lisbon by sailing from Baltimore straight east across the Atlantic Ocean. A plane could also reach Lisbon by flying straight east from Baltimore.

The shortest route

Strangely enough, the best way to reach Lisbon from Baltimore is not by going straight east. There is a shorter route. In order to understand why this is so, you might like to do the following.

On your classroom globe, find Lisbon and Baltimore. Both cities lie just south of the 40th parallel. Take a piece of string and connect the two cities. Let the string follow the true east-west direction of the 40th parallel. Now, draw the string tight. Notice that it passes far to the north of the 40th parallel. The path of the tightened string is the shortest route between Baltimore and Lisbon. The shortest route between any two points on the earth is called the great* circle route.

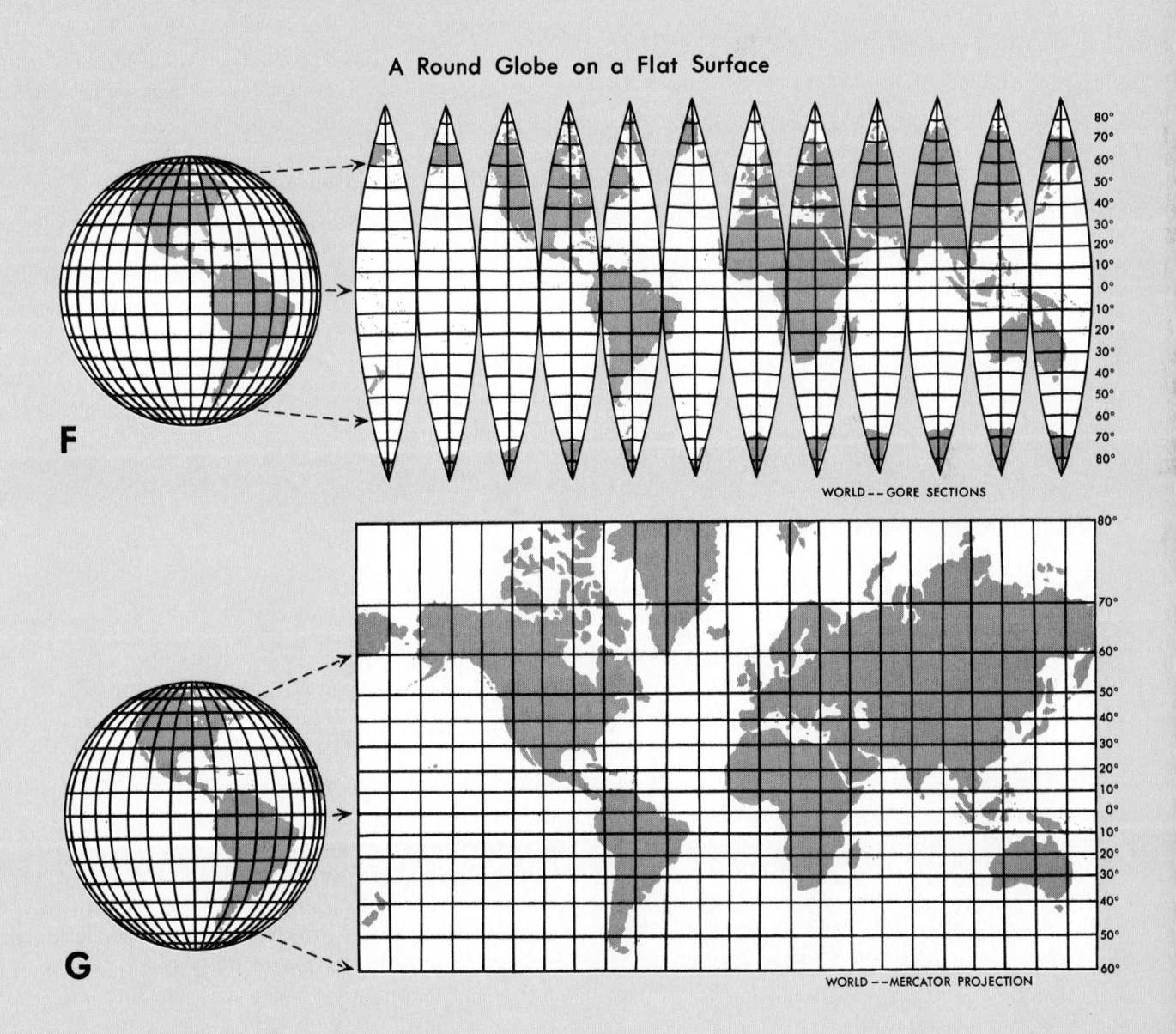

A Round Globe on a Flat Surface

F

WORLD -- GORE SECTIONS

G

WORLD -- MERCATOR PROJECTION

13

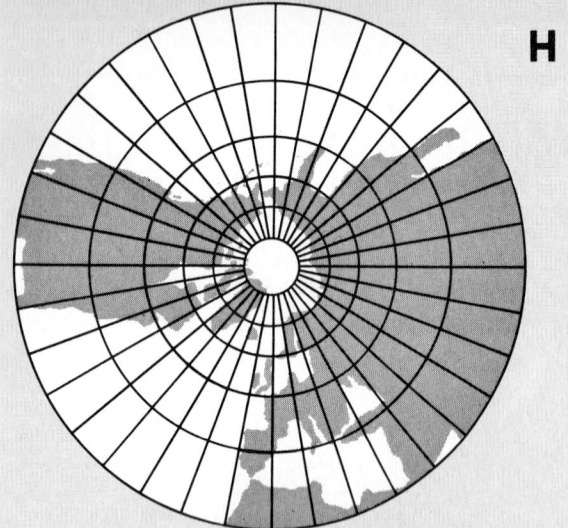

GNOMONIC PROJECTION

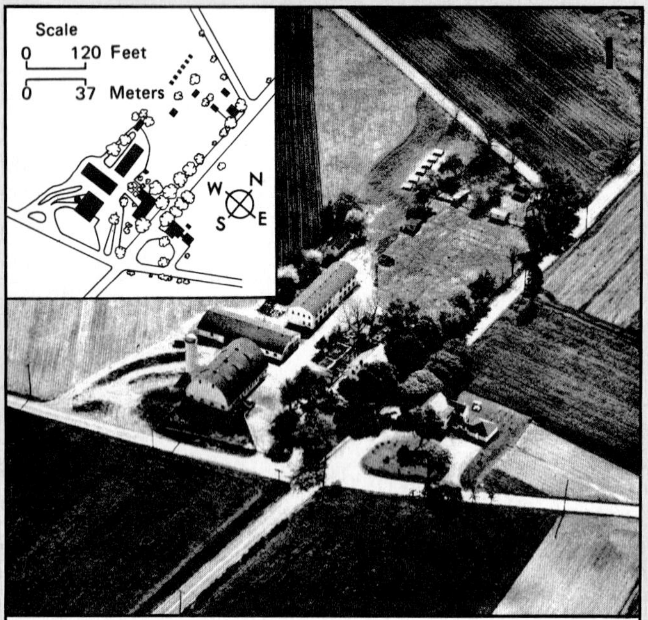

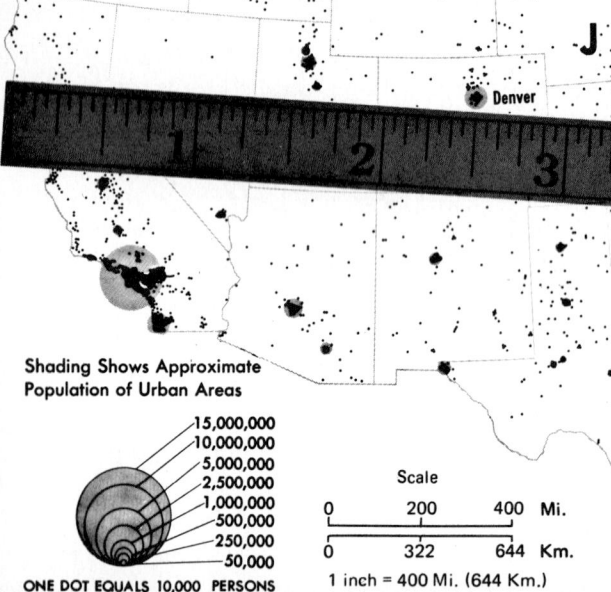

The gnomonic (nō mon′ ik) projection

Using a globe and a piece of string is not a very handy or accurate way of finding great circle routes. Instead, sailors and fliers use a special kind of map called the gnomonic projection. (See drawing H, at left.) On this kind of map, the great circle route between any two places can be found simply by drawing a straight line between them.

Special-Purpose Maps

Maps that show part of the earth

For some uses, we would rather have maps that do not show the whole surface of the earth. A map of a very small part of the earth can be drawn more accurately than a map of a large area. It can also include more details.

Drawing I, on this page, shows a photograph and a map of the same small part of the earth. The drawings on the map that show the shape and location of things on the earth are called symbols. The small drawing that shows directions is called a compass* rose.

Maps for special purposes

Maps can show the location of many different kinds of things. For instance, a map can show what minerals are found in certain places, or what crops are grown. A small chart that lists the symbols and their meanings is usually included on a map. This is called the key.

Symbols on some geography maps stand for the amounts of things in different places. For instance, map J, at left, gives information about the number of people in the southwestern part of the United States. The key tells the meaning of the symbols. In this case the symbols are dots and circles.

On different maps, the same symbol may stand for different things and amounts.

14

Each dot on map J stands for 10,000 persons. On other maps, a dot might represent 5,000 sheep or 1,000 bushels of wheat.

There are other ways of giving information about quantity. Different designs or patterns may be used on a rainfall map to show the areas that receive different amounts of rain each year.

Relief Maps
The roughness of the earth's surface

From a plane, you can see that the earth's surface is rough. You can see mountains and valleys, hills and plains. For some uses, globes and maps that show these things are needed. They are called relief globes and maps.

Since globes are three-dimensional* copies of the earth, you may wonder why most globes do not show the roughness of the earth's surface. The reason for this is that the highest mountain on the earth is not very large when it is compared with the earth's diameter. Even a very large globe would be smooth nearly everywhere.

In order to make a relief globe or map, you must use a different scale for the height of the land. You might start with a large flat map. One inch on your flat map may stand for a distance of 100 miles (161 kilometers) on the earth. Now you are going to make a small copy of a mountain on your map. On the earth, this mountain is two miles (3.2 kilometers) high. If you let one inch stand for this height on the earth, your mountain should rise one inch above the flat surface of your map. Other mountains and hills should be copied on this same scale.

By photographing relief globes and maps, flat maps can be made that show the earth much as it looks from an airplane. Map K, at right above, is a photograph of a relief map. Map L is a photograph of a relief globe.

Topographic maps

Another kind of map that shows the roughness of the earth's surface is called a topographic, or contour, map. On this kind of map, lines are drawn to show different heights of the earth's surface. These are

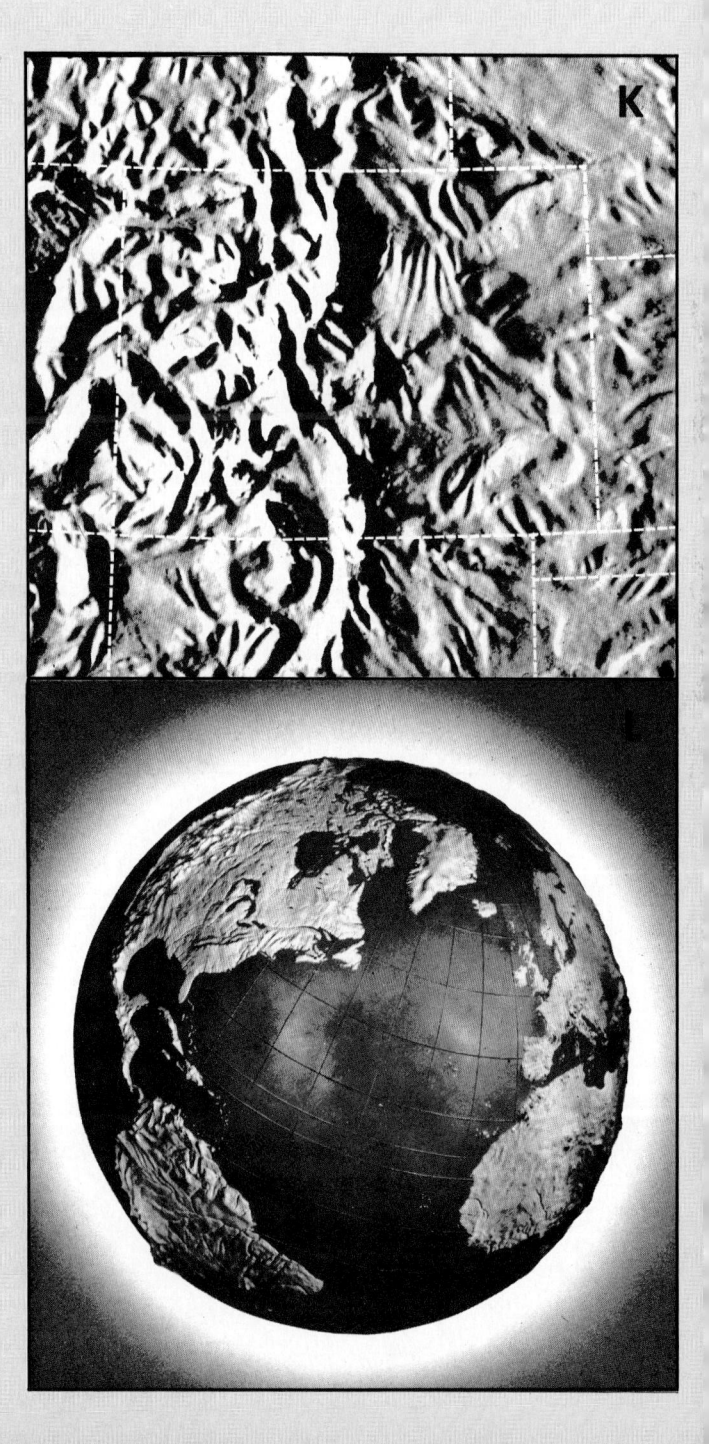

15

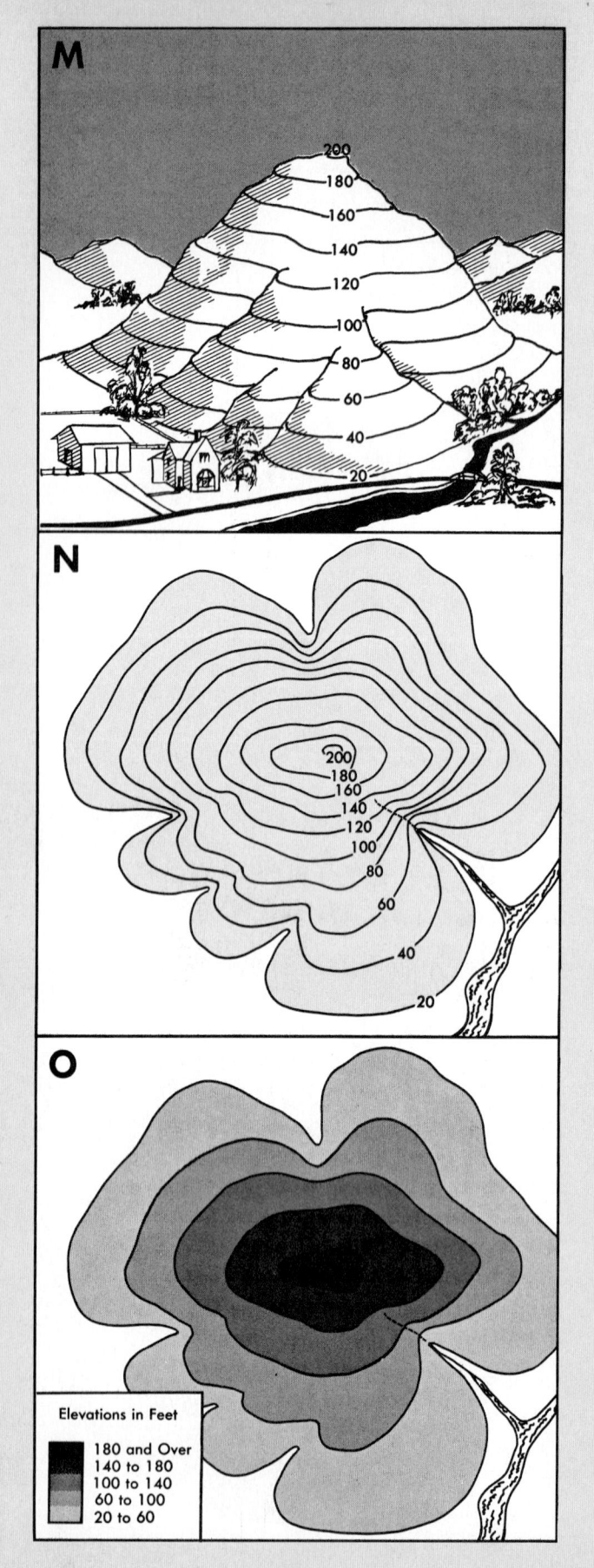

called contour lines. The maps on this page help to explain how topographic maps are made.

Map M is a drawing of a hill. Around the bottom of the hill is our first contour line. This line connects all the points at the base of the hill that are exactly twenty feet above sea level. Higher up the hill, another contour line is drawn. It connects all the points that are exactly forty feet above sea level. A line is also drawn at a height of sixty feet. Other lines are drawn every twenty feet until the top of the hill is reached. Since the hill is shaped somewhat like a cone, each contour line is shorter than the one just below it.

Map N shows how the contour lines in the drawing of the hill M can be used to make a topographic map. This map gives us a great deal of information about the hill. Since each line is labeled with the height it stands for, you can tell how high the different parts of the hill are. It is important to remember that land does not really rise in layers, as you might think when you look at a topographic map. Wherever the contour lines are far apart, you can be sure that the land slopes gently. Where they are close together, the slope is steep. With practice, you can picture the land in your mind as you look at such a map. Topographic maps are especially useful to people who design such things as roads and buildings.

On a topographic map, the spaces between the contour lines may be filled in with different shades of a color. If a different shade of brown were used for each different height of land shown in map N, there would be ten shades. It would be very hard for you to tell these different shades of brown apart. Therefore, on map O, at left, black and four shades of brown were used to show differences in height of forty feet. The key shows the height of the land represented by the different shades. On some topographic maps, different colors are used to stand for different heights.

16

Needs of People

All people on earth must meet certain needs in order to be healthy and happy. Scientists who study human beings tell us that these basic needs are the same for everyone. It does not matter if you are rich or poor . . . tall or short . . . fat or thin . . . dark-skinned or light-skinned. You have the same basic needs as everyone else.

There are three kinds of basic needs. These are: physical needs, social needs, and the need for faith.

Physical Needs

Some basic needs are so important that people will die or become seriously ill if they fail to meet them. These are called physical needs. They include the need for each of the following:
1. air
2. water
3. food
4. protection from heat and cold
5. sleep and rest
6. exercise

Although all people share these needs, they do not all meet them in the same way. How do you meet your physical needs?

Social Needs

People also have social needs. They must meet these needs in order to have a happy and useful life. Social needs include:

An outdoor concert in Louisville, Kentucky. All people on earth have certain basic needs. Some of these are called social needs. For example, feeling that you belong to a group is a social need. Do you think the members of this orchestra have a feeling of belonging to a group? Why do you think this? What are some other basic needs that all people share?

1. Belonging to a group. All people need to feel they belong to a group of people who respect them and whom they respect. Belonging to a family is one of the main ways people meet this need. What can the members of a family do to show that they love and respect each other? How do the members of your family help one another?

Having friends also helps people meet their need for belonging to a group. What groups of friends do you have? Why are these people your friends? Do you suppose young people in other countries enjoy doing the same kinds of things with their friends as you enjoy doing with your friends? Why? Why not?

2. Goals. To be happy, every person needs goals to work for. What goals do you have? How can working toward these goals help you have a happy life? What kinds of goals do you think other young people in our country have?

3. A chance to think and learn. All people need a chance to develop and use their abilities. They need opportunities to find out about things that make them curious. What would you like to learn? How can you learn these things? How can developing your abilities help you have a happy life?

4. A feeling of accomplishment. You share with every other person the need for a feeling of accomplishment. All people need to feel that their lives are successful in some way. What gives you a feeling of accomplishment? Can you imagine what life would be like if you never had this feeling?

The Need for Faith

In addition to physical and social needs, all people also have a need for faith. You need to believe that life is precious and that the future is something to look forward to. You may have different kinds of faith, including the following:

1. Faith in yourself. In order to feel secure, you must have faith in your own abilities. You must feel that you will be able to do some useful work in the world and that you will be generally happy. You must believe that you can work toward solving whatever problems life brings to you. How do you think you can build faith in yourself?

2. Faith in other people. You also need to feel that you can count on other people to do their part and to help you when you need help. What people do you have faith in? What do you think life would be like without this kind of faith?

3. Faith in nature's laws. Another kind of faith that helps people face the future with confidence is faith in nature's laws. The more we learn about our universe, the more certain we feel that we can depend on nature. How would you feel if you couldn't have faith in nature's laws?

4. Religious faith. Throughout history, almost all human beings have had some kind of religious faith. Religion can help people understand themselves and the world they live in. It can bring them joy, and it can give them confidence in times of trouble. Religion can also help people live together happily. For example, most religions teach people to be honest and to love and help their neighbors.

Meeting Needs in Communities

No person can meet his or her needs alone. Only by living and working with others can a person have a happy, satisfying life. For this reason, people everywhere on earth have always lived in communities.

Over the years, people have followed certain ideas or ways of living that help them to live together in communities. We call these the "great ideas." In other parts of this book, you can discover how the great ideas have helped people in the United States to meet their basic needs.

Great Ideas That Built Our Nation

People have been living in America for thousands of years. During this time, they have always met their needs in communities. No one can meet his or her needs all alone. Only by living and working with other people can a person have a happy, satisfying life.

In order to make community life successful, people have developed certain ways of living. We call these the "great ideas." Let us examine ten great ideas that have been important in our country's history.

cooperation	using tools
loyalty	division of labor
freedom	exchange
rules and government	language
using natural resources	education

What great ideas do you think are illustrated by the pictures on this page?
1. Cutting timber in a western forest.
2. The city of Los Angeles, California.
3. A factory worker in Rhode Island.

Exploring the moon. The astronaut is driving a lunar roving vehicle on the moon. At left is the lunar module that brought him to the moon from a spacecraft circling high overhead.

Cooperation

A Great Idea

Working together is called cooperation. This is one of the great ideas that helped build our nation. For example, the early settlers in America needed to cooperate. They worked together to provide the food they needed. In what other ways do you think the early settlers cooperated with one another?

How is cooperation important to communities today? What are some important jobs that require cooperation? What are some other examples of cooperation in the community where you live? Do you think our country could have sent astronauts to the moon if people had not worked together on the space program? Explain.

Loyalty
A Great Idea

People discovered long ago that in order to live together successfully in a community, they had to be loyal to each other. People were willing to do unpleasant or difficult tasks simply because they felt a strong sense of loyalty to their community. Members of families had to be loyal to each other in order to have a happy family life.

In every truly successful community on the earth today, people are usually loyal to each other. They are loyal to their community, their country, and their leaders. Do you think the astronaut shown on page 20 is loyal to our country? What are some things you can do to show that you are loyal to our country? Do you think that the leaders of a community should be loyal to the people? Why do you think this?

The people in successful communities are also loyal to their ideas and beliefs. Most people in our country, for example, are loyal to the principles of democracy, and to the ideas of freedom, justice, and equality. In addition, they are loyal to their religious faith.

Boy scouts looking at a statue of Abraham Lincoln. Lincoln was president of our country during the Civil War.* Why do you think Lincoln is honored today? Is it partly because of his loyalty to certain principles, such as the idea of freedom for all people? Explain your answer.

Do you think boy scouts need to be loyal to certain persons and ideas? Is loyalty important to organizations such as the Boy Scouts of America? Why? Why not?

*See Glossary

Freedom
A Great Idea

The idea of freedom has been important to Americans since the early days of our country's history. Many of the settlers who came to America from Europe during the 1600's and 1700's were seeking more freedom than they had in their homelands.

By the middle of the 1700's, there were thirteen British colonies along the Atlantic coast of North America. During the 1760's and early 1770's, Britain began to take away some of the freedoms the colonists had enjoyed. On July 4, 1776, representatives of the thirteen colonies approved the Declaration of Independence. In this famous document, the colonists declared

Minutemen fighting British troops at Concord, Massachusetts. Minutemen were American colonists who fought to gain freedom from British rule during the Revolutionary War. They were called minutemen because they could be ready for battle in only a few minutes. Why did the colonists want to be free from British rule? You may wish to do research to discover answers to this question.

The White House, the home of our country's president. In the United States, all citizens are free to take part in electing the president and other government leaders.

their freedom from British rule. They set up a new nation called the United States of America.

At the time our country was founded, there were many people here who did not enjoy all the same rights and freedoms as other Americans. For example, most black people lived in slavery. They were forced to work all their lives for white masters. The Civil War* finally led to the ending of slavery throughout the United States.

For a long time after the founding of our country the freedom of women was limited in certain ways. For instance, women could not vote in elections or testify as witnesses in a court of law. A married woman had no right to any property of her own. Any wages that she earned became the property of her husband.

Gradually women began to gain more rights and freedoms. One state after another passed laws giving married women the right to own property. The Nineteenth Amendment to the Constitution, which became law in 1920, guaranteed to women throughout the United States the right to vote.

Today most Americans enjoy a large amount of freedom. For example, they are free to live where they please and to work at jobs of their own choosing. They can express their ideas freely without fear of punishment. They are also free to worship God in their own way, or not to worship at all if they so desire.

Are there any people in the United States today who do not enjoy as much freedom as other Americans? Who are they? What is being done to help these people gain more freedom?

Rules and Government
A Great Idea

People in every community need to follow rules in order to live together successfully. Why is this true? What kinds of rules do people in your own community follow? How do these rules make life safer and more pleasant for everyone? What would it be like to live in a community that had no rules?

In every community, there must be a person or a group of persons to make the rules and see that they are carried out. In other words, all communities need some form of government. Who makes the rules in your local community? Who enforces the rules that these people make?

Although every successful community has some form of government, not all governments are alike. The United States is a democracy. This means that its citizens have a share in governing themselves. Do you think it is important for people to take part in their own government? Why do you think this?

A committee meeting in California. These men and women are all members of the California legislature, which makes the laws for that state. Do you think laws are necessary? Why? Why not?

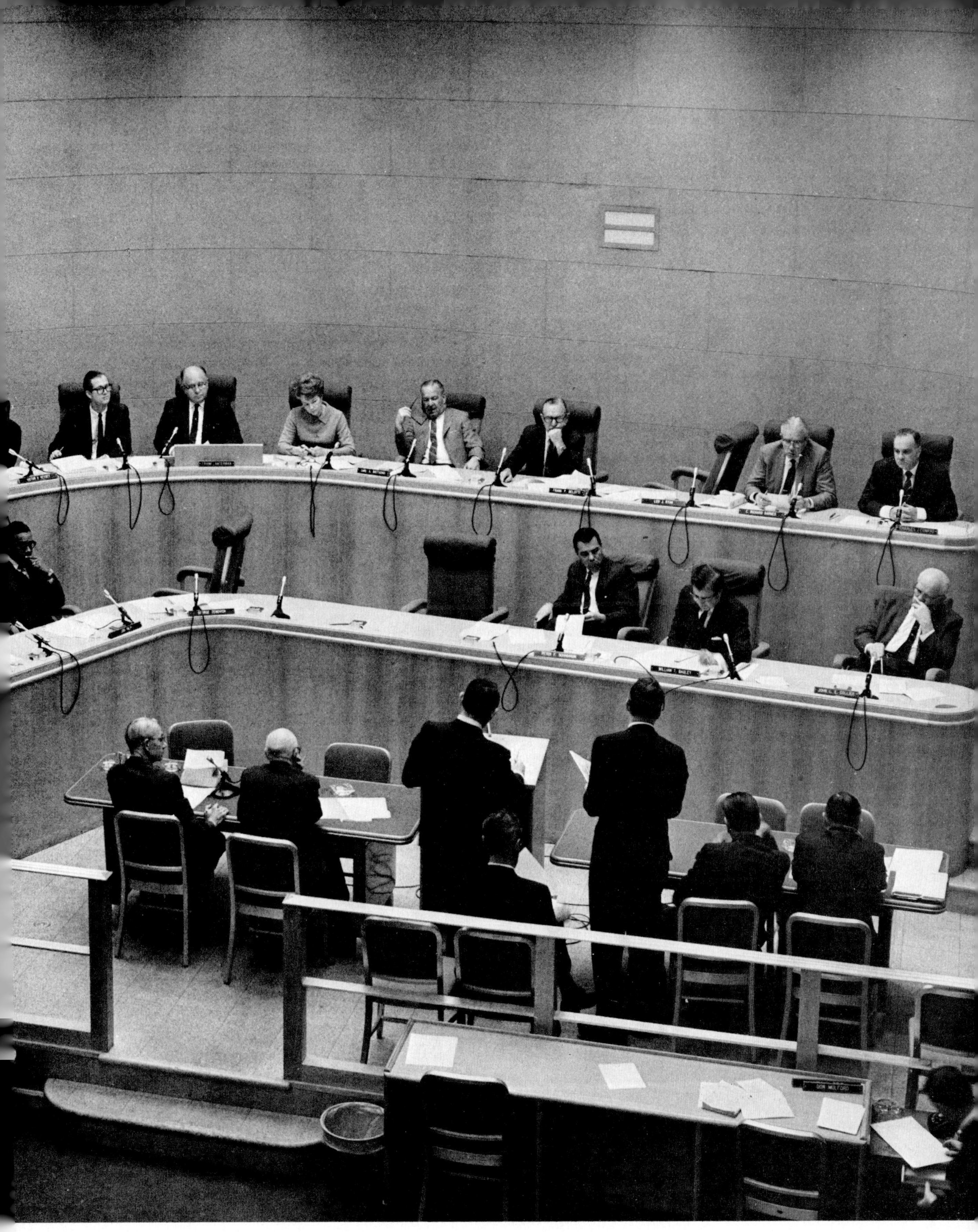

Pouring melted steel into molds in a Pennsylvania steel plant. Many important products are made from steel. Do research to discover what mineral resources are used in making steel.

Using Natural Resources
A Great Idea

The picture above shows a farmer growing crops in an irrigated* field in the West. In growing crops, farmers use certain natural resources. By "natural resources" we mean any gifts of nature that people use to meet their needs. Some important natural resources are listed below. Which of these do you think farmers use?

air	water	wild animals
soil	sunshine	wild plants
	minerals	

Over the years, people in various parts of the world learned how to make greater use of the earth's resources. The world's first farmers began to use soil, sunshine, and rain to grow crops. They also began to raise animals for food. Later, people began to use different metals for making tools and weapons.

Today, we use hundreds of natural resources in meeting our needs. Stone and trees are just as important to us as they were to earlier people. We use these materials both in building and manufacturing. Farmers today use sunshine, soil, and water, just as early people did. Minerals such as coal and iron ore are among our most valuable resources. What are some natural resources that are used by people in your community?

A lumber mill in Florida. Lumber is one of the many valuable products we get from forests.

People have always depended on the earth's resources to help them in meeting their needs for food, clothing, and shelter. Early people hunted wild animals for food and for skins to make clothing. They added to the food supply by gathering the fruits, seeds, and roots of wild plants. These early people lived in caves or built shelters from tree branches, mud, or animal skins. They used wood, stones, bones, and shells to make tools and weapons. Compared to people who lived later, however, the people of early times made very little use of the natural resources in the world around them.

Using Tools
A Great Idea

A tool is anything that people use to help them do work. Some tools, such as hammers and shovels, are very simple. Other tools are large or complicated. Tools that have a number of moving parts are called machines. What kinds of tools do you have in your home? How do these tools help the members of your family to meet their needs?

The early settlers who came to our country brought with them several important kinds of tools. Among these were guns and axes. With their rifles, the settlers killed wild animals to get meat for food and skins for making clothing. They also used guns

A huge scoop used for mining phosphate* rock. This scoop is pulled across the phosphate rock deposit to gather up large amounts of the mineral. Then a giant crane lifts the filled scoop and empties it into a bin. Do you think it would be possible to produce large amounts of minerals without the use of tools such as these? Explain.

Cutting down trees in colonial days. The early settlers in America used axes to clear the land so they could grow crops. They used the logs for building cabins.

to protect themselves from unfriendly Indians. With their axes, they chopped down trees in the forests so they could use the cleared land for growing crops. Axes were also used to cut logs for building cabins.

Today people in our country use many kinds of modern machines to produce the goods they need. Many of these machines are very complicated and are run by electricity. Do you think that people who use modern machines can have more goods to enjoy than people who use only a few simple tools? Why do you think this?

A worker in a textile factory in Hawaii. In a factory, the work is divided among people who do different jobs. This is known as division of labor.

Division of Labor

A Great Idea

In every community, not all the people do exactly the same kind of work. Instead, they work at different jobs. For example, some people earn their living by farming. Others work in factories or offices. Dividing up the work of a community among people who do different jobs is known as division of labor. By using division of labor, people are able to obtain more goods and services than they could if they tried to meet all of their needs by themselves. Why do you suppose this is so?

Division of labor also makes it possible for each person to work at the job he or she can do best. For example, this textile worker (see picture above) is very skillful at his job. He also enjoys it very much. He probably would not like to do some other kind of work that did not require the skills he has learned. On the other hand, the people who produce the food, appliances, and other things he buys might not enjoy the kind of work he does.

Division of labor also helps people produce many useful things that one person working alone could not produce. Do you think it would ever be possible for one person to make and use all of the many tools needed to manufacture such things as automobiles and refrigerators?

This photographer is preparing to take a picture of some handbags for a magazine advertisement.

The people shown below are members of a hospital operating team. Like the photographer, they provide a service instead of helping to make a product. Other people who perform services are teachers, lawyers, telephone operators, and police officers.

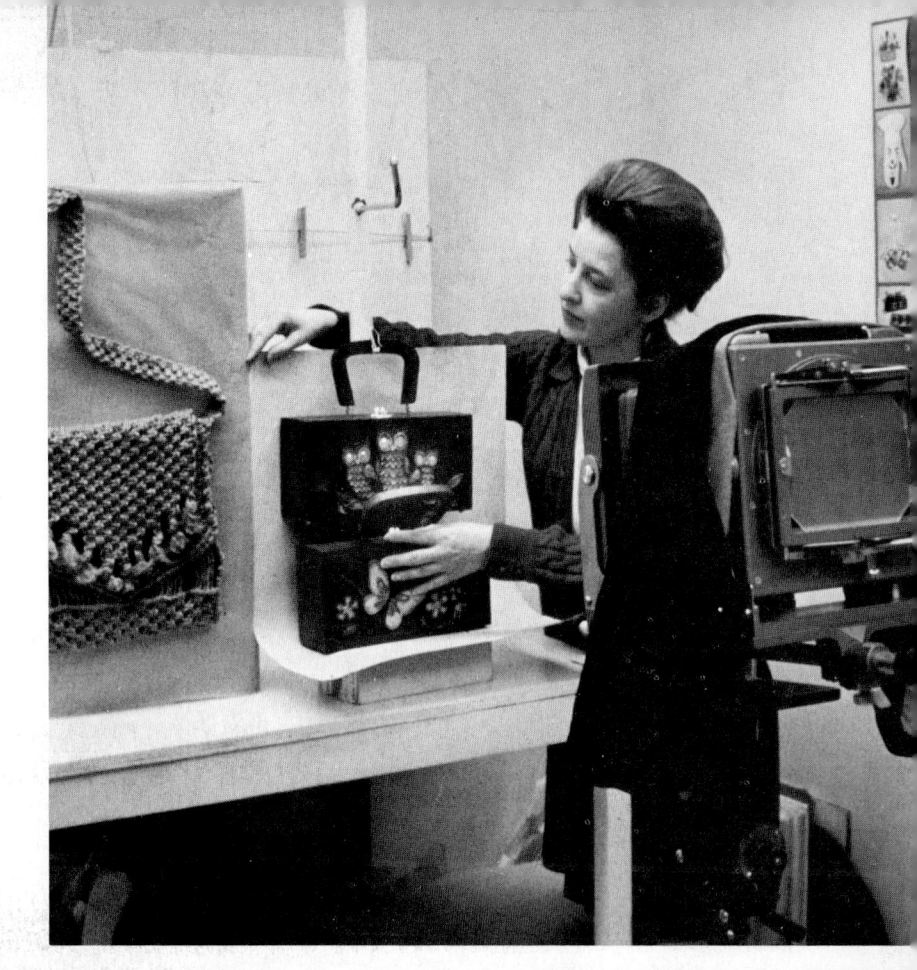

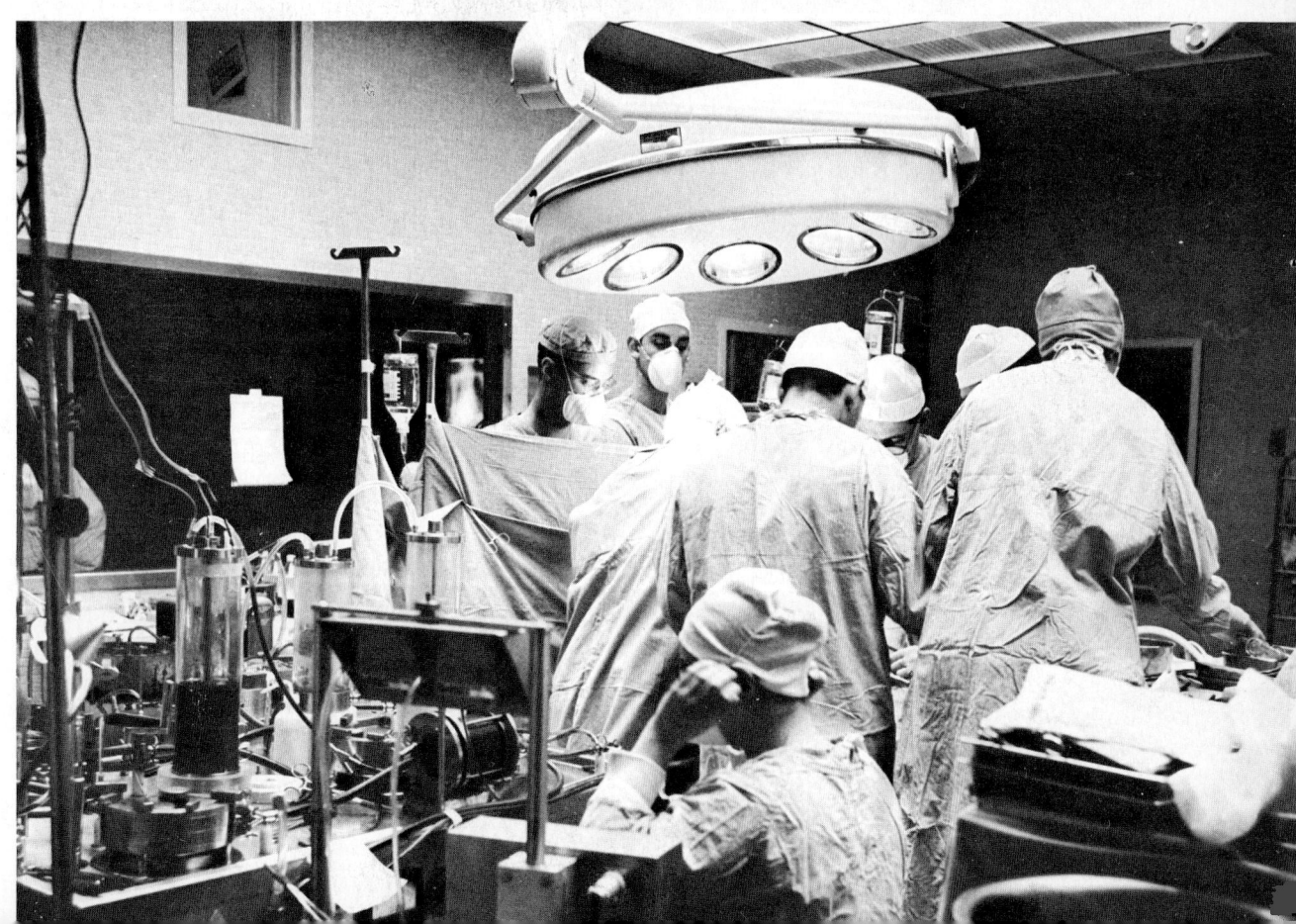

Shopping for food. What will this woman give the store in exchange for the things she needs? Do you think it would be possible for her to get these things without using the idea of exchange?

Exchange
A Great Idea

When people use division of labor, they need to exchange goods and services with each other. In this way, they can get goods and services they do not produce themselves. What would it be like to live in a community where people did not use the great idea of exchange? Explain.

In early times, people often traded goods and services directly with each other. Today most people work at jobs where they earn money. They use this money to buy the goods and services they need. Do you think money makes it easier to carry on exchange? Give reasons for your answer.

Language
A Great Idea

Throughout history, people have felt the need to communicate with each other. In order to work together, people need to share their ideas and feelings. Early people communicated in several ways. For example, they smiled, frowned, made gestures with their hands, and drew pictures. Their most important way of communicating, however, was by speaking. Scientists who have studied the beginnings of language believe that all human beings—even those who lived in earliest times—have had some form of spoken language.

Human beings did not develop written language until about five thousand years ago. Writing made it possible for people to store information so that it could be used at a later time. Writing also enabled people to communicate over long distances. Today, almost every language in the world can be written as well as spoken.

Every day, you use language to communicate with others. You talk with your family and your friends. On school days, you talk with your teachers and the other members of your class. You write notes and letters. You write out much of your schoolwork. Do you think it is important to use spoken language in such a way as to communicate clearly with other people? Why do you think this? Do you think it is important to be able to put your thoughts and feelings into writing? Explain.

People in New York City's Chinatown. What does this picture tell you about language in our country?

Education
A Great Idea

In every community, the older people pass on their ideas and skills to the younger people. This is one kind of education. Do you think it would be possible to have a successful community without education? Why? Why not?

In early times, parents taught their children most of the things they needed to know. Today, most American children get a large part of their education in school. Do you think education is important for every person? Why do you think as you do?

High school students in a science class. In most parts of the world, young people receive much of their education in school. Do you think education is important for everyone? Why? Why not?

Word List
(Glossary)

Complete Pronunciation Key

The pronunciation of the word is shown just after the word, in this way: **Iroquois** (ir′ ə kwoi). The letters and signs used are pronounced as in the words below. The mark ′ is placed after a syllable with a primary or strong accent, as in the example above. The mark ′ after a syllable shows a secondary or lighter accent, as in **electronic** (i lek′ tron′ ik).

a	hat, cap	j	jam, enjoy	u	cup, butter
ā	age, face	k	kind, seek	u̇	full, put
ã	care, air	l	land, coal	ü	rule, move
ä	father, far	m	me, am	ū	use, music
b	bad, rob	n	no, in		
ch	child, much	ng	long, bring	v	very, save
d	did, red	o	hot, rock	w	will, woman
		ō	open, go	y	young, yet
e	let, best	ô	order, all	z	zero, breeze
ē	equal, see	oi	oil, voice	zh	measure, seizure
ėr	term, learn	ou	house, out		
		p	paper, cup		
f	fat, if	r	run, try	ə	represents:
g	go, bag	s	say, yes	a	in about
h	he, how	sh	she, rush	e	in taken
		t	tell, it	i	in pencil
i	it, pin	th	thin, both	o	in lemon
ī	ice, five	TH	then, smooth	u	in circus

abstract. Refers to a painting or a sculpture that does not look like a person or an object. Instead, the work of art represents the artist's ideas or feelings about a subject.

Aleutian (ə lü′ shən) **Islands.** A long chain of islands that are part of Alaska. The Aleutians extend southwestward into the Pacific Ocean.

Aleuts (al′ ē üts). A group of people who live on the Aleutian Islands and in other parts of Alaska. Their language and customs are similar to those of the Eskimos. Many Aleuts earn their living by fishing, raising sheep, or hunting fur seals. See **Aleutian Islands.**

alewife. A fish of the herring family. It is found along the Atlantic coast and in the Great Lakes. Alewives are sometimes used for food. They are also made into products such as oil and fertilizer.

alfalfa. A plant with cloverlike leaves. Hay made from alfalfa is used as food for farm animals.

altitude. Height above the level of the sea. For example, a mountain that rises 10,000 feet (3,050 meters) above sea level has an altitude of 10,000 feet.

ammonia (ə mōn′ yə). A colorless gas with a sharp smell. The ammonia used for cleaning around the house is really ammonia dissolved in water. Ammonia is an important chemical used in industry. It is used in making products such as fertilizers and explosives.

ancestors. People from whom one is descended. They include your grandparents, great-grandparents, and others farther back in your family.

anchovy (an′ chō vē). A very small fish, used mainly in sauces and relishes.

35

annex. To make one territory part of another.

Appalachian (ap/ə lā/chən) **Plateau.** The westernmost section of the Appalachian Highlands region. See **plateau**.

aqueduct (ak/ wə dukt). A canal, tunnel, or large pipe for carrying water. An aqueduct usually carries the water from a river or a lake to the place where it is to be used.

Arab. Refers to a group of people who live mainly in northern Africa and Southwest Asia. Arabs speak the Arabic language. Most of them follow the religion of Islam. See **Islam**.

architecture. The art of designing buildings.

astronaut. A pilot or a crew member of a spacecraft.

atomic energy. Energy that is stored in atoms. See **atoms**.

atoms. Pieces of matter too small to be seen except with a special microscope. When atoms are split or combined in certain ways, great amounts of energy are released. This energy can be used for many purposes, including the production of electricity.

automation. The use of machinery that needs only a few, if any, people to run it.

bale. A large bundle of material that is squeezed together and tied with rope, wire, or straps.

basic chemicals. Common chemicals that are produced in large amounts for use in industry. Ammonia and certain strong acids are examples of basic chemicals. See **chemicals**.

basin. An area of land that is largely surrounded by higher land. Also, the total area of land that is drained by a river and its branches.

bauxite (bôk/ sīt). An ore that is the chief source of aluminum. See **ore**.

bearings. Objects such as metal balls and rollers that enable one part of a machine or a mechanical device to slide smoothly over or around another part. Ball bearings are used in roller-skate wheels, for example.

bill. A suggested law to be voted on by a legislature. See **legislature**.

bituminous (bə tü/ mə nəs) **coal.** Another name for high-grade soft coal. This is the most plentiful and important type of coal.

blackout. A period of time during which electricity is cut off from an area.

blast furnace. A furnace in which iron is made from iron ore. It is called a blast furnace because a strong blast of air is blown into the bottom of the furnace.

bluegrass. Any one of about 200 kinds of grass with bluish green stems and blue flowers. The best known is Kentucky bluegrass, a useful lawn and pasture grass.

boll (bōl). The seed pod of a plant such as cotton. The white fibers found in cotton bolls are used to make cotton cloth.

borates. A group of certain chemicals that are somewhat like salt. Several borates are found in nature as minerals. A common borate is called borax. It is used for softening water and for cleaning. See **chemicals**.

breakwater. A wall built in the water to protect a harbor or a beach from waves. Breakwaters are usually built of stone and concrete.

British Parliament. See **parliament**.

Buddhism (bud/ iz əm). A religion founded in India about 2,500 years ago. It teaches that selfishness is the cause of all sorrow, and that brotherly love among all people is the way to happiness.

butte (būt). A flat-topped hill that rises steeply from the land around it. A butte is somewhat like a mesa, but smaller. See **mesa**.

cancer. A serious disease marked by a harmful growth or growths in the body.

Cancer, Tropic of. See **Tropic of Cancer**.

candidate. A person who seeks a job or an office, such as president. Each candidate in an election hopes to get the most votes.

canyon. A valley with high, steep sides.

capital. A city that serves as the center of government for a country or a state. In economics, "capital" refers to wealth that is used to produce more wealth. Money, factory buildings, and machines are important forms of capital.

capitol. A building in which lawmakers meet. When spelled with a capital "C," this word means the building in Washington, D.C., where the United States Congress meets. See **United States Congress**.

Capricorn, Tropic of. See **Tropic of Capricorn**.

carbon. A common substance found in nature in many different forms. A diamond is pure carbon. So is graphite, the black writing material in your pencil. Anthracite, a high-quality coal, is almost entirely carbon. Carbon is found in all living things, in many kinds of rock, and in petroleum.

cash crops. Crops that farmers raise to be sold, rather than to be used by themselves and their families.

Celsius (sel′sē əs). Refers to a scale for measuring temperature. On the Celsius scale, which is part of the metric system, 0° represents the freezing point of water and 100° represents the boiling point. To change degrees Celsius to degrees on the Fahrenheit scale, multiply by 1.8 and add 32. See **metric system** and **Fahrenheit**.

centimeter (sen′tə mē′tər). A unit in the metric system for measuring length. It is equal to about .39 inch. See **metric system**.

cession. The giving up of territory by one country to another.

chemicals. Substances that are made when two or more substances act upon one another. Examples are salt, soda, ammonia, and aspirin.

chemist. A person who studies, tests, or makes chemicals. A chemist usually works in a laboratory. See **chemicals**.

cholera. A disease caused by polluted food or water. Early settlers who traveled west often had to use whatever food or water they could find. Many became sick or died.

Christianity. A religion that is followed by more people than any other religion in the world. It is based on the teachings of Jesus Christ, who lived nearly two thousand years ago. There are three main branches of Christianity. These are the Roman Catholic Church, the Eastern Orthodox churches, and the Protestant churches.

circumference (sər kum′ fər əns). The distance around something, such as a circle or a ball.

citrus fruit. Any of several kinds of fruit. Oranges, grapefruit, lemons, and limes are some of the common citrus fruits.

civil rights. The rights and freedoms that belong to a person as a member of a community, a state, or a country. There are many different civil rights. Among them are the right to speak freely and to attend the church of one's choice. Others are the right to own property, the right to a fair trial, and the right to get a job or a place to live without discrimination. (See **discrimination**.) Sometimes the right to vote is also thought of as a civil right.

Civil War, 1861-1865. A war between the northern and southern parts of our country. The northern states were called the Union. The southern states were called the Confederacy. The Union won the Civil War.

climate. The average weather conditions of a given place over a period of many years.

coke. A fuel made by roasting coal in special ovens from which the air has been shut out.

coking coal. Coal that is good for making coke. See **coke**.

colonial. Refers to a certain period of time in the history of the United States. The colonial period began when the first European colonies were started in America. It lasted until the thirteen British colonies became the United States.

colony. A settlement outside the country that controls it. In American history, usually means any one of thirteen colonies along the Atlantic coast. These colonies were started by people from England in the 1600's and 1700's. Later, the thirteen colonies became the United States.

commercial (kə mėr′ shəl). Having to do with business or trade.

communicate. To share ideas and feelings with other people. Speaking and writing are two of the most important ways of communicating.

communication. Sharing ideas and feelings with other people. Speaking is the main way in which we communicate with people who are near enough to hear us. Writing helps us communicate with people who are not close by. Other means of communicating over a distance include such things as the telegraph, radio, and television.

Communist. Refers to certain countries in which the government controls industry, farming, trade, education, and most other activities. The word Communist also refers to political parties and to people who favor such a system of government control.

compass rose. A small drawing put on a map to show directions. Here are three examples of compass roses:

PRONUNCIATION KEY: hat, āge, cãre, fär; let, ēqual, tėrm; it, īce; hot, ōpen, ôrder; oil, out; cup, pu̇t, rüle, ūse; child; long; thin; ᴛʜen; zh, measure; ə represents a in about, e in taken, i in pencil, o in lemon, u in circus. For the complete key, see page 35.

complicated. Made up of a number of different parts.

composer. A person who writes music.

computer. A machine that stores information and uses this information to solve difficult problems.

concrete. A hard, strong material that is used for such things as buildings and roads. Concrete is made by mixing cement, sand, gravel, and water. This mixture becomes hard as it dries.

conservation. Saving or protecting something so it will not be wasted. For example, forests and soil need to be conserved.

conserve. To protect or keep safe.

constitution. A set of rules telling how a country or a state is supposed to be governed. When this word is written with a capital "C," it usually means the Constitution of the United States. Our Constitution was adopted in 1788. It has been in use ever since.

conterminous (kən tèr′mə nəs) **United States.** The forty-eight states of the United States that are enclosed by an unbroken boundary. The word conterminous means "having the same boundary."

continent. One of the six largest land areas on the earth. These are Eurasia, Africa, North America, South America, Australia, and Antarctica. Some people think of Eurasia as two continents—Europe and Asia.

Continental Congress. A meeting of leaders from the colonies in America that later joined together to form the United States. There were two Continental Congresses. The First Continental Congress met in 1774 to discuss the quarrel between the colonies and Great Britain. The Second Continental Congress met in 1775, soon after the Revolutionary War began. On July 4, 1776, it approved the Declaration of Independence. For several years after this, the Second Continental Congress served as the government of the United States.

conveyor belt. A moving belt, usually made of canvas, rubber, or metal, that carries things from one place to another.

cowhand. A person who takes care of cattle.

crop rotation. A way of farming in which different crops are raised on the same land in different years.

crude oil. Petroleum as it comes from the ground.

cultivate. To break up the soil around the roots of growing plants, mainly for the purpose of killing weeds. Also, to prepare and use land for growing crops.

Declaration of Independence. A public statement made by leaders of the American colonies on July 4, 1776. This statement said that the colonies were independent, or free, of Great Britain.

Delmarva Peninsula. A peninsula along the Atlantic coast of the United States. It is about 180 miles (290 kilometers) long and 70 miles (113 kilometers) across at its widest part. Most of the state of Delaware and parts of Maryland and Virginia lie on this peninsula.

democracy. A country in which people govern themselves. The people choose their leaders and make decisions by majority vote. See **majority.**

density of population. The average number of people per square mile, square kilometer, or some other unit of area, in a given place. Density of population may be found by dividing the total number of people in an area by the number of square miles or other units of the area.

depressed area. An area where many of the people are unable to find jobs.

descent. Birth or ancestry. For example, we might say that a certain person born in the United States is of French descent. This means that some or all of that person's ancestors were born in France.

diameter (dī am′ə tər). A straight line that joins opposite sides and passes through the center of something, such as a circle or a ball. Also, the length of such a straight line.

diesel (dē′ zəl) **engine.** A kind of engine often used in trucks and trains. Instead of gasoline, it burns a petroleum product called diesel oil.

discrimination. Keeping rights and freedoms from people because they belong to certain groups. Usually, people are discriminated against because they belong to minority groups. (See **minority group.**) Although women are not a minority group, they have also suffered from discrimination.

District of Columbia. A piece of land set apart as the home of the federal government of the United States. The District of Columbia lies in the eastern part of our country, between Maryland and Virginia. It is not part of any state. Washington, our national capital city, covers the entire area of the District of Columbia.

drift mine. A type of mine in which a tunnel is dug into the side of a hill.

drought (drout). A long period of dry weather.

dry farming. A way of farming used in areas where there is little water. Dry farmers in these areas raise crops that need little moisture. They leave part of their land idle, or fallow, each year. This lets the soil store up moisture.

Dutch. People from the Netherlands. (See **Netherlands.**) Also, the language spoken by these people.

Eastern Orthodox (ôr′ thə doks). Refers to one of the three main branches of Christianity. (See **Christianity.**) Most of the churches that belong to this branch are in western Asia and eastern Europe. Eastern Orthodox also refers to the members of these churches.

ecology (ē kol′ ə jē). Refers to the relationships living things (plants, animals, and human beings) have to each other and to their environment. Also, the study of these relationships. See **environment.**

electric power. Electricity.

electric power plant. A plant that uses machines called generators to produce electricity. The generators are run by other machines called turbines, which are usually powered by steam. Turbines may also be powered by the force of falling water.

electron. The smallest possible amount of electricity.

electronic (i lek′tron′ik). Refers to certain kinds of electrical devices, such as vacuum tubes and transistors. Also refers to products that use such devices. Radios, television sets, and computers are examples of electronic products.

electron microscope. A microscope is a special tool used by scientists for making very tiny things look larger. An electron microscope is different from a regular microscope in that it uses a beam of electrons instead of light to show the shape of an object. See **electron.**

energy. Power, or force, that can be used to do work. In earliest times, people used only their own muscles to do work. Since then, they have learned to use many other sources of energy. Some of these are wind, flowing water, and fuels such as coal, oil, and natural gas.

engineer. A person who plans or builds such things as machinery, bridges, and roads.

engineering. The kind of work that engineers do. See **engineer.**

environment (en vī′ rən mənt). Everything that surrounds living things and influences their growth and development. The environment of a person includes such things as air, sunlight, water, land, plants, animals, and other people.

equator (i kwā′ tər). An imaginary line around the earth, dividing it into a northern half and a southern half.

equinox (ē′ kwə noks). Either of two times of the year when the sun shines directly on the equator. They take place about March 21 and September 22. At these two times, day and night are each twelve hours long everywhere on the earth.

Erie Canal. A canal in New York State. It connected the Hudson River, near the city of Albany, with the port city of Buffalo, on Lake Erie. It was finished in 1825. In the early 1900's, the Erie Canal became part of a larger system of canals called the New York State Barge Canal.

erosion. The wearing away of the earth's surface by the forces of nature. These forces include falling rain, running water, ice, wind, and waves. Erosion may be helpful to people, as when soil is formed from rock. Or it may be harmful, as when rich soil is washed away.

Eskimos. Certain people who live in the far northern parts of North America and eastern Asia. The Eskimos in Alaska include two groups. These are the Inuit and the Yupiit. Many Eskimos earn their living by hunting and fishing. Others have jobs in factories and offices.

essay. A piece of writing that usually tells what the writer thinks about a subject.

etcher. An artist who uses acid to make a design or a picture on a metal plate. The plate is then inked and used to print copies of the design or picture.

Eurasia (yu̇ rā′ zhə). The largest continent on the earth. It is sometimes thought of as two separate continents—Europe and Asia. See **continent.**

evaporate (i vap′ ə rāt). To change from a liquid to a gas or vapor. For example, when the water on a wet sidewalk disappears, it is said to evaporate. The water changes into a gas called water vapor, which mixes with the air.

explosives. Substances that can be exploded. For example, the gunpowder used in firecrackers is an explosive.

PRONUNCIATION KEY: hat, āge, cãre, fär; let, ēqual, tėrm; it, īce; hot, ōpen, ôrder; oil, out; cup, pu̇t, rüle, ūse; child; long; thin; ₮Hen; zh, measure; ə represents a in about, e in taken, i in pencil, o in lemon, u in circus. For the complete key, see page 35.

export (ek spôrt′). To send goods from one country or region to another, especially for the purpose of selling them. These goods are called exports (eks′pôrts).

fallow. Farmland on which no crop is being grown is said to be fallow.

Fahrenheit (far′ ən hīt). Refers to a scale for measuring temperature in which the freezing point of water is represented by 32° and the boiling point by 212°. See **Celsius**.

federal. A system of government in which the constitution gives great powers to the central government to govern the country, yet leaves control of local affairs to the states. The national government, as separate from the governments of the states, is called the federal government.

feedlot. A place where cattle are kept while being fattened for market.

fertile. Good for producing crops.

fertilizer. A substance that farmers add to their soil. The fertilizer helps the soil produce more and better crops.

fiber. A thread or a threadlike part.

fiction. Novels, short stories, and other writings that tell about people and happenings that are not real.

Filipino (fil′ ə pē′ nō). Refers to people from the Philippines or people whose ancestors were from the Philippines. See **ancestors**.

First Continental Congress. See **Continental Congress**.

fission. The splitting or breaking apart of atoms in a way that releases large amounts of energy. See **atoms**.

fossil. The remains or traces of a plant or an animal that lived long ago. For example, an animal bone that has turned into rock is called a fossil. The fossil fuels—coal, oil, and natural gas—were formed from the remains of plants and animals that lived millions of years ago. Over the years, the forces of nature changed these remains into the fuels we take from the earth today. Sometimes you can actually see the pattern of a fern in a piece of coal.

foundry. A place where melted metal is poured into hollow forms called molds. When the metal cools, it hardens into the desired shape. Then the mold is removed.

freeway. A broad highway that is designed to carry heavy traffic at high speeds. Freeways have no traffic lights or crossroads.

French and Indian War, 1754-1763. A war in North America. In this war, Great Britain and its American colonies defeated the French. Indians fought on both sides. As a result of the war, Great Britain took over most of the land that the French had claimed in North America.

frontier (frun tir′). An area that lies between settled lands and the wilderness.

fusion. The combining of atoms in a way that releases large amounts of energy. See **atoms**.

generator. A machine used to make electricity. In electric power plants, the generators are usually run by other machines called turbines. The turbines are run by the force of steam or of falling water.

Georgian (jôr′ jən) **style.** A style of building much used in Britain and its colonies in the 1700's and early 1800's. A house built in the Georgian style was usually very impressive. It had a central doorway, often with tall columns. On each side of the doorway were the same number of windows.

gin (jin). A machine that separates cotton fibers from seeds and other materials. The fibers are pulled through holes that are too small to let the seeds and other materials through.

glacier (glā′ shər). A mass of ice that moves slowly down a slope or valley.

Great Britain. A large island that lies off the western coast of Europe. It includes three parts—England, Scotland, and Wales. Long ago, these were three countries with different rulers. Wales was joined to England during the 1500's. Then, in 1707, England and Wales were united with Scotland to form the kingdom of Great Britain. The ruler of Great Britain also ruled the British colonies in America. Later, the northern part of Ireland became part of the kingdom of Great Britain. Today, the official name for this country is "The United Kingdom of Great Britain and Northern Ireland."

great circle. Any imaginary circle around the earth that divides its surface exactly in half. The equator, for example, is a great circle. The shortest route between any two points on the earth always lies on the great circle that passes through them.

Great Lakes. Five huge lakes in the central part of North America. These are Lakes Superior, Michigan, Huron, Erie, and Ontario.

Great Lakes-St. Lawrence Waterway. A great inland waterway that includes the St. Lawrence

River, the five Great Lakes, and several smaller connecting waterways. The system of canals, dams, and locks on the St. Lawrence between Lake Ontario and the city of Montreal, Canada, is known as the St. Lawrence Seaway. See **lock**.

Great Plains. A part of our country that is made up of broad, level plains. It lies east of the Rocky Mountains and extends from Canada to Mexico.

Great Valley. A long chain of valleys in the eastern part of the United States. The Great Valley forms a large part of the Appalachian Ridges and Valleys section of the Appalachian Highlands.

gristmill. A mill for grinding grain.

groundwater. Water that soaks into the ground and collects in layers of soil and rock. This is the water that supplies wells and springs.

growing season. The period of time when crops can be grown outdoors without danger of being killed by frost.

guided missile. A kind of rocket that can be used to carry bombs to enemy countries during a war. Some guided missiles are directed by radio signals sent from the ground. Others are guided by an electronic device inside the missile. See **electronic**.

hardwood. Refers to trees that have broad leaves, rather than needles. Oaks and maples are examples of hardwood trees.

hectare (hek′ tär). A unit in the metric system for measuring area. It is equal to about 2.47 acres. See **metric system**.

Huguenots (hū′ gə nots). The name given to the Protestants in France during the 1500's and 1600's. The Huguenots were often made to suffer by French Roman Catholics. Thousands of Huguenots were put in prison or killed. Many fled to other countries. See **Protestant** and **Roman Catholic**.

humid (hū′ mid). Refers to air that contains a large amount of moisture.

hydrochloric acid. A strong, colorless acid. It is widely used in industry for cleaning metals. It is also used in dyeing and in food processing.

hydroelectric (hī′ drō i lek′ trik). Refers to hydroelectricity. See **hydroelectricity**.

hydroelectricity (hī′ drō i lek′ tris′ ə tē). Electricity produced from waterpower.

hydrogen bomb. A very powerful bomb. In this kind of bomb, atoms are combined in a way that releases large amounts of energy. See **atoms**.

hypotheses (hī poth′ ə sēz). Possible answers or solutions to a problem. Sometimes hypotheses are called "educated guesses." A hypothesis may turn out to be wrong. But it helps us find the right answer.

illustrate. To explain or to show more clearly with diagrams, maps, or pictures.

immigrant. A person who moves into a country or region with the purpose of making a new home there.

immigration. Moving into a country or region with the purpose of making one's home there. Also, the movement of immigrants into a country or region.

import. To bring goods into a country or region from another country or region, especially for the purpose of selling them. These goods are called imports.

income. The money a person or a business makes during a given period of time. For example, a person's yearly income might include wages for a job plus profits from a business. See **profit**.

indigo (in′ də gō). A plant from which a deep-blue dye is made. Also, the name of the dye.

insurance. A means of protection that provides money in case of illness, accident, or some other event.

Intracoastal (in′ trə kōs′ təl) **Waterway.** A protected water route used by boats along the Atlantic and Gulf coasts of our country. It includes rivers, bays, and canals.

invest. To use money for the purpose of making more money.

iron ore. A rocklike mineral that contains enough iron to make it worth mining.

Iroquois (ir′ ə kwoi). A group of Indian tribes that once lived mostly in what is now lower Canada and central New York State.

irrigate. To supply dry land with water. Ditches, canals, pipelines, and sprinklers are common means used to irrigate farmlands.

irrigated truck farm. A vegetable farm to which water is supplied by such means as ditches, canals, pipelines, and sprinklers. See **truck farm**.

PRONUNCIATION KEY: hat, āge, cãre, fär; let, ēqual, tėrm; it, īce; hot, ōpen, ôrder; oil, out; cup, put, rüle, ūse; child; long; thin; ᴛHen; zh, measure; ə represents a in about, e in taken, i in pencil, o in lemon, u in circus. For the complete key, see page 35.

irrigation. The act or practice of irrigating. See **irrigate.**

Islam (is′ ləm). One of the world's major religions. Islam was founded by an Arabian prophet named Mohammed, who was born in A.D. 570. According to this faith, there is only one God, called Allah, and Mohammed is his prophet. Followers of Islam are called Moslems, or Muslims.

Jew. A member of a group of people held together for more than three thousand years by their history and their religious faith. The history of the Jews began in southwestern Asia, probably about 1900 B.C. The Jewish faith, called Judaism, is one of the world's major religions. See **Judaism.**

Judaism (jü′ dā iz əm). One of the world's major religions. It is based on the teachings of the Old Testament, and on the Talmud, which is an interpretation of these teachings. Followers of Judaism are called Jews. The main beliefs of Judaism are that there is only one God, that God is good, and that God wants people to follow his laws. Two other major religions, Christianity and Islam, grew out of Judaism.

jury. A group of persons who serve in a court of law. The jury studies the facts and decides whether or not the person charged with a crime is guilty.

kaolin (kā′ ə lin). A fine, white clay used to make chinaware.

kerosene. An oily liquid that is usually made from petroleum. One hundred years ago, many people used kerosene as a fuel in lamps and stoves. Today, kerosene is used mainly as a fuel in jet airplanes.

Korean War, 1950-1953. A war between North Korea and South Korea, two countries in eastern Asia. The United Nations sent soldiers to help South Korea. Many of these soldiers were Americans. See **United Nations.**

kilometer (kə lom′ ə tər). A unit in the metric system for measuring length. It is equal to about .62 mile. See **metric system.**

labor union. A group of workers who have joined together to deal with their employers on such matters as higher wages and better working conditions.

Latino. A person who was born in Latin America or whose ancestors were Latin Americans. Latin America includes all of North and South America south of the United States. For example, people from Mexico, Cuba, and Puerto Rico are Latinos.

latitude. Distance north or south of the equator, measured in units called degrees.

legal. Refers to anything that is allowed by law. Also refers to anything having to do with the law or courts of law.

legislature. A group of persons who have the power to make laws for a state or a country.

Lent. A special period observed by many Christian churches before Easter. People often give up certain foods or say extra prayers during this time.

levees. High, wide walls made of earth or concrete. They are built along rivers or lakes to prevent flooding.

lignite. A low-grade coal that is about half carbon and half water. (See **carbon.**) When lignite is burned, it gives off less heat than coal that contains more carbon.

lint. The long fibers obtained from the cotton plant.

livestock. Farm animals such as cattle, hogs, sheep, horses, and chickens.

lock. A section of a canal or river that is used to raise or lower ships from one water level to another. Gates at each end permit ships to enter or leave the lock. When a ship is in the lock, the gates are closed. The water level in the lock is raised or lowered to the level of the part of the canal or river toward which the ship is going. Then the gates in front of the ship are opened, and the ship passes out of the lock.

majority (mə jôr′ ə tē). Usually, any number over half. The term "majority vote" refers to a way in which groups of people make decisions. In this system, important questions are decided and people are elected to office by the largest number of votes.

Manhattan. One of the five boroughs into which New York City is divided. The Borough of Manhattan consists mainly of an island, also called Manhattan, that lies at the mouth of the Hudson River. It also includes several very small islands nearby.

manufactures (man′ yə fak′ chərz). This word usually means goods that are produced in factories. Sometimes, fact tables show dollar figures for manufactures. These figures represent the value added to goods or raw materials by factories in a certain area. The value added is figured out in an interesting way. From the amount of money received from the sale of goods, the cost of the materials needed to make them is subtracted. The amount of money left is the value added by the factories.

Mediterranean (med′ə tə rā′nē ən) **Sea.** An inland sea about 2,330 miles (3,749 kilometers) long. It lies south of Europe, west of Asia, and north of Africa.

menhaden (men hā′ dən). A fish found along the Atlantic and Gulf coasts of the United States. Menhaden are chiefly used to make fertilizer, cattle feed, and oil.

mesa (mā′sə). A small plateau that rises steeply from the land around it. (See **plateau**.) A mesa has a flat top. Mesa is a Spanish word that means table.

mesquite (mes kēt′). A spiny, low-growing tree with long roots. It grows in the southwestern part of the United States and in other dry lands. Parts of the mesquite plant are eaten by cattle.

meter. In the metric system, the basic unit for measuring length. It is equal to 39.37 inches. See **metric system**.

metric system. A system of measurement used in many countries throughout the world, especially in science. In this system, the meter is the basic unit of length.

metropolitan (met′rə pol′ə tən) **area.** A thickly populated area that includes at least one large central city. Besides the central city, a metropolitan area usually includes several smaller towns and settled sections.

Midwest. A part of the United States. The Midwest includes the states of Illinois, Indiana, Iowa, Michigan, Minnesota, Missouri, Ohio, and Wisconsin.

mineral. Any of certain substances found in the earth. Diamonds and coal are examples of minerals.

minority (mə nôr′ə tē) **group.** A group of people who differ in race, religion, or national origin from the people who make up the largest group in a country or a region.

missile. A weapon, such as a bomb or rocket, that travels through the air without a pilot. Missiles may be guided by radio signals from the ground. They may also be guided by an electronic device within the missile. See **electronic**.

missionary. A person who is sent out by a religious group to persuade other people to follow the same religion.

mohair. The long, silky hair of the Angora goat. Also, yarn or cloth made of mohair.

mold. A hollow container in which something can be shaped. For example, liquid Jello is poured into a mold. After it has become solid, it may be turned out in the shape of the mold.

monuments. Objects or structures, such as buildings, put up to keep people or events from being forgotten.

mural. A picture, usually very large, that is painted on a wall.

national origin. Generally refers to the country where a person was born, or where one's parents or grandparents were born.

natural resources. Useful things found in nature, such as soil, water, trees, and minerals. See **mineral**.

Nazi (nät′sē). Refers to a political party in Germany called the National Socialists. This undemocratic party controlled the country from 1933 to 1945. Adolf Hitler was leader of the National Socialists and dictator of Germany. Under his leadership, Germany tried to gain control of much of the world. See **World War II**.

Netherlands. A small country in northwestern Europe. The Netherlands is often known as Holland, although this name really refers only to part of the country.

newsprint. An inexpensive, coarse paper made mostly from wood pulp. It is mainly used for newspapers.

Nobel Prize. Any one of several prizes given each year for important work in such fields as science, writing, and world peace.

nonfiction. Writing that deals with real people and events.

nonmetallic minerals. Minerals that do not provide metals. (See **mineral**.) Examples of nonmetallic minerals are sulfur and limestone.

novel. A long story, usually telling about people who did not really live and events that did not really happen.

novelist. A person who writes long stories, called novels. Usually, the people in a novel did not really live, and the events did not really take place.

nuclear (nü′ klē ər). Refers to the production or use of atomic energy. See **atomic energy**.

PRONUNCIATION KEY: hat, āge, cāre, fär; let, ēqual, tėrm; it, īce; hot, ōpen, ôrder; oil, out; cup, put, rüle, ūse; child; long; thin; ᴛʜen; zh, measure; ə represents a in about, e in taken, i in pencil, o in lemon, u in circus. For the complete key, see page 35.

Old State House. A building in Boston where the government leaders of the Massachusetts Bay Colony met. Later, the Old State House served as the first capitol for the state of Massachusetts. (See **capitol**.) This building is now used as a museum.

ore. Rock or other material that contains enough metal to make it worth mining.

Oregon Trail. The main route taken by the pioneers who traveled westward in the mid-1800's to settle in what is now the state of Oregon. This trail went from Independence, Missouri, to the Willamette Valley in Oregon.

oxygen (ok′sə jən). A colorless, odorless, tasteless gas. It makes up about one fifth of the air we breathe. Combined with other substances, oxygen is found in all plants and animals. It is also found in water and in many kinds of rock.

parliament (pär′lə mənt). In some countries, a group of people who make the laws. In many ways a parliament is like the Congress of the United States. When "parliament" is spelled with a capital "P," it usually means the parliament of Great Britain.

pasteurize (pas′chə rīz). To heat a liquid such as milk to a high temperature and then cool it rapidly. This process kills harmful germs.

patchwork. Pieces of cloth of different colors and shapes, which have been sewed together. Also, anything that looks like patchwork.

patchwork quilt. A warm covering for a bed. The top is made from patches of cloth, of different colors and shapes. These have been sewed together.

peninsula (pən in′ sə lə). An area of land that is almost surrounded by water. It is connected to a larger area of land.

petrochemicals (pet′ rō kem′ ə kəlz). Chemicals obtained from petroleum or natural gas. Petrochemicals are used in making hundreds of products, such as paint, fertilizer, and synthetic rubber. See **chemicals**.

petroleum. Also called oil. A thick oily liquid that comes from the earth. Petroleum may be dark brown or greenish black in color. Gasoline and many other useful things are made from petroleum.

phosphate rock. A kind of rock that contains chemicals needed by plants. It is ground up and used in making fertilizer. See **chemicals**.

Piedmont (pēd′ mont) **Plateau.** A section of the Appalachian Highlands that extends from New York into Alabama. Most of the land in the Piedmont is gently rolling or hilly.

Pilgrims. A group of English colonists who came to America in 1620. The Pilgrims had left England because they had not been allowed to worship God as they pleased. They started a colony called Plymouth in what is now Massachusetts.

planet. The earth or any one of the other heavenly bodies that move around the sun. The nine main planets are Mercury, Venus, Earth, Mars, Jupiter, Saturn, Uranus, Neptune, and Pluto.

plateau (pla tō′). A large, generally level area of high land.

plywood. A material made by gluing together thin sheets of wood.

polio. A short form of the word poliomyelitis. This is a serious disease that causes fever and weakness of the muscles. Some people die from polio and some become lame.

pollute. To make something dirty or impure.

pollution. Making something dirty. For example, air or water may become polluted.

population. The total number of people living in any particular place. See **density of population**.

potash. See **potassium salts**.

potassium salts. A group of certain chemicals, many of which are found in nature as minerals. Most of them are commonly referred to as potash. Potassium salts are used in making fertilizer, medicine, photographic supplies, and many other products. See **chemicals**.

prairie. A large area of level or rolling land covered with grass. A prairie usually has no trees.

prejudice. An opinion that is formed without knowing all the facts. The dislike for a person just because he or she belongs to a different group is a common kind of prejudice.

process. A method or way of doing something, or the steps taken to get a thing done. Also, to treat foods or other substances in some special way to make them more useful. For example, corn is said to be processed when it is canned or made into cornflakes.

produce (prə düs′). To make or to raise. For example, factories produce manufactured goods. Farms produce crops and livestock.

profit. The money earned by a business. It is the amount of money taken in, minus the money spent in running the business.

Protestant. Refers to one of the three main branches of Christianity. Also, a member of any one of the many different Protestant groups, such as the Methodists, Baptists, or Presbyterians. See **Christianity**.

prune. To cut off dead or useless parts of a tree, bush, or other plant. Usually, a plant is pruned to give it a better shape or to aid its growth.

Puerto Rico (pwer′ tō rē′ kō). An island about 1,000 miles (1,609 kilometers) southeast of Florida. The United States has had control of Puerto Rico since 1898. Today, this island governs itself with the help of the United States.

Puget-Willamette (pū′ jit wə lam′ ət) **Lowland.** A long valley in the western part of Oregon and Washington. It is about 350 miles (563 kilometers) long and 50 miles (80 kilometers) wide.

Pulitzer (pū′ lit sər) **Prize.** Any one of several prizes given each year in the United States for good work in such fields as newspaper writing, literature, music, and cartooning. The prizes are named for Joseph Pulitzer (1847-1911), a newspaper editor and publisher. Pulitzer left a large amount of money for these prizes.

pulp. A soft, damp material usually made from wood or rags. It is used in making paper.

purify. To make pure or clean.

pyrites (pī rī′tēz). Various minerals that include sulfur combined with metals such as iron, copper, and nickel. Both copper and nickel may be produced by smelting ores that contain pyrites, but it is not practical to obtain iron in this way. (See **smelting.**) A gas formed during the smelting process is used to make sulfuric acid, which is an important industrial chemical. The gas is also used in refrigeration.

quarry (kwôr′ē). An open pit in the earth from which stone is taken for use in building.

rain shadow. An area is said to lie in a rain shadow if mountains shelter it from moist winds. When moist winds rise to go over mountains, they are cooled and lose moisture in the form of rain or snow. By the time they have crossed the mountains, they are drier. As the winds move down to the lower land on the other side of the mountains, they become warmer. This causes them to take up moisture instead of losing it. Thus the land in the rain shadow is drier than the land on the other side of the mountains.

raw materials. Substances that can be manufactured into useful products. For example, iron ore is the main raw material needed for making iron and steel. Many manufacturing plants use steel as a raw material for making machinery and other metal products.

raw sugar. A form of sugar obtained from the juice squeezed from sugarcane. It is yellowish brown in color because the sugar crystals are covered with a thin film of molasses. Raw sugar is refined to produce the white sugar sold in stores.

recession (ri sesh′ən). A time when business activity slows down and many people are put out of work.

refinery. A place where useful products are made from something found in nature. For example, petroleum is made into gasoline, kerosene, and other useful products in a refinery.

research. A careful search for facts or truth about a subject.

reservation. An area of land owned by the government and set aside for some special use. Especially, an area set aside for use by Indians.

reservoir. A lake that stores large amounts of water until it is needed. The water may be used in homes, in manufacturing, or for farming. A reservoir may be a natural lake. Or it may be a lake formed by a dam on a river.

responsibility. Duty. Something that a person ought to do because it is the right thing to do, such as obeying the law.

retail (rē′tāl). Refers to stores that sell goods directly to the people who will use the products. Grocery stores and department stores are examples of retail stores.

Revolutionary War, 1775-1783. A war between Great Britain and thirteen British colonies in America. The colonies won the war and became states in a new country. This was the United States.

rickets. A disease of children in which the bones are not straight. It is caused by a lack of sunlight or a lack of vitamin D in the diet.

Roman Catholic. Refers to a church that is one of the three main branches of Christianity. Also refers to members of this church. See **Christianity.**

rosin. A hard, brittle substance that is made, along with turpentine, from the sap of living pine trees or from dead pinewood. Rosin is used in products such as paint, varnish, and soap.

PRONUNCIATION KEY: hat, āge, cãre, fär; let, ēqual, tėrm; it, īce; hot, ōpen, ôrder; oil, out; cup, pùt, rüle, ūse; child; long; thin; ᴛHen; zh, measure; ə represents a in about, e in taken, i in pencil, o in lemon, u in circus. For the complete key, see page 35.

sagebrush. A low, bushy plant with grayish green leaves. Sagebrush grows in the western part of the United States. It is sometimes used for fuel. It is also used as winter feed for sheep and cattle.

Scandinavia. A large area in northern Europe that includes the countries of Norway, Sweden, and Denmark.

scientist. An expert in some branch of science. A scientist makes an orderly study of natural laws and facts about nature.

scrap. Metal that is thrown away. Steel scrap is often used to replace part of the iron ore needed to make steel. Each ton of steel scrap used saves two tons of iron ore.

sculptor. An artist who makes figures or statues, usually of marble, wood, metal, or some other hard material.

sculptures. Works of art that are three-dimensional. (See **three-dimensional**.) For example, a statue made of marble, wood, or some other hard material.

sea level. The level of the surface of the sea. All surfaces on land are measured according to their distance above or below sea level.

Second Continental Congress. See **Continental Congress**.

segregation (seg′ rə gā′ shən.) In the United States, the separation of black people from white people, either by law or by custom. Under segregation, blacks generally attend separate schools, eat in separate restaurants, and sit in separate sections of buses. In many cases, they also live in separate sections of cities.

shale. A kind of rock that was probably formed from clay.

silage (sī′lij). Chopped green cornstalks or other plants that have been stored in a silo. A silo is an airtight building, usually shaped like a cylinder. Silage is used to feed cattle or other livestock.

slag. The waste material that is produced when ore is smelted to obtain metal. See **smelt**.

slate. A dark-colored rock, usually bluish gray, that splits easily into thin layers. Slate is used to make shingles, blackboards, and other items.

slum. A crowded, run-down part of a city or town. Most of the people who live in slums are very poor.

smallpox. A serious disease from which many people once died.

smelt. To separate the metal from the other materials in ore by melting the ore in a special furnace.

smelter. A place where smelting is done. Also, a furnace in which ore is smelted. See **smelt**.

smelting. The process by which metal is obtained from ore.

social scientist. A person who is skilled in any of the social sciences. These are sciences that deal with people. They include history, geography, and economics.

solar system. Our sun and the planets and smaller heavenly bodies that revolve around it.

solstice (sol′ stis). Either of two times of the year when the direct rays of the sun are farthest from the equator. This occurs about June 21 and about December 22.

South. A region of the United States, which includes Alabama, Arkansas, Florida, Georgia, Kentucky, Louisiana, Mississippi, North Carolina, South Carolina, Tennessee, and Virginia. "South" also refers to the states that opposed the Union in the Civil War. See **Civil War**.

Soviet Union. Short name for the Union of Soviet Socialist Republics, or U.S.S.R. Also called Russia. This country is located in Eurasia. See **Eurasia**.

State Supreme Court. In most states, the highest court of law.

standard of living. The way of living in a community or a country that people think of as necessary for a happy, satisfying life. In a country with a high standard of living, many different goods and services are thought of as necessary for most of the people. In a country with a low standard of living, many of these same things are enjoyed by only a few very wealthy people.

steam engine. An engine that is run by steam. To produce the steam, water is heated by burning a fuel such as coal or oil. Steam engines are often used to run trains and ships. They are also used in power plants to produce electricity.

stock. The total capital of a corporation. (See **capital**.) The stock of a company is usually divided into small portions called shares. A person may buy one or more of these shares. He or she then owns part of the business.

strike. The stopping of work by a group of workers. The purpose of a strike is usually to force a business to pay higher wages or provide better working conditions.

strip-mining. A way of digging up minerals that are deposited in flat strips near the surface of the earth. To reach these deposits, the layers of soil and rock that lie on top of the minerals must be removed.

suburb. An outer part of a city, or a smaller community near a city.

sulfuric (sul fyůr′ ik) **acid.** A heavy, colorless, oily liquid. It is used in refining petroleum and in making fertilizers, chemicals, steel, and plastics.

Supreme Court. The most important court of law in the United States. It meets in the nation's capital, Washington, D.C. The Supreme Court has nine judges, who are called justices. Their job is to make sure that our country is being governed according to the rules in the Constitution. See **constitution.**

suspension bridge. A bridge hung from thick wire ropes called cables. The cables are fastened to high towers on each side of the water or gap to be bridged.

synthetic (sin thet′ ik). Refers to certain substances such as plastics and nylon, developed to replace similar natural materials.

terminus. The end of a transportation route.

textile. Cloth, or the thread used to make cloth.

three-dimensional (də men′ shə nəl). Refers to anything that has height, length, and width.

thresh. To separate the grain from the husks and stems of the plant.

tinplate. Thin sheets of steel that have been coated with tin.

tobacco. A plant that is used mainly for making products such as cigars and cigarettes. In recent years, scientists have discovered that the use of tobacco products is harmful. They have reported that smoking helps to cause cancer, heart trouble, and other serious diseases.

treaty. An agreement, usually in writing, between two or more nations.

Tropic of Cancer. An imaginary line around the earth, about 1,600 miles (2,574 kilometers) north of the equator.

Tropic of Capricorn. An imaginary line around the earth, about 1,600 miles (2,574 kilometers) south of the equator.

tropics. The part of the earth that lies between the Tropic of Cancer and the Tropic of Capricorn. The weather in the tropics is generally hot all year round. See **Tropic of Cancer** and **Tropic of Capricorn.**

truck farm. A farm on which vegetables are raised to be sold. One meaning of the word "truck" is to trade things. Formerly vegetables often were traded for other products.

try. To bring a person before a judge or jury in a court of law. The judge or jury decides whether or not the person is guilty of breaking a law.

turbine. An engine commonly run by the force of water or steam striking against blades. Turbines are used to run electric generators. See **generator.**

turpentine. An oily liquid prepared from the sap of living pine trees or from dead pinewood. It is often used for thinning paints and varnishes.

Union. The United States of America. During the Civil War, the northern states were called the Union. See **Civil War.**

United Nations. An organization of countries from all over the world. It was started in 1945 to work for world peace. About 150 countries now belong to the United Nations.

United States Congress. The lawmaking, or legislative, branch of the United States government. It is made up of the Senate and the House of Representatives.

United States Supreme Court. See **Supreme Court.**

Upper Peninsula. The northern part of the state of Michigan. It lies mainly between Lake Superior and Lake Michigan.

uranium (yů rā′ nē əm). A very heavy, silver-white metal. It is important as the source of certain materials used to produce atomic energy. See **atomic energy.**

urban. Having to do with cities or large towns.

victim. A person who is harmed by something or someone.

Vikings. People who lived along the seacoast in Scandinavia about one thousand years ago. (See **Scandinavia.**) The Vikings were fine sailors and fierce warriors. They often invaded other countries in northern Europe. Some of them settled on the islands of Iceland and Greenland.

volcano. An opening in the earth's crust through which melted rock, called lava, and other materials are forced to the surface. These materials often build up to form a hill or mountain, also called a volcano.

weather. The condition of the air or atmosphere at a given time and place. A description of weather includes such things as wind, sunshine, temperature, and moisture. The average weather conditions of a particular place

---

PRONUNCIATION KEY: hat, āge, cāre, fär; let, ēqual, tėrm; it, īce; hot, ōpen, ôrder; oil, out; cup, pút, rüle, ūse; child; long; thin; ᵺen; zh, measure; ə represents a in about, e in taken, i in pencil, o in lemon, u in circus. For the complete key, see page 35.

over a long period of time make up its climate.

West Indies. A large group of islands in the Atlantic Ocean. They lie between the United States and South America. The West Indies got their name because Columbus thought he had reached lands in eastern Asia called the Indies.

wholesale. Having to do with selling large amounts of goods to businesses for resale. For example, a wholesale hardware company might buy a large amount of hammers from the manufacturer. The wholesale company would then sell the hammers to hardware stores throughout our country. These hardware stores, which sell the hammers to the people who are going to use them, are called retail stores. See **retail**.

wood pulp. See **pulp**.

World War I, 1914-1918. A war that was fought in many parts of the world. On one side were the Central Powers. These were Germany, Austria-Hungary, Turkey, and Bulgaria. They were defeated by the Allies. These included Great Britain, France, Russia, Japan, the United States, and other countries.

World War II, 1939-1945. A war that was fought in many parts of the world. On one side were the Allies, which included the United States, Great Britain, the Soviet Union, France, and many other countries. On the other side were the Axis Powers, which included Germany, Italy, and Japan. The Allies defeated the Axis Powers.

X-ray. A ray that can go through substances that light cannot go through. X-rays can be used to photograph such things as broken bones inside the body.

yucca (yuk′ə). Any of several plants of the lily family that grow in warm, dry areas. Some yucca plants are short but others are as tall as trees. The leaves of the yucca are usually stiff, narrow, and pointed. Yucca flowers are white.

Acknowledgments

Grateful acknowledgment is made to the following for permission to use the illustrations found in the Thinking Aids section of this book:

A. Devaney, Inc.: Page 26
Alpha Photo Associates, Inc.: Pages 21 and 27
Camera Hawaii: Page 30
De Wys, Inc.: Page 23
Field Enterprises: Pages 22-23, painting by Frederick Coffey Yohn
Grant Heilman: Page 34
H. Armstrong Roberts: Pages 31 (lower) and 33
Kaiser Steel Corporation: Page 19 (lower left)
Louisville Chamber of Commerce: Page 17
Magnum Photos, Inc.: Page 31 (upper)

NASA: Page 20
Shostal Associates, Inc.: Page 19 (upper left and lower right)
Sirlin Studios: Pages 24-25
Texasgulf: Pages 28-29
The Fideler Company: Page 29 by Adrian Beerhorst
United States Department of Agriculture, Soil Conservation Service: Pages 26-27
United States Department of Interior, Bureau of Reclamation: Page 32

Grateful acknowledgment is made to Scott, Foresman and Company for the pronunciation system used in this book, which is taken from the Thorndike-Barnhart Dictionary Series. Grateful acknowledgment is made to the following for permission to use cartographic data in this book: Creative Arts: Bottom map on page 15; Base maps courtesy of the Nystrom Raised Relief Map Company, Chicago 60618: Top map on page 15; United States Department of Commerce, Bureau of the Census: Bottom map on page 14.